THE CANBERRY TALES

Salacious Satire from the Culture Wars

ROWAN DEAN

Published by:
Wilkinson Publishing Pty Ltd
ACN 006 042 173

PO Box 24135, Melbourne, Victoria, Australia 3001
Ph: 03 9654 5446
enquiries@wilkinsonpublishing.com.au
www.wilkinsonpublishing.com.au

A catalogue record for this book is available from the National Library of Australia

ISBN(s): 9781925927818: Paperback

Design by Spike Creative Pty Ltd
Ph: (03) 9427 9500
spikecreative.com.au

Printed and bound in Australia by Ligare Pty Ltd.

f WilkinsonPublishing
⊙ wilkinsonpublishinghouse
🐦 WPBooks

To Sasha
who encouraged me to confabulate

These articles all first appeared in the *Australian Financial Review Weekend* newspaper between 2017 and 2021. My sincere thanks to Michael Stutchbury, Kevin Chinnery and the *AFR* team for their continuous support and kind permission to reprint. Any resemblance of any of the characters in this book to anyone dead or alive is purely satire.

CONTENTS

INTRODUCTION

For over a decade in the late 1300s the talented courtier Geoffrey Chaucer penned his *Tales of Caunterbury* or—as they are more commonly known—*The Canterbury Tales*. Written in Middle English verse as well as prose, these engaging, informative and often bawdy yarns are loosely strung together, built around the neat premise of a story-telling competition between a troupe of pilgrims travelling from London to Canterbury. Thus we have 'The Cook's Tale', 'The Knight's Tale', 'The Wife of Bath's Tale' and so on. Much like Boccaccio's *The Decameron*, this narrative structure gives us wonderful glimpses and insights into the lives, customs, loves and libidos of an exhilarating range of colourful characters from the period, from nobility to commoner and everything in between.

Critically, *The Canterbury Tales* was written during a crazy and turbulent time in English history. Paper, and thus written communications, was a recent invention—the Twitter of its day, perhaps? Some of Chaucer's friends were executed—surely the ultimate form of cancel culture. Fake religions and fraudulent religious indulgences abounded, much like the climate and woke cults of our era. Greed, corruption and abuse were rife; a king was deposed; a plague had decimated the land—I think you get my drift.

For the last decade, I have penned a weekly satirical column for the *Australian Financial Review Weekend*. For that honour and that privilege, I thank the Editor-in-Chief Michael Stutchbury and Opinions Editor Kevin Chinnery. Political satire is a joy to write and hopefully a pleasure and a delight to read. In compiling this selection from 2017–2021, I have concentrated on the columns where the humour still resonates and does not overly rely on the reader being aware of the topical events of whatever it was that occurred in Canberra, the nation's capital, or within politics that particular week.

The columns are in chronological order, with a brief description of the events that prompted them, and I trust that the narrative flows in a smooth and compelling manner, although some readers may prefer simply to dip in and out of the stories in a random fashion.

Regular readers of the column will also no doubt be familiar with the helpful and observant interventions of my ed., as well of course of my trusted assistant, Ms Rowena, a talented young lady who has provided me with inspiration, insights and close physical companionship.

Above all, I fondly hope that the humourous characters and political peccadilloes of our modern world jump off the page in all their inglorious colour and breathtaking absurdity.

So put up your feet, grab a tankard of your favourite ale, and allow me to entertain you with my Canberry Tales.

2017—the Year of Waffle

Having only won legitimacy as prime minister in his own right by a single seat the previous year, and in the process having lost the Coalition fourteen seats won by Tony Abbott, Malcolm Turnbull sets out on his inevitable journey to being forever remembered as one of Australia's most unlamented prime ministers. Key to this process are two fundamental Turnbull traits: a unique ability to dither and waffle on any decision-making or policy reform combined with a well-honed narcissism and paranoia as regards his colleagues.

He begins the year by ratifying the Paris Agreement on the same day as Donald Trump, who has promised to pull out of Paris, is sworn in as the 45th US president (a victory predicted by this author and virtually nobody else among Australian commentators).

Over the course of the year Australians will be forced to endure the same-sex marriage debate, as well as contemplate the ridiculous decision to purchase French nuclear submarines and retrofit them with diesel engines, which no doubt thrilled our maritime enemies.

Bill Shorten believes he is destined for the Lodge with Chris Bowen by his side. Bill Leak dies of a heart attack and Gillian Triggs is awarded a free speech prize.

But the drumbeat of 2017 and 2018 is of course the march of endless bad news polls for Malcolm Turnbull…

Prime Minister Malcolm Turnbull, already floundering in the opinion polls, informs Australians that he is the happiest Prime Minister Australia has ever had.

Happy is the head that wears the PM's crown

7 January 2017

Malcolm Turnbull repeatedly tells us that 'I may not be the best Prime Minister we've had, but I'm the happiest.' But is he right? In this world exclusive, *The Fin*'s Canberra correspondent Professor Rowena Bipolar-Blackdog looks at the long history of manically depressed Australian prime ministers:

Sir Robert 'Misery Guts' Menzies: the source of Menzies' deep unhappiness is usually attributed to his shocking long-term memory lapses. Time and again over decades Menzies would completely forget that he had already been elected in numerous landslides and would insist on doing it all over again. Menzies also had this strange affection for the mysterious 'forgotten' people who, in his unhappy state of mind, were the Liberal Party base and the backbone of the country. Most subsequent PMs, including the current one, have naturally dismissed such a foolish notion.

'Happy' Harold Holt: with his ironic Aussie nickname of 'Happy' (from back when Australians weren't afraid to call redheads 'bluey' and

Aborigines 'chalky'), Holt was of course one of our unhappiest prime ministers. He hid this unhappiness by always being photographed with a great big beaming smile on his face and a couple of well-endowed sheilas under each arm, one of whom was sometimes his wife. In the end, 'Happy' was so unhappy that he persuaded the Chinese to kidnap him in a submarine and smuggle him off to a new life in swinging '60s Shanghai.

Sir John 'Grizzleface' Gorton: clearly, as a decorated war hero who miraculously survived not one but three horrific air accidents and went on to become a hugely popular politician who was then handed the prime ministership on a plate, Gorton should have been extremely happy with his lot in life. However, the one event that plunged him into deep depression was the fact that he lost 15 seats to Labor and nearly wiped out the government's entire majority in the 1969 election—a disastrous 'victory' historians agree has only ever been equalled once (on 2 July 2016).

Billy 'Moaning' McMahon: like Holt, Sir Billy hid his profound unhappiness with the human condition by always being photographed, even on state visits, with a beautiful blonde in a miniskirt by his side. Who actually was his wife. McMahon's unhappiness stemmed from always being viewed by the public as a devious schemer who stabbed his own PM in the back to steal the job for himself and then had no idea what to do with it—a feat historians agree has only ever been equalled once (in 2015–17).

Gough 'Sourpuss' Whitlam: with his booming voice, charismatic looks, and messianic popularity, Whitlam should have been the very personification of '70s Aussie sunny optimism. However, Whitlam harboured an unhappy secret which plagued his entire career: he couldn't add up. Before long, the wealthy Australia he had inherited from the Liberals was so broke that Gough tried to borrow cash from a bunch of crooked Pakistanis. Finally he was booted out, which added to his unhappiness but, ironically, left mainstream Australia ecstatic.

Malcolm 'Malcontent' Fraser: An old-style elitist, Malcolm grew up believing he was destined to become prime minister, priding himself on his great oratorical flourishes and personal magnetism. Yet, bizarrely, when he became PM Malcolm waffled around, couldn't make up his mind about anything, and didn't bother with any urgently needed economic reforms. Tragically, Malcolm's unhappiness came from the fact he had joined the wrong party, and would have far preferred to have been PM of a touchy-feely leftie party fighting for climate change, gay marriage and a republic, which is what his wife always wanted him to do. (You sure you've got the right Malcolm here?—ed.)

Robert 'Joyless' Hawke: top bloke. Top Rhodes scholar. Top union boss. Top beer guzzler. Waltzed into Parliament. Won four elections. Won the America's Cup. Gave everybody the day off. Most successful Labor leader ever. Unhappy? Hardly.

Paul 'Undertaker' Keating: Deeply unhappy throughout his entire life for one reason only (see above).

John 'Po-face' Howard: much like his hero Menzies, clearly the reason for John Howard's long-term unhappiness is the fact that people kept handing him stunning election victory after stunning election victory. He also made Australia prosperous; remains respected and admired on the world stage; and gets mobbed wherever he goes.

Kevin Rudd: so unhappy he started eating his own earwax.

Julia Gillard: felt so unhappy about being PM that she salved her conscience by donating $300 million of Australian taxpayers' money to the Clinton-affiliated Global Partnership for Education and then agreed to chair its board.

Tony Abbott: was extremely happy as PM and doing a great job until he got stabbed in the back by his closest colleagues who then went on to wipe out his majority.

Malcolm Turnbull: Happily living in exciting times of innovative, agile jobs and growth with continuity and change. For the time being, at least…

Australia Day weekend arrives with all the usual hysterics. And Donald Trump is sworn in.

Torture

27 January 2017

Newly sworn-in US President Donald Trump announces that he intends to bring back torture. Should we do the same here? And if so, using which techniques? In this world exclusive, *The Fin*'s sadism and torture expert Fraulein Rowena Torquemada de Sade identifies Aussie-style tortures that might come in handy:

The Aussie Day Date Changer: an intense form of psychological torture, the Date Changer requires the subject to sit in front of an angry, agitated crowd of Indigenous, flag-burning activists and nominate a new date for Australia Day. To add to the mental anguish, the proposed new national day must not only offend no minority groups whatsoever (best to avoid those tricky anniversaries such as the genocide of the Armenians or the enslavement of the Falun Gong), but it must also include a public holiday at the end of January because Aussies like their long weekends. Hours of exquisite self-flagellation.

The Australian of the Year Selection Technique: if the Date Changer fails to crack the prisoner, then force him or her to nominate next year's Australian of the Year. Having your fingernails and toenails ripped out with a pair of rusty tongs is less stressful. To increase the pain factor significantly, force the prisoner to repeatedly watch former Australian of the Year David Morrison's exposition on why the word 'guys' is bad or former Australia of the Year Adam Goodes on why he's ashamed to be Australian. They'll soon be begging you for mercy.

The Soap Box: a cruel twist on the above. Tell your worthy stem cell scientist that he or she is Australian of the Year, place them on a pedestal for 12 months without respite, get the ABC and the media to fawn all over them, and then see how long they can resist before turning into a patronising, climate-preaching, LGBTIQ-worshipping, republican luvvy.

The Turnbull Process: designed to crack even the toughest nut, the Turnbull Dithering Technique has been formulated by a group of psychologists specialising in sadomasochistic human responses to rational decision-making functions within the conscious mind. Over an extended period of time (the torture can be drawn out over many months, or even years) a number of so-called 'attractive options' are repeatedly placed 'on and off the table' in front of the desperate prisoner. These may include tantalising rewards such as food, drink, human contact, a GST, or negative gearing. They'll soon collapse into a dithering wreck.

Q&A: a variation on the standard 'good cop/bad cop' interrogation technique favoured by law enforcement authorities around the world, Australia's own 'Q&A' has been uniquely developed in an underground bunker in Ultimo over many years of trial and terror. After first being stripped of all dignity in the notorious 'Green Room' whilst being force-fed cold pizza and warm beer, the subject is frogmarched into a large blacked-out studio and strapped in a chair on a so-called 'panel' in front of glaring lights and a hostile, baying crowd. Questions are then thrown in a seemingly random fashion by a friendly sounding 'host' until the subject is reduced to a quivering mess of bedwetting political correctness eager to confess that climate change is real, we need a republic, Australia was invaded and gay marriage is a human right.

Trawling the US Studies Centre Archives: mental torture doesn't come any more sophisticated than this. The prisoner must sift through

12 months of written reports, in-depth studies, newspaper articles, radio and TV interviews, public debates, emails, texts, voice messages and any other material produced by the 30 taxpayer-funded academics at the $21 million a year US Studies Centre at Sydney University and produce one single sentence or phrase that predicted or supported the possibility of a Trump election victory.

The Bowen Knot: more effective than ropes, shackles, handcuffs, etc.—simply force the prisoner to explain Chris Bowen's grasp of economics. He'll be tied up in knots for weeks before eventually strangling himself on his own inconsistencies.

The Reliably Efficient Torture (RET) method: a uniquely South Australian/Victorian form of sensory deprivation, this systematic torture involves the subject putting all his money into a business (such as a pharmacy, smelter or perishable goods) and then randomly and frequently cutting off all power and plunging the prisoner into total darkness. Then dramatically ramp up the pain directly onto the individual's bank balance by applying increasingly frequent and even greater 'power shocks' and blackouts until the subject is finally broken, or at the very least broke.

The Honours Torture: if none of the above tortures have succeeded in reducing your prisoner to a quivering, dry-retching, sobbing human being, and time is running out, then simply whisper into his or her ear that the following individuals all received the highest honours on Australia Day this year; Julia Gillard for services to the economy, Martin Parkinson for dedication to climate change, and Ahmed Fahour for running our postal services. Then sit back and watch the subject scream uncontrollably and tear their own hair out.

A former prime minister is appointed Chair of a mental health charity.

Lakeside lunatic asylum

25 March 2017

The world of political depression was rocked to its core this week by news that former prime minister Julia Gillard has been appointed chairperson of mental health organisation Beyondblueties.

'Oi am deloyted to accept moi friend Jiff Kunnut's koind offer to reploice him as the moin person in Orstraya in charge of mental health,' said a clearly deloyted, er, delighted Ms Gillard to an enrapt press conference of mental health experts. 'Normally Oi don't loik men in blue tois but in Jiff's case Oi am prepared to moik an exception.'

Ms Gillard is believed to have been hand-picked for the job due to her lengthy experience diagnosing imaginary mental disorders such as sexism and misogyny during her three-year stint as head nurse at the notorious Lakeside Lunatic Asylum in Canberra. The asylum is buried deep underground and can house up to several hundred patients at a time in its notorious 'Green' and 'Red' twin chambers.

Critics of the institution claim that Nurse Gillard was responsible for inflicting a series of highly dubious and extremely costly research programmes upon not only unsuspecting inmates but the nation as a whole. 'The sums involved were mind-blowing,' complained a former colleague, Dr Wayne Springsteen of 4 Surplus Row, Nambour. 'They did my head in.'

'It was like the lunatics had taken over my asylum,' complained a former inmate, Kevin, a drifter of no fixed abode. 'Which is exactly what she did. I've been wandering around in a daze ever since and I'm incapable of landing even the most menial of jobs. They won't even let me scrub the dunnies at the UN.'

But Nurse Ratshit remains unapologetic:

'Moi good friend Kevin was a dangerous psoichopath suffering from severe narcissism with delusions of being the Proim Minister of Orstraya which was of course moi job. Oi had no choice other than to get Little Sammy, Smurky Burky and Fat Howzie to pin him down so Oi could perform an emergency lobotomy on his spoinal chord with the sharpest knoife Oi could foind.'

Nurse Gillard remains convinced that her controversial approach to mind control allowed an entire generation of women and young girls to discover they were inflicted with severe bouts of non-existent male oppression. 'These girls are now so oppressed they feel they have no choice other than to go and jump off the Wage Gap,' explained one expert.

'Oi clearly established through moi extensive research programme that when a man in a blue toi looks at his watch when Oi am spoiking then he is clearly suffering from acute misogyny,' explained Ms Gillard to a jubilant crowd of nutcases at the Sydney Opera House. 'And Oi will not be lectured to about sexism and misogyny boi this man, Oi will not. And Oi sincereloi hope that Mr Rabbit has a poice of paper and is wroiting out his own job prescription,' she added, to thunderous applause from a group of wailing, hysterical feminists.

However, other experts believe that evidence published in her autobiography *Moi Story* suggests that Nurse Gillard herself suffered from repeat bouts of paranoia and self-delusion, indulging in extreme flights of fancy where she imagined herself to be a happily married woman living in a quaint cottage in Canberra charmingly called 'The Lodge' with her own private hairdresser/boyfriend ensconced in a man shed at the bottom of the garden. 'It was all part of the fantasy,' claims one psychologist. 'She even imagined she would be Headmistress of the Entire World if she gave enough taxpayers' dollars to the Clinton Foundation.'

CT scans are believed to indicate that the Left side of Nurse Gillard's brain is abnormally enlarged, likely to have been brought on through years of unhealthy exposure to student undergraduate politics and hardcore union affiliations. 'On occasions, those close to Nurse Gillard could be spotted in the middle of the night hiding her medication in a brown paper bag and burying it in the garden,' admitted her former boyfriend.

Beyondblueties was established by former Victorian premier Jiff Kunnut after he lost his marbles thanks to an intercepted phone call with fellow Victorian Andrew P. Cock in 1987.

In a clear case of Munchowards-by-Proxy, an audibly deranged Mr Kunnut can be heard accusing another man identified only as Little Johnny of 'going off his brain'. Mr Kunnut then accuses the man of being an unprintable four-letter word, before admitting that he himself is 'going berserk'.

Mr Kunnut explained that he was standing down from Beyondblueties for mental health reasons and to spend more time with his id.

In an effort to apportion blame to everyone other than himself, Prime Minister Malcolm Turnbull sets up an internal Liberal Party review of what went wrong in the 2016 election—the election where the Coalition barely scraped back in and lost 14 of the seats won by Tony Abbott, the man Mr Turnbull had ruthlessly deposed in 2015 (see this author's previous book 'Way Beyond Satire').

Who cruelled my marvellous election victory?

8 April 2017

A post-mortem review of what went wrong in the Liberal Party's 2016 election campaign was handed yesterday to the federal executive of the party. A leaked copy has been obtained by *The Fin*'s investigative reporter Rowena Depe-Throte.

Prologue: In this comprehensive and no-holds-barred Committee Report, ex-Premier of NSW Barry O'Farrell and I undertook an exhausting evening of acute analytical processes as we enjoyed a rather tasty bottle of Grange that Baz happened to have lying around in order to offer a fearless, forthright and, er, sober analysis of all the major strategic and tactical flaws that completely screwed up what should have been a marvellous victory by the great Malcolm, oops, sorry, we agreed, no names, no pack drills, by, er, The Great Communicator himself.

Accordingly, whilst avoiding pointing the finger at any one particular individual we have listed without fear or favour all the major causes of this disgraceful stuff-up by Tony Nutt, er, by, I mean by He Who Shall Remain Nameless But Must Resign Forthwith. We have also identified several Key Areas of Strategic Failure going back many, many years, for which no one person can solely be held responsible because there were of course three of them; Tony, Peta and Joe.

History: The roots of the disastrous 2016 election campaign can be traced back to a sequence of cataclysmic decisions and events by the Party that took place in 2009, when a man identified only as Old Onion Breath Himself disgracefully and treacherously stabbed the hugely charismatic and talented then-Leader of the Opposition in the back and to the horror of Lucy and myself, er, sorry, scratch that, um, to the horror of all progressive and enlightened members of the Liberal Party, mounted a hard right-wing coup that led to a series of disastrous policy errors such as giving that goose Phil the Greek a knighthood, winking lecherously at a radio host during an interview with my own hand-picked hooker, er, I mean with some random member of the public who happened to be a sex worker, and then repulsively eating an onion as if it were an apple. All of these ultra-conservative, fringe, alt-right, Trumpian, neo-con, populist, Hansonite policies combined to create a perfect storm of simultaneous events which necessitated an urgent party room ballot to realign the party with its correct leadership team of Lucy and… I mean, er, with what historians now rightly call The Restoration of the Sensible Centre. As was widely acclaimed at the time by every single one of my and Lucy's handpicked, objective and unbiased members of the ABC and the mainstream media, this exciting, innovative and agile leadership style coupled with my immense personal popularity and single-minded clarity of thought was clearly destined to deliver a richly deserved historic landslide victory of the type not seen since I won, or rather, would have won if it hadn't been rigged by that bastard Howard, the 1999 Republican Referendum. Such a victory, we can all agree, would have echoed down through the annals of Liberal Party history thanks to my firm yet flexible, decisive yet cautious, single-minded yet complex, inspirational yet measured, fair but balanced advocacy of economic leadership that the nation has yearned for ever since the disastrous 2014 fat-man-with-a-cigar-who-we-shipped-off-to-the-seppos Budget.

Strategy: Despite Tony Nutt's, er, despite an Unnamed Person's chronic inability to follow even the most basic steps as outlined in the clear-headed and powerful strategic advice that Lucy and, er, that the Prime Minister's Office artfully designed, it is clear that the Key Insight, developed with the help of our brilliant political strategist guru, that the Liberal base had nowhere else to go so we could screw over as many little old ladies and super-annuants as we possibly could, was self-evidently a critical insight and no blame whatsoever can be apportioned in this Report to anything to do with Crosby Textor, got it?

Implementation: That was delicious, don't suppose you've got another bottle handy do you Baz? Excellent! POP! Now, where were we? Hang on, I'll switch the tape back on. There! So, in conclusion it's clear to this Committee that the Implementation of the Key Insight was flawed from the very start. This can be seen in the fact that not enough effort was put in by Tony Nutt, er, by any Unnamed Persons to adequately promote the exciting and innovative new Turnbull Coalition Team logo which Lucy designed herself on the back of a silk embroidered designer napkin which we had flown in from Milan. The dramatic, eye-catching, seductive, powerful circular device, with its subliminal graphic echoes of Italianate sophistication and crisp palette, wherein the pale blue of modern Liberalism was complemented by a delightfully soft progressive yellow, and with its symbolic circular motifs invoking memories of Presidential Valour and Wimbledon Prowess (tape runs out).

A popular Human Rights guru wins a major award.

Free speech at the Fiberty Awards

6 May 2017

The world of freedom of expression was rocked to its core this week by news that Human Rights Commissioner Gillian Triggerwarnings has been awarded this year's coveted Fiberty Australia Free Speech Award.

In a tight race that included deceased Indian guru Mahatma 'Turn-the-other-cheek' Ghandi, deceased Robben Island inmate Nelson 'Truth and Reconciliation' Mandela, deceased French satirist Francois-Marie 'I'll die for your right to say what the hell you want' Voltaire, deceased African-American soap-box orator Martin Luther 'I-have-a-dream' King, deceased English philosopher John Stuart 'Do-no-harm' Mill, deceased Vanity Fair columnist Christopher 'Make-mine-a-double' Hitchens and deceased Aussie larrikin cartoonist Bill 'Righto-what's-his-name-then?' Leak, the judges were unanimous that Ms Triggerwarnings was the stand-out winner.

Said a spokesperson for the coveted Victorian Free Speech Award: 'Obviously I am not at liberty to say what I really think about why the Free Speech jury gave the award to Ms Triggerwarnings ahead of all the other seemingly worthier contestants of differing ethnic backgrounds, because someone might be offended, humiliated, insulted or even intimidated by what I say about them, even though, of course, they're all dead. But the last thing I want is to be hauled up in front of some Commission or other and hounded to my, er, I mean to their grave.'

But others were quick to praise the choice of the judges. 'Clearly, in this woman you have a candidate who has taken Voltaire's famous dictum and given it a brand new and highly innovative twist. This is an exciting development in the evolution of free speech in contemporary Australia. But on another level, we were particularly impressed by the way Ms Triggerwarnings encapsulates the idea of being able to say whatever you want at any given time to any Senate committee and then being free to completely change your story at a later date. This is the very essence of freedom of expression.'

Not everybody, however, was convinced that Ms Triggerwarnings genuinely deserved the award. Said one irate Free Speech judge who agreed to speak freely about free speech on the strict condition of his name not being in any way associated with his own words for fear of legal or government reprisals: 'No comment. And if you dare quote me on that or anything else I'll sue the pants off you.'

Ms Triggerwarnings was busy listening to a family conversation around an ordinary kitchen table when she received the exhilarating news of her award, although it wasn't actually her own kitchen table or her own family. 'At the Human Rights Commission we are currently investigating exciting new ways of monitoring every kitchen table in the land to ensure that free speech remains exactly what we say it is,' she explained.

A major energy company starts running ultra-woke ads.

The coal miner's marketer

9 September 2017

One day in a Sydney energy giant's boardroom.

'Well, thank you all for coming to this brainstorming thingummybob today, it shouldn't take too long, but I'd...'

'We haven't said 'Welcome to Country' yet, Andy.'

'Oh, er, yeah, um, well of course not, Skye, I, um... that is to say before I begin today's, ah, Marketing and Branding Innovative Diverse Digital Strategic Planning Session, I think we should, er, give thanks to the, um, Bennelong Peoples of the, er, Barangaroo Nations upon whose lands, we, ah, anyway... let's get cracking, I can't be late for my next meeting.'

'But we also need to take a quiet moment to reflect upon Gaia and the inconvenient truth that the mining of fossil fuels is directly responsible for the devastating hurricanes destroying the ancient native cultures of the Caribbean as we speak and all the damage that mankind has inflicted upon the natural world.'

'Of course, Tony, I, ah...'

'White mankind in particular.'

'Privileged white mankind to be specific.'

'Old privileged white mankind, actually.'

'Straight old privileged white mankind if we're going to be honest, Andy. Much like you.'

'Um, sure, yes, er, too right... anyway, anybody got any ideas for the new branding campaign? We're making squillions out of these renewables subsidies and the whole RET malarkey so I guess we can afford to splash out on a couple of TV ads. I've been thinking we need a more inclusive spokesperson for the brand.'

'What's wrong with the coal miner with the dirty face in the hard hat standing next to the open-cut coal mine that we've always used? I mean, that's the honest...'

'Oooooh, no no no! We need to update to a far more sensitive and culturally competent image than that. I was thinking, maybe an innovative young man with a beard?'

'Can he look like Chris Martin from Coldplay?'

'I'm loving it already!'

'With glasses and an open-neck shirt!'

'Nice!'

'Can he have a chai latte in one hand?'

'Turmeric I hope. Fair trade.'

'Perfect.'

'And an iPhone in the other hand, of course. With an app on it, showing how he can save heaps on his electricity bills.'

'Woah! Steady on there. Not so fast...The app won't really do very much, Andy. But everybody wants an app these days, they're sooooo cool.'

'Well, alright then. So long as...'

'He can say "Let's be honest, things need to change..."'

'That's good. I like honesty. It's one of our brand values. It says so in the brand guidelines booklet.'

'How about some windmills in the background?'

'Now you're talking!'

'Can he have a cool manbag over one shoulder?'

'Because he's transitioning?'

'Well, er, slow down, I mean, of course we are all transitioning out of fossil fuels to renewables but not for bloody decades...'

'I mean hormonally transitioning. Don't be so judgmental, Andy! This is 2017 after all and even energy company brand ambassadors should be allowed to express their gender fluidity.'

'Well, I think the manbag says that already, doesn't it?'

'Good point.'

'Which brings me to our logo. Nobody knows what our silly initials stand for anyway, so I was thinking we should update them. Remember how BP swapped from British Petroleum to Beyond Petroleum? That was friggin' genius! Totally fooled all the idiot greenies, er, sorry, I mean all those who are compassionately concerned for the survival of our planet and ensuring a sustainable future. Those bastards made a bloody fortune out of simply changing the meaning of one goddam lousy initial! Wish we had an ad agency who could do stuff like that!'

'Let's change our own initials!'

'How about we become "Australia's Greenest Luvvies"?'

'I like it.'

'Or what about "Australia's Gaian Lobby"?'

'Now you're talking.'

'Or what about "Actively Gay Lefties"?'

'Certainly got a ring to it.'

'We could re-do our logo in an all-inclusive yet beautifully diverse palette of rainbow colours!'

'Genius!'

'How about we make an ad showing how we make electricity out of rainbows!'

'Well, er, I'd have to check with our technical team first, but, er...'

'Of course we can, Andy! It's just sunlight filtered through water vapour. It's how we harness the power of mother nature to ensure a greener, safer, more tolerant world for transgender children, refugees and oppressed minorities!'

'That's so beautiful, Skye! We show our support for multiculturalism and the Yes campaign and solve the energy crisis all in one go!'

'Andy?'

'Yeah, whatever. But you'll have to excuse me, I've got my "Extraordinary Financial Profitability Update Thanks to Making Squillions out of the Renewables Scam" meeting scheduled for 12.30 in the Champagne and Cigar room at Rockpool. Can't afford to miss that one.'

So what did you do in the Great Culture War, er, Daddy?

23 September 2017

Confused about where you stand in the Culture Wars? Can't tell your compassions from your convictions? Your right-wing ideology from your left-wing idiocy? Your luvvies from your swivel-eyed loons? *The Fin*'s very own Sensible Centrist has devised a Cultural Competency Questionnaire to help you decide on which side of the cultural trenches your political affinities lie.

Simply choose a) or b) depending on what feels most logical to you.

The high cost of my electricity bill is due entirely to:

a) an extremely complex network of inter-connectivity and regional environmental co-ordinates that rely upon a matrix of co-functioning multi-coagulated energy generating systems disastrously undermined by economic variables related to privatisation processes that have bled consumers dry whilst greedy developers have been allowed to plate wooden telegraph poles and wires in solid gold at the same time as ripping coal out of the ground and dumping it onto the Great Barrier Reef which is what happens when you don't allow socially-aware controlled market forces to bring down the cost of wind and solar power pumped uphill to a giant battery.

b) renewables.

The same-sex marriage debate has turned ugly because:

a) when you are talking about two people who love each other and the basic fundamental human rights enshrined in every United Nations Universal Declaration of Equality that 'love is love' so any two loving persons can share a bottle of bubbly and a lifetime in the sack together and besides they could always adopt or get a surrogate or find a lesbian couple to do it with, er, anyway it is imperative that those of us who do have a voice speak out against racism and white oppression and shout 'We are proud to be gay!' at the top of our voices from every single rooftop (except in Iran, obviously—ed) in order to tackle this grotesque hate speech which oozes out of every pore of every low-life festering effin' Christian sicko who should be made to march naked down the middle of Oxford Street with a giant YES tattooed with a rainbow-coloured hot poker onto each of their miserable homophobic buttocks or at the very least they should lose their job.

b) some people say marriage is between a man and a woman.

Donald Trump is:

a) a sleeper Soviet agent who is about to destroy the entire planet in a nuclear Armageddon brought on by his constant tweeting of provocative insults which have only served to antagonise the peace-loving leader of a small, impoverished nation who has done nothing other than strive to help his people live a better life after decades of colonial racism and imperialist oppression by firing a couple of harmless rockets into the sea and who now has to suffer a giant wall being built along his border which he also has to pay for but this is exactly the sort of unhinged behaviour you'd expect from a man who boasts about raping reality TV stars and stood in front of the statue in Charlottesville of some slave killer where he gave a Nazi salute to a thousand white supremacists and told them to assassinate all the black actors in Hollywood.

b) not doing a bad job, all things considered.

January 26 is:

a) the day that marks the beginning of one of the very worst episodes of genocide, mass-murder, infanticide and racial oppression the world has ever seen of an entire peaceful, united nation of, er, First Nations all living harmoniously together in a paradise of good-will and compassion before they were thrown into poisoned wells in plague-infested blankets by a group of pillaging Anglo-Celtic botanists and cartographers whose statues are a sick reminder of this violent stain upon our national identity just as I described in my best-selling book sorry I said I wanted two sugars not one in my latte what time am I due in make-up?

b) Australia Day.

Safe schools are where:

a) young, confused and vulnerable children are protected from the despicable, cruel and deeply offensive taunts of disgusting bullies and monsters who tease them in the most abusive fashion by calling them vile names simply because they choose to express their own unique cultural identity by exploring without fear or artificial stereotypes the myriad gender options available to them that flourish in an environment of imagination and self-expression as they learn to love the body they were wrongly born into through the spiritually-fulfilling act of pretending to be gay.

b) kids don't trip over playing footy on the asphalt.

The ABC is:

a) a brave bastion of cultural awareness, diversity and multicultural inclusive independence and compassionate broadcasting surrounded by a sea of crass, grasping, populist, overly-commercialised, sensationalist right-wing, free market propaganda and moronic shock jock scare-mongerers.

b) unwatchable.

Bill Shorten is:

a) useless.

b) useless.

2018—the Year of Reckoning

With the MeToo movement in full flight, it was only a matter of time before the accusatory finger was pointed at prominent Australians, particularly in the acting profession. With same-sex marriage now safely tucked in bed, the Turnbull government wonders what on earth it can do next and the Prime Minister decides he'll have to find a way to bring about his climate change nirvana.

With sex on their brains, the Canberra press gallery uncover a shocking scandal which involves a senior minister leaving his wife and, er, marrying someone else who is going to have his baby. Malcolm Turnbull doesn't hesitate and immediately invokes a strict Bonking Ban on his ministers and their staffers.

Meanwhile, that sound Mr Turnbull hears growing ever louder is the approaching death toll of the thirtieth bad news poll in a row, the justification he gave for rolling Tony Abbott.

In August, the axe falls. Peter Dutton challenges, Turnbull panics and calls a spill, Scott Morrison wins (and nobody votes for the sheila in the red shoes).

Horror rocky show

13 January 2018

The worlds of *#MeToo* and Hollywood's feminist 'Time's Up' anti-sexual harassment movement were rocked to their cores this week when a group of young Aussie starlets pointed their fingers at our very own alleged superstar sexual predator. The salacious scandal centres around Craig McLachlan, who has been replaced by understudy Adam Rennie in *The Rocky Horror Show*. The flamboyant former heartthrob has been accused of attempting to grope an innocent young actress under the sheets in a cult musical about a flamboyant sexual predator who gropes innocent young women under the sheets.

Coming to the rescue of offended snowflakes everywhere, *The Fin*'s very own 'sweet transvestite' Rowena O'Brien has rapidly re-imagined the show for a more puritanical and enlightened, socially-aware and woke audience.

Plot: Two budding young starlets have a breakdown when they realise their career prospects have gone flat because they don't have any acting talent, but luckily they spot a light in the darkness ('There's a light, over at the Weinstein's place!'). They knock on a mysterious hotel room door only for it to be opened by a masturbating mogul in a shower robe called 'the Creature' who invites them in and asks for a massage ('Touch-a-touch-a-touch me! I wanna meet Ha-arvey! You can rub me up and oil me down, down, down!'). He promises to turn them into perfect Hollywood specimens by placing their most appealing naked body parts on a large casting couch. In the end it all goes horribly wrong when their careers fade and they need a virtuous new cause to jump onto. In the spectacular climax the entire Twittersphere goes into meltdown and all the riff raff join in singing the popular feminist refrain—Let's do the 'Time's Up' again!

Here are some of the highlights from the new adapted lyrics:

Adam Rennie stood in, The day sex became sin
And we tweeted where we stand.
And Craig McLachlan was there, Without his underwear
Harvey Weinstein had wandering hands.
Then something went wrong, For Geoffrey and Don
They got caught in a celluloid jam.
And at a deadly pace, It came from cyberspace
And this is how the message ran:
(Chorus) Me Too fiction! Double standards!
We'll build a hashtag, See tabloids fighting
Reese is moping, Forbidden groping
At the late night, double standards, Golden Globes.
I knew Leo Di Caprio, Was over a barrel
As Tarantino took to the hills
And I really got hot, When I saw Ridley Scott
Reshoot every scene where Kevin was billed.
Woody Allen said prudes, Made him sound crude
And robbed him of his comedy skills.
But 'when world's collide', said George Pell to his bride
'I'm going to give you some terrible thrills' (Glad you got Pell in there,
good for ticket sales —Prod.)
Me Too Fiction! Double Standards!

We'll build a hashtag, See tabloids fighting,

Here comes Oprah, to slay The Groper

At the late night, double standards picture show,

I want to go,

To the late night double standards Twitter show,

Me Too! Me Too!

To the late night, double standards Golden Globes.

It's astounding, trolls are hounding, madness takes its toll

But listen closely, all you snowflakes, the gals have grabbed control

I remember, creating a hashtag

Closing the pay gap, doing a cash grab

Let's do the Time's Up again, Let's do the Time's Up again

It's just a swipe to the left, And then a click to the right

With your hands on your tweets, You bring your knees in tight

But it's the Oscar thru-ust, That really drives them insa-a-ane

Let's do the Time's Up again, Let's do the Time's Up again

It's so dreamy, my virtue will free me

So you can all see me, yes, Me Too!

In another dimension, with my noblest intentions

Let's do the Time's Up again

With a bit of a mind flip, And a very large pay slip

My career will soar again

We preach meritocracy, To hide our hypocrisy

Let's do the Time's Up again, Let's do the Time's Up again

Well I was walking down the street just a-having a think

When a snaky producer gave me an evil wink

He asked me upstairs which was no surprise

He had a pickup line and a mogul's eyes

He offered to cast me, as I felt his hand

Then he made me a star, just as I'd planned
Let's do the Time's Up again, Let's close the Pay Gap again

Casting sessions for the new, more puritanical and enlightened version of the show will take place in the shower cubicle of Rowena's penthouse suite. Robes optional.

A bizarre family cult are discovered living in filth and Australia's finest pop stars express outrage that Cory Bernardi has included them on his alternative iTunes music list for Australia Day.

Rock charts

20 January 2018

The world of strange and mysterious cults was rocked to its core this week following the discovery of a bizarre 'family' living in their own ideological filth in an otherwise normal-looking House of Horrors in a pretty suburb of Canberra. Thirteen intellectually-malnourished Greens senators, MPs and staffers, ranging in mental ages from two to 29, were discovered shackled to a set of outdated and irrational policy ideas after one of them managed to escape and alert the media via a doorstop interview. When questioned by authorities, the ideological parents of the group, Richard and Sarah, remained adambandt—er, sorry, typo—adamant that they had done nothing wrong and insisted that changing the date of Australia Day was the nation's 'top priority'.

The parents have been charged with torturing mainstream Aussies by inflicting unnecessary economic pain and neglecting the truth with fantasies about the ongoing genocide and slaughter of Indigenous Australians.

'We were astonished to find out some of them are actually adults,' explained one horrified local voter. 'But they've been deprived of living in the real world for so long that they look and behave like a bunch of three-year-olds.'

'They were supposedly schooled at universities to at least undergraduate level,' said one baffled onlooker, 'but most of the MPs and certainly all of the staffers lack even the most basic knowledge of life in the real world.'

'Many of them don't even know what a proper job is,' a police spokesperson confirmed.

Experts believe the father of the group, Richard, who is rumoured to have once had a fixation with underpaying his au pair girls, was guided by his fervent belief in quasi-religious concepts such as climate change, social justice and re-introducing death duties.

Disturbing photos have emerged of the entire family all lined up together reading from the same song sheet on the steps of Parliament pretending to pass themselves off as a group of normal Australians.

The horrific discovery came after the eldest member of the family, Lee-Rhianna, escaped and fled back to Russia. Authorities revealed that in keeping with their fundamentalist environmental beliefs, the entire family are only allowed to wash once a year.

In other disturbing news this week, a bevy of mainstream rock musicians vented their displeasure at being included on Cory Bernardi's iPod compilation to celebrate Australia Day.

Said Derryn Gayes, a solo artist whose career has sadly never reached the dizzying heights he enjoyed before he foolishly disbanded his hit group Savage Boredom: 'The idea that somebody should want to sully my serious artistic reputation by playing one of my greatest ditties on a day that symbolises the ongoing slaughter and genocide of not only the entire First Nations but also Planet Earth by catastrophic climate change thanks to Donald Trump and the fascist, racist, transphobic policies of the Australian Conservatives is why I immediately seized this opportunity of jumping on the Invasion Day bandwagon.'

A spokesperson for Mr Gayes' record company was keen to remind fans that his long-awaited new solo album, tentatively titled 'Truly, Madly,

#MeToo' would be released very soon.

However, the controversy immediately escalated as other pop stars were quick to recognise a rolling publicity bandwagon and leap onto it.

Said Bernardi Faffing, a solo artist whose career has sadly never reached the dizzying heights he enjoyed before he foolishly disbanded his hit group Powdertoes: 'The idea that some prissy pop star whose biggest mistake was disbanding his silly little boy group should get all this amazing publicity out of this Cory Bernardi Australia Day malarkey is why I immediately phoned my agent and insisted that we send out some tweets about my strong stance against the ongoing slaughter and genocide of, er, who was it again?'

A spokesperson for Mr Faffing's record company was keen to remind fans that his long-awaited new solo album, tentatively titled 'My Unhappiness (that the Barrier Reef is Dying)', would be released very soon.

By late last night the backlash against Mr Bernardi's iPod song choices had intensified.

Said Jimmy Booze, a solo artist whose career has sadly never reached the dizzying heights he enjoyed before he foolishly disbanded his hit group Cold Fizzle: 'The idea that all these other has-beens are grabbing the headlines over the latest inner-city, latte-sipping, lefty fad when of course everybody knows that is my speciality is an absolute disgrace which is why I refuse to allow my hit song 'Working Class Man' to be played on Australia Day by Cory Bernardi's revolting bunch of redneck, racist, homophobic, blue-collar, coal-digging, carbon-emitting, flag-waving, er, working class men.'

A spokesperson for Mr Booze's record company was keen to remind fans that his long-awaited new album, tentatively titled 'The Last Wave of Publicity', would be released very soon.

According to a left-wing newspaper, Crocodile Dundee is politically incorrect.

That's not oppression, this is oppression

27 January 2018

The world of world-wide Aussie blockbusters was rocked to its core this week following the shock discovery by a reporter on a leading left-wing newspaper that Australia's most successful movie of all time, *Crocodile Dundee*, was in fact vulgar, sexist, homophobic, racist, misogynistic, transphobic… and worse, not even funny.

Strewth! With news that a modern sequel is in the offing, *The Fin's* own progressive scriptwriter Rowena Dundean offers up a more enlightened and compassionate version of the classic Aussie tale to soothe the nerves of a new generation of young Australians.

In the new script, which has the working title of *Snowflake Dundee*, a young virile lad called Mick who grows up in the harsh Aussie Outback has to wrestle not only with crocodiles but also with his own identity. One day he mentions to his mentor, Willy, who runs the local pub, that he 'feels like a girl'. But Willy misunderstands him completely and introduces him to an attractive young female reporter, Sue, in khaki shorts and a tank top who happens to be in the Outback doing an in-depth story on the impact of catastrophic climate change on Indigenous cultures, and the inter-related effects of colonial sexism and racism on the complexity of First

Nations language structures, for the Guardian. When Mick puts his hand on her knee, all hell breaks loose and she immediately grabs her iPhone and tweets #MeToo.

Her editor, sensing a great story, instructs a hit squad of journalists to fling as much mud at the predatory Mick as they can find in order to thoroughly destroy his professional reputation and hopefully sell some newspapers. This they are able to do quite literally, when Sue accidentally posts a video on Facebook of Mick clearly harassing and abusing a large Indigenous female crocodile by leaping on top of her and forcing her face down into the mud in front of a large wooden sign that says 'Beware of Predators'.

Mick is so ashamed by all the publicity that he wanders off into the bush to go walkabout. Sue secretly follows him, also hoping to gain further insights into the impact of rising sea levels on kangaroo culling.

But in the meantime, Sue discovers that she has completely got the wrong impression of Mick and when he said he felt like a girl, it was because he felt like a girl. Sue decides the two of them have to travel to the big city together where she can introduce him to her friend Roz who is running a compulsory Safe Schools program courtesy of the Daniel Andrews Labor government.

Together, they set off on their great adventure, although Sue refuses to allow Mick to bring his smelly leather hat with the horrible crocodile teeth around the rim with him because it offends her as a vegan.

Once they get to Melbourne, Mick is confused and disorientated but naively follows Sue's lead and eagerly immerses himself in traditional neo-Marxist survival techniques, such as breast-binding and penis-tucking, two skills which he masters with ease. Echoing one of the original film's most memorable scenes, when Mick finally gives in and agrees to undergo gender reassignment surgery the doctor whips out the necessary medical implements and says 'that's not a scalpel, this is a scalpel'. At which point Mick faints.

Sue decides that she and Mick need a safe space where they can escape from the madness of the real world without fear of being triggered by offensive books like *To Kill A Mockingbird* and politically incorrect films like *Crocodile Dundee* whilst they explore each other's gender fluidity, so they rent a terrace together in St. Kilda on Airbnb where they lie on the sofa and watch an ABC Australia Day special on the evil threat of One Nation, Cory Bernardi, Tony Abbott and Donald Trump to the success of Australian multiculturalism. When Sue switches on Triple J's Hottest 100, Mick instantly dozes off.

When Mick wakes up he finds he's in the middle of a typical Melbourne home invasion, as a gang of thugs rampage through the house stealing anything they can and smashing everything to bits. (Casting note from Screen Victoria—please ensure appropriate multicultural mix of actors in the gang, i.e. Caucasians, Chinese, Vietnamese, Italian and Greek.) Sue is nowhere to be seen but Mick thinks he can hear her being triggered in the bathroom. When Mick tries to explain to the gang of aggressive young North African Muslim men that their anger stems from the fact that they are suffering from the mental trauma of centuries of imperialism and racism at the hands of the while male patriarchy and Western oppression, the leader of the gang whacks him over the head with a crowbar and says 'that's not oppression, this is oppression'. The End.

Hundreds of top-secret Cabinet documents are found in a Canberra secondhand junk shop. And the Department of Foreign Affairs and Trade enthuses on social media about the Muslim 'modest fashion market' of hijabs and 'burqinis'.

Daft virgins

3 February 2018

The world of secret cabinet files was rocked to its core this week by the startling news that a bunch of secret cabinet files were found locked in a secret filing-cabinet that had been sold off cheap to top secret cabinet files recyclers Steptoe and Son Pre-loved Filing Cabinets, Fyshwick, Canberra, before being flogged to the ABC.

In keeping with the highest standards of professional journalism, *The Fin*'s top recycling journalist, Rowena Defiled, has filed an exclusive scoop about secret plans she found in a recycled government recycling bin on the pavement outside the Department of Foreign Affairs and Trade, known as DFAT.

The files contain top secret research findings for creative marketing proposals to further extend DFAT's product range following its successful launch into the global rag-head trade (isn't that 'rag-trade'?—ed).

Focus groups of young, diverse, multicultural Australian women have confirmed that a new brand name 'Department of Arabic Fashion Traders' is more fitting (unlike the new line in women's hijabs—ed).

A budget of over a million dollars has been awarded to Mustafa Halal-logos and Co. to design a more appropriate and inclusive logo for the Department's exciting new acronym, DAFT.

The files also reveal a comprehensive set of exciting new DAFTwear advertising ideas designed to enhance the Department's 'fashion diplomacy' by appealing to cashed-up consumers in the global 'emerging modesty market'. These include:

Daft Prayer-pads: fed up with getting down on your knees with your bum in the air five times a day? Think of the strain this puts on your joints! But now you can kneel in Aussie designer comfort with DAFT's cushy new range of specially patented (and padded!) DaftPads. Strap 'em on under your DAFTwear robes and nobody will know the difference! So now you can spend as many long hours every day as you like face down— just don't forget to pray for peace!

Accessorise your hijab: one often over-looked aspect of the exciting emerging modest fashion market is the desire of young women in certain parts of the world to spontaneously tear off their hijab and wave it around provocatively in the air! Hours of fun! And you're bound to attract the attention of the menfolk! So why not accessorise your Daft Hijab (check out our new Opera House range at daft.com) with one of our special brand of DaftSticks? Fashioned from 100% Chinese-crafted selfie sticks, the revolutionary new range of DaftSticks come pre-fitted with a special telescopic attachment so you can still carry on waving your hijab through the bars on the window of your cosy new underground accommodation!

Schoolgirl nets: fed up with trying to catch an entire classroom of Christian schoolgirls in one go without half of them running away to escape?!? With our new tough and flexible DaftNets, fashioned exclusively from genuine recycled and environmentally-friendly Tasmanian trawler driftnets, you'll be amazed how quick and easy it is to round-up an entire 'school' of girls in one clean sweep and cart them off deep into the nearest jungle of your choice!

FGM dolls: loads of fun for the old crones in your family, and particularly those men who are so concerned that you might actually grow up one day and have too much fun in your married life! Why not distract them with a selection from our new range of DaftDolls? Aussie-designed DaftDolls come with their own female genital mutilation plastic surgical kit, needle and thread, removable bits and bobs, and detailed instructions on how to smuggle your daughter out of the country on a 'cultural exchange' visit so that the operation can be performed for real without DOCS ever finding out! A lifetime of fun! (Legal disclaimer: may also result in a lifetime of agony, infection and no fun whatsoever.)

DaftKnives: in today's complicated and crazy world of modern jihad, certain ancient multicultural activities such as decapitating Syrians can be a blunt and bloody affair, let's face it! But no longer. With a brand-new set of stainless steel, Aussie-Barbeque style designer DaftKnives, you'll never be without the sharpest utensils you'll ever require for all those messy medieval tasks. But wait, there's moor! Each set of DaftKnives comes with a free box of matches in case you urgently feel the need to roast an infidel alive in his cage. Hours of fun for the whole family! (Caution: some proscribed activities may be illegal under international law.)

DaftVirgins: why wait until you get to the Pearly Gates? With our enticing new range of 72 Inflatable Virgins, you can collect all the heavenly delights you could possibly require whilst still enjoying life here on Earth. DaftVirgins come in a range of shapes and sizes, with ages, er, sorry, we mean sizes, ranging from a zesty, youthful nine to a more mature and fulsome eighteen. Collect the whole set!

A well-known Greens MP is forced to apologise to a conservative Senator for potentially defamatory comments made about actions during the Iraq war.

Bandting together

10 February 2018

This week, following urgent requests from concerned readers, *The Fin*'s highly acclaimed sustainable and compassionate etymologist Professor Rowena Handsome-Young explores the unusual philology and usage of the word 'bandt'.

Bandt of Brothers: famous war TV mini-series in which a motley group of Greens senators and MPs (known as 'Cowardly Company') are forced to bandt together for a long march through the institutions. Over ten gruelling episodes the series details their exploits fighting Australia's interminable and bloody Culture Wars. Starting with extreme neo-Marxist training at the notorious Campus Melbourne, they learn to battle their way into parliament by making increasingly ridiculous and absurd comments in front of live TV cameras, such as 'It's true coz I saw it on Sea Patrol' and 'that man is a war criminal'. The central character, Major Richard Di Natale, manages to keep his household together throughout the entire series by paying his au pairs well below the minimum wage.

Bandt on the run: classic Paul McCartney album which tells the story of a rock 'n' roll bandt who are 'stuck inside these four walls, sent inside forever' after they refuse to apologise for defaming a decorated war hero by calling him a war criminal and are sent to prison. As the music crescendos, the protagonist attempts a daring escape with a six-word apology but falls flat on his face in front of the 'jailer man' and, more worryingly, 'Sailor Sam'. Lyrics include ideological references to climate change and renewables, when the 'rain explodes with a mighty crash' and the MP, a rooftop solar panel devotee, 'falls into the sun'.

Sergeant Molan's Lonely Hearts Club Bandt: another classic McCartney song and Beatles album about a lonely new senator who is attacked by a group of nasty Greens who like to eat 'marshmallow pies', 'go upstairs and have a smoke', then 'blow their minds out… getting high with a little help from their friends'. Characters in the concept album include a mysterious 'girl with kaleidoscope eyes' who hasn't got the faintest clue about her own superannuation policy. The album, much like the group's policies, is rumoured to have been heavily influenced by hallucinogenics.

Bandt-Aid: a quick six-word apology that you hastily stick over an open sore hoping to stop the bleeding. If bleeding persists, see your lawyer.

The Bandt Played On: famous popular gay pride song known for its poignant chorus: 'Adam would waltz with a strawberry blonde, And the Bandt played on, He'd glide cross the floor with the boy he adored, And the Bandt played on, But his brain was so loaded it nearly exploded, Jim Molan shook with alarm, Adam went on Sky but had to apologise, As the Bandt played on.'

Bandticoots: often confused with rodents, these small, omnivorous pests are a nuisance throughout our inner-cities, but are most commonly found lurking at taxpayers' expense along the shores of Lake Burley Griffin. These parasitic creatures require a wide variety of fictitiously threatened habitats, from 'disappearing' coral reefs and 'rising' sea levels to 'melting' ice-caps, in order to have any hope of survival.

Bandtwagon: colloquial expression for any cheap political stunt or lefty fad, such as gay marriage, changing the date of Australia Day, or 'war crimes', that brainless undergraduate politicians with zero credibility or genuine policy proposals eagerly jump onto in order to get interviewed on the nightly news.

Bandty-legged: genu varum (also called bow-leggedness and tibia vara) is a varus deformity marked by (outward) bowing at the knee, which means that the lower leg is angled inward (medially) in relation to the thigh's axis, giving the limb overall the appearance of an archer's bow. This common inner-city deformity is caused by deficiencies in diet, such as too much frothy milk in coffee, a lack of red meat and an excess of greens.

Bandtpass filter: an electronic circuit within the human brain that allows absurd and ill-informed concepts to pass unhindered into those lobes that form speech patterns during live TV interviews. Also blocks thought patterns at more logical or common-sense frequencies from ever entering the brain.

Bandtsaw: is a saw with a long, sharp blade consisting of a continuous bandt of toothed metal. They are used principally in branch-stacking, lopping unwanted commie Greens senators, and backstabbing for the leadership when Di Natale least expects it.

Bandtwidth: this word has a number of meanings but since the popularisation of the internet generally refers to the volume of information per unit of time that a transmission medium (like an internet connection) can handle, which in the case of the Greens-supported NBN, is virtually zero.

Bandteau bra: perfect for gender fluidity homework, Safe Schools tutorials or after school-hours breast-binding, this strapless style of self-supporting padded bra also comes with side openings for easy access.

Barnaby Joyce gets caught up in a 'sex scandal'.

Star-crossed lovers

17 February 2018

As Canberra's shadowy world of sleazy affairs and ill-fated lovers comes under scrutiny, *The Fin*'s own scarlet lady, Rowena de Pompadour, explores history's most famous star-crossed lovers.

Barnabeo and Vikkilet: the ultimate tale of forbidden love between two rival families, the Cabinets and the Staffers. Shakespeare's clever use of constantly switching between comedy and tragedy is what gives this, his greatest work, such poignancy. Tragic moments such as Barnabeo's tear-jerking 'My Wife and Four Daughters' soliloquy are immediately punctured by laugh-out-loud absurdist scenes such as Friar Malcolm's Morality Code, a classic piece of bawdy Elizabethan satire. The play itself ends very badly, with the lovers running away together to Maguire's Motel and Trailer Park in Armidale where they decide to fatally poison the Coalition's opinion polls with a potion reluctantly given to them by the 'inept' Apothecary Signor Turnbull himself. In the end, Barnaby has had enough and declares 'a plague o' both your houses of parliament! They have made worms' meat of me!' So saying, he resigns, the Nats lose his seat in a landslide, and the 'fool's paradise' of a Turnbull government is over.

Mark Barnaby and Vikkeopatra: possibly the most famous couple that ever lived, these lovers ruled the world of tabloid newspapers for an entire fortnight in the ruthless, intolerant age of MeToo. Alas, their love proves too great for the world, as Mark Barnaby is torn between duty and love; between his responsibility to the Coalition and his flat in Armidale; between the by-election he conquered and his passion for Vikkeopatra's short skirts and tank tops. Complex, charismatic, and fierce, Vikkeopatra is a mother-to-be, a lover, a Tabloid Queen. Meanwhile, terrified of his own short-comings and inept leadership, Gaius Malctavian stirs up animosity against the couple, partly because he hasn't a clue what else to do and partly because Lucius Turnbullus tells him to, or else! During a panicky press conference Malctavian introduces a new Morality Code to come into immediate effect, leading Barnaby to declare 'The worm is not to be trusted...' When Malctavian's entire Cabinet breaks into open rebellion (because most of them are currently bonking their own staffers) the opinion polls collapse. Devastated, Malctavian falls on his sword and Barnaby falls back into bed.

Vikki the Great and Barnaby Potemkin: Time: Mid-winter, 2017. Place: Winter Ball, Canberrovitch, on the frozen shores of Lake Burli-Griffinski. Walking into the glitzy ballroom is Barnaby Potemkin, whip in one hand and wife in the other. But young ambitious staffer Vikki is already smitten. She persuades Barnaby to move her into Matt Caravaggio's dacha as a 'senior media adviser'. Then when Barnaby Potemkin is declared a dual Russian-Austrian citizen, she gets him to create another fictitious job, but for slightly less money. After Barnaby gets re-elected, he and Vikki move in together under the protection of a local Count who owns a motel. Despite the fact that Barnaby Potemkin is a buffoonish character with a ruddy face, is several decades older than her, and is an uncouth bumpkin with wandering eyes, the two become secret lovers. But fate has other plans...

Prince Beetroot and Mrs C: one of history's most tragic and heartfelt apologies was delivered early in 2018 during a radio address to a stunned public by His Stuttering Royal Highness Prince Beetroot: 'I-I have found it i-impossible to carry the h-heavy burden of responsibility and to dis-discharge my d-duties as leader of the N-N-Nats as I would wish to do without the help and s-support of my s-senior media advisor, Mrs C-c-c-c...' Prince Beetroot, heir to the House of Tony Windsor, is often portrayed as a hapless and forlorn character who gave up one of the most coveted and cushiest positions on earth – Deputy PM in a Coalition government—all for the sake of a young media adviser. Forced to abdicate by a furious Queen Lucy for breaking her husband's sacred Morality Code (even though it didn't exist at the time) the Prince and his mistress are exiled to spend the rest of their lives partying as tabloid celebrities in a luxury rent-free apartment in Armidale.

Barnaby Abelard and Vikeloise: Vikeloise is a bright, gifted media adviser in 12th century Paris who wants most of all to answer the question of career advancement. Barnaby Abelard offers to tutor her, and although he is 20 years her senior, the two fall deeply in love. Soon Vikeloise is pregnant. A scandal is imminent, so the couple flee to Armidale. The local priest, a crusading zealot called Malcolm, finds out and is furious, and in a hastily-organised doorstop interview introduces a brand-new Morality Code. The fired-up tabloids threaten to lynch them both, so Vikeloise takes refuge in a nunnery (as a highly-paid media adviser) but Barnaby's career is, alas, castrated. Or is it...?

A dark festival of disturbing satanic rituals takes place as Barnaby Joyce is forced to resign following his 'sex scandal'.

Dark Mofo

24 February 2018

Following *The Financial Review Magazine*'s excellent coverage of Dark Mofo, the creepy orgy of satanic and other pagan art forms that takes place annually in Hobart, *The Fin*'s own edgy creative director, Rowena Moaner-Gallery offers up her own truly gruesome conceptual pieces to really excite the luvvy crowds.

The Slaughtered Bull: a magnificent piece of dark performance art in which the entire Coalition Cabinet is invited to participate. To the accompaniment of a strange and discordant acapella choir of ministerial howlings, a former prime minister is dragged in front of the captive audience and slowly dismembered on a large, urine-soaked wet bed. As chunks of his sinister Sydney Institute speech are read out aloud, calling for a cut in the annual rate of immigration, the audience, led by a mysterious Belgian soloist and the famous 'Smirking Man of the Shire', are invited to join in a frenzied free-for-all; first by shrieking with laughter and finally by ripping the former PM limb from limb and rolling around in his bloodied carcass. Not for the faint-hearted.

Dark and Dangerous Polls: drawing heavily on 2015's hugely successful collaborative show-stopper '30 polls trajectory', in which a volunteer from the Lodge is publicly crucified immediately after his 29th bad poll, this latest re-interpretation requires a new volunteer from the

Lodge to fabricate the most implausible and laughable excuses that he (or his wife) can think of in order to avoid meeting the same grisly fate.

The Second Woman: a midnight screening of the highly pornographic documentary about the perverse love life and sexual peccadillos of a man in a large hat who leaves his wife and four daughters for a femme fatale seductress known only as The Senior Media Adviser. The screening includes a salacious viewing of the entire series of original News Corp front pages and punning headlines detailing the sordid affair read aloud by a nondescript and bland Nationals MP picked at random from the backbench. At the end, the audience are invited to pile on the humiliations, make up their own sexual harassment claims, form a lynch mob and throw beetroots at him until the man in the hat also agrees to go to the backbench.

Poo Machine: an extraordinary sculptural artwork that replicates the gastroenterological journey food takes, beginning at mastication and ending several hours later in defecation, complete with the authentic smell. Visitors are invited to view the 'feeding' twice a day, where a staff member places gigantic wads of billions of taxpayers' dollars into the so-called 'Ultimo' receptacle. Visitors gasp in amazement as the money is greedily ingested, slowly passing through a range of hardcore leftwing bureaucratic processes before it emerges at the other end of the machine as faecal sludge, or 'ABC programmes' as they are euphemistically called. If they can stomach it, audiences are then invited to participate in the excretionary process themselves by holding their noses and watching an entire episode of *Q&A*.

On Darkness: one of the most realistic artistic installations yet undertaken by Dark Mofo, this year it will not only be Tasmania but the entire state of South Australia that is plunged into darkness for weeks on end. Designed by our inspirational installations guru Jay Weathersick, and curated by world-renowned 'con' artist Elon Musksticks, the entire state is powered for at least three and a half seconds by the world's largest toxic lithium sculpture (especially designed to resemble a plausible energy policy) powered entirely by gigantic stacks of taxpayer subsidies and retirees' electricity bills.

Nude Solstice Swim: in which cabinet ministers and their staffers are invited to participate in a nude frolic across Lake Burly Gropin'. The object is for the ministers to experience the unfamiliar act of 'sexual self-restraint' and to 'purify' themselves in the freezing cold waters whilst resisting the natural temptations of the flesh in keeping with monastic practices of abstinence in the modern workplace.

Lucy Says: deeply disturbing surreal performance art where the Prime Minister of the day ignores his colleagues and instead gets his wife to run the country.

*The Russians poison a couple on a park bench as, to the consternation
of colleagues, Bill Shorten flip flops again on Adani. And a bank tells its
staff what words they can and cannot use.*

Assassination/Unhelpful words

10 March 2018

The world of political assassinations and intrigue was rocked to its core
this week when a man believed to be the leader of the Opposition was
found slumped on a park bench in the seat of Batman. Experts believe the
'sleeper agent' had been poisoned by a disgruntled element within his own
party to punish him for double-crossing them in his support for the Adani
coal mine.

The man, who had a bright greenish foam oozing out of every orifice,
was rushed to intensive care where he continued twitching violently
from left to right and mouthing incoherent and self-contradictory
sentences. Medics initially suspected a form of highly toxic nerve agent
had destroyed the man's neural pathways when he started gibbering in an
unfamiliar language saying 'wiv', 'uvver' and 'enviramennly-stackup' until
it was pointed out that was his normal speech pattern.

Authorities refuse at this stage to speculate who administered the
deadly man-made gas, believed to be a concentration of politically-
charged CO_2 developed in a James Cook University lab from molecules of
powdered bleached coral, although intelligence experts are keen to explore

the theory that a 'hit squad' of rogue CFMEU and MUA thugs disguised as a Chinese woman in a pie shop may have spiked his pie.

Investigators are busily tracing the man's final movements, including a mysterious $17,000 snorkelling trip in a helicopter funded by a millionaire neo-Marxist ad man passing himself off as a tax-free 'conservation charity'.

Others point to the presence in Canberra recently of a dangerous KGB cell, rumoured to comprise notorious Soviet agents 'Albo' Albania, 'Tanya' Plebiscite and Ms Moneypenny-Wong, all of whom had both the opportunity and the motive to administer the fatal dose.

Meanwhile, the federal Labor party also remains in a self-induced coma, with scientists pointing to the presence of a clear, colourless, tasteless and odourless chemical called Shortin which paralyses opinion polls and fatally drains all credibility and integrity out of the helpless victim.

In other news this week, NAB's Diversity and Inclusion Council released a new handbook outlining what words and phrases are no longer appropriate for a modern, successful, dynamic corporation to allow in the workplace. The Council's Chairthingy, Dr Kon Henry, explained to an enrapt audience of diverse CEOs and inclusive Human Resources officers, that in the modern era of 'social purpose', certain old-fashioned words, ideas and attitudes are now defunct. In this 'cut-out-and-pin-on-the-office-latte-machine' guide, *The Fin*'s economics expert, Rowena d'Alberici, has compiled a complete dossier of words your staff must never be permitted to utter, even in jest.

Profit: this is a highly offensive and objectionable word which we believe has no place in the modern workplace, as it suggests that some business or corporate tasks may be undertaken for the express and noxious purpose of attempting to create wealth by exploiting your workforce's culturally diverse and inclusive skills-set.

Toil: a completely inappropriate word to employ anywhere near your, er, employees, this demeaning and aggressive word carries with it

Victorian-era connotations such as 'blood, sweat and tears', which imply the highly objectionable expenditure of additional effort or energy outside your HR-mandated working guidelines.

Trickle-down: a vile and disgusting concept from a long-forgotten era when a business or corporation would attempt to hang on to some of the money it made on the erroneous grounds that it would re-invest that cash in a larger and/or better-paid workforce.

Merit: an insulting and deeply divisive word that suggests some people are better equipped than their fellow diverse and inclusive workmates to perform certain tasks and therefore should be employed on that peculiar basis, rather than be selected for the obvious reason that they are a woman, gay, transgender, brown-skinned or, preferably, all of the above.

Competitive/competition: a terrifyingly non-inclusive sentiment, the idea that business can in some way be compared to a sports competition resulting in 'winners' and 'losers' is so obsolete and offensive that it beggars belief that there are still individuals out there who cling onto such a repugnant view.

Success: unfortunately, too many managers (old white anglo-saxon males, predominantly) still confuse the idea of success in the workplace, taking it to mean fiscal rewards gathered through the dubious acquisition of market share (itself a dangerous concept from an HR perspective) with the far more successful social reward of a warm, fuzzy, happy, delightfully inclusive and culturally tolerant workplace. To be safe, we recommend banning the word 'success' altogether.

Survival: a vulgar term whose crassness can be immediately discerned by the fact the word frequently pops up in various non-inclusive and demeaning 'reality TV shows', the word is doubly offensive due to its racist links to Charles Darwin's deplorable Victorian-era concept of the 'survival' of the 'fittest', thereby reducing the complexities of the modern, dynamic, socially-purposeful workplace to little more than barbaric animalistic behaviour.

Following a week of chaos, Malcolm Turnbull is dumped as Liberal leader and Prime Minister in favour of Scott Morrison, defeating challenger Peter Dutton by 45 votes to 40. Josh Frydenberg is elected deputy leader.

Ad man gets the top job

25 August 2018

Finally, Australia has a Prime Minister with a solid advertising background. But how can Scott Morrison apply the tricks of the trade he learned in his years as Marketing Director of Tourism Australia to the benefit of the country he now leads? *The Fin*'s own marketing and advertising expert, Rowena Groin-Transfer, takes a look at how our 30th Prime Minister's expertise in the dark arts of creative advertising slogans could serve Australia well.

'Where the bloody hell are you?' In this fresh and innovative new ad campaign, a bikini-clad Laura Tingle wanders around the beautiful, pristine Australian coastline looking for the million or so Liberal voters who have deserted the party in droves. With her cute girl-next-door looks and Aussie twang, Laura is the perfect embodiment of the innocence and friendly openness of the mythical Australian swinging voter as she casually strolls from one unmanned polling booth to the next in search of someone—anyone!—who will hand her a Liberal 'how-to-vote' card. As she pops into her local bank, she discovers an elderly group of retirees trying to draw money out of their superannuation accounts only to find they are completely empty! Laura's frustration grows as she visits

beautifully filmed popular tourist destinations around the country but the mythical 'grey nomads' are nowhere to be seen because they can no longer afford the holiday they'd been promised their super would pay for. In the dramatic closing scene, the camera pulls back to reveal a sweeping shot of dozens of retirement villas on a cold chilly night with all the electricity and lights switched off so that typical Aussie retirees can meet their Paris commitment.

'Throw another PM on the barbie.' If there's one thing people from all around the world know about Australia, it is our laid-back, friendly habit of cheerfully tossing a discarded PM onto the scrap-heap at least once a year. In this delightful ad, a laconic, smirking Scott Morrison warns potential tourists of the natural dangers down under, from getting wet in the surf to getting dumped by your own party.

'You oughta be congratulated.' A revamp of the classic '80's margarine ad written and performed by the multi-award winning MoSco agency and the legendary creative duo of Alan Morrison and Scott Johnson, this typically jaunty jingle and cheesy visuals takes a look at the everyday life of a cheerful, smiling Treasurer as he goes about his business dramatically cutting into excessive government spending and profligacy with an extra blunt butter knife. 'You stopped the boats and stopped illegal immigration. You stole half of our superannuation. No one else can do, a budget just like you, you oughta be congratulated.'

'Liberal One Day, Labor-lite The Next.' Capturing the sunny optimism of a famous 1990's tourism slogan for Queensland, this new modern Liberal party slogan perfectly embodies the breezy, lazy sameness of every single moment in Canberra, in which one day merges effortlessly into the next and the policies of the two major parties remain completely indistinguishable from each other. Bliss.

'A hard-earned thirst'. With its earthy visuals and sweaty atmosphere of smoky backroom deals and weekends spent working the numbers, this

timeless TV ad conjures up the hard-earned work of a Treasurer forced to work day and night to help himself to the fruits of hard-working Aussie retirees who've worked year in year out to get their hard-earned super only to discover the government has nicked it. The lyrics capture the poignancy and heartache of a typical leadership challenge: 'You can get it wheeling, you can get it dealing, you can get it just after noon. Matter of fact I've got it now. A leadership thirst needs a big cold spill. And the bitterest cold spill is Lib. Liberal Bitter.'

'*100% Pure New Leader.*' Imagine the beautiful sunny uplands of a pristine new Australian political landscape basking in the purity of its renewable energy targets and bounteous, abundant gifts of nature such as an unlimited supply of coal, gas, uranium, er, hang on, wrong script, are we still in Paris or not? Is the NEG dead or not? Are we building a new coal-fired power station or not? Josh? Josh?

'*How do you feel?*' Another from the classic MoSco stable, in which a former hero of the conservative side of politics has to wrestle with the impossible dilemma of keeping the party together despite his own acts of treachery and betrayal of his core supporters. 'How do you feel, when you get the job, from the lefty mob, and conservatives squeal? How do you feel, when you've got to try, to put all behind, and get the party to heal? And the climactic answer: 'I feel like a reshuffle' never fails to bring back fond memories. Or even possibly Tony Abbott.

Former prime minister Malcolm Turnbull licks his wounds and disappears into oblivion in New York City. (Or does he?)

Mal goes to NYC

1 September 2018

Malcolm Turnbull and his wife Lucy are off to New York for six weeks in order to avoid the hassle of having to hand out 'how-to-vote' cards in dreary old Wentworth. But six weeks is a long time for a man with as many talents as our former PM to spend hanging around in a foreign city. How on earth will he fills his days? *The Fin*'s New York entertainment correspondent Rowena Bigg-Apples offers some helpful tips:

A visit to the Meat Packing District: If you've always been handy with a knife and don't mind getting a little blood on your hands, what better place for you to pick up a few new modern butchering techniques than a day spent in this famous New York neighbourhood? You have to get up early, but part of the fun is seeing your own handiwork hanging up in the window afterwards. You can even give the carcasses their own names— like Tony, Brendan, Peter etc.

A tour of Trump Towers: More popular than ever, a trip to Trump Towers is a must for any serious visitor to New York these days. What a pity you didn't bother when you had the chance back in 2016 but were too busy taking selfies with Barack Obama instead! Still, take the subway to 53rd/5th Avenue and you'll see this magnificent 58 story skyscraper in front of you. Once inside the splendour of the Atrium allow yourself a few quiet moments to contemplate the baffling success of a single-minded politician whose enviable popularity is built entirely on the fact that he eschews all forms of political correctness and who has brought his country's economy roaring back to life by pulling out of Paris.

The Battery: Also known as Battery Park, this splendid 25-acre park is located at the southern end of Manhattan. The Battery is named after the giant battery that the world's most successful entrepreneur Elon Musk installed as back up for New York's amazing renewable energy windmills and solar panels which these days give New Yorkers their abundance of clean, green energy. The giant battery can power the entire city of New York in the event of a blackout for approximately 0.000000001 seconds! (Just kidding, it's not really named after a giant battery. Nobody would ever buy a story as silly as that.)

Grand Central Terminal: What better metaphor for the terminal state you left your political party in and of course the inescapable fact that you've reached the end of the line and your political journey is well and truly over.

Central Park: Beautiful and romantic, no trip to New York is complete without a stroll or a carriage ride through Central Park. But do be careful! Avoid speaking to any strangers (such as random Aussie voters) or you might get mugged by reality.

The Theater of Disappearance at the Met: A must-see for the curious tourist, this intricate installation features detailed replicas of hundreds of objects that have mysteriously disappeared from history! Objects depicted include the Australian Liberal party's massive majority originally won in a landslide by Tony Abbott at the 2013 election that has inexplicably vanished, the trust and confidence the Australian electorate had in the Liberals and the belief that they were morally better than Labor—gone!— the lowest energy prices in the world—gone!—record low Australian government debt and your own political popularity. Not a trace of them to be found!

Rockefeller Centre: From the famous Observation Deck with its banks of binoculars you can gaze down across many of New York's most famous buildings, including peering into the office windows of your old firm, the world-famous merchant banking mob who have made billions of dollars out of promoting such beneficial and important projects as the highly lucrative trading of carbon credits which of course relies primarily on leaders of governments around the world ratifying laws to 'combat catastrophic climate change'.

Tickets to Hamilton: Broadway's finest musical about the most extraordinary figure in the history of politics; a young boy who grew up destined to become the greatest Prime Minister Australia would ever know, but who despite his extraordinary talents of innovation and agility and phenomenal popularity and commitment to renewable energy was betrayed by a sinister right wing cabal of climate deniers disguised as Sky News 'after dark' chat show hosts which brought this brilliant political leader crashing to (is this right—ed?) (No, it's not—Rowena).

A trio of academics release hoax peer-reviewed papers designed to highlight the decline in modern academic standards.

Hoax

6 October 2018

The world of academic hoaxes was rocked to its core this week as three top academics admitted that a series of fake papers that they had written as a joke and then submitted to leading research journals had been favourably peer-reviewed and published as authentic scientific papers. In this exclusive expose, *The Fin*'s science correspondent, Professor Rowena Sokal-Hoakes, reveals some of the most famous scientific hoax papers and analyses the 'nutty and absurd' theories designed specifically to fool gullible academics.

'We are all doomed (except me)' by Professor Timothy Flannelshirts, I.P.C.C., U.N, Institute of Global Climate Studies, Batchelor of Possum Defecation Patterns in the Lower Hawkesbury (1998), University of Hawkesbury River Flats: In this hilarious paper, the hoaxer posits the ludicrous idea that the entire planet is facing imminent catastrophic destruction due to the preponderance of a mysterious invisible gas emitted by farting cows. With a straight face, the author claims that within a few years as the deadly Flatulent Bovine Gas makes its way into the Upper Troppo-sphere the rivers will all run dry, the dams will all be cracked and empty, the North and South Poles will turn to mush and the world's oceans will rise by up to thirty metres flooding coastal habitats with drowning polar bears and dehydrated defecating possums from New

York to San Francisco to London to Hong Kong (except, oddly, the Lower Hawkesbury, where the author expects real estate waterfront property prices to boom thanks to a scientifically-acknowledged counter-effect known as Flannel's Lower Hawkesbury Global Warming Real Estate Oscillation Index).

'*Trumble's Snowy Turbines Perpetual Motion Theorem' by Professor Lucy Turbine with research assistance from Mr Malcolm Turncoat Emeritus Batchelor of Spills and Political Judgment, University of Cooma, Snowy Mountains (currently Visiting Fellow at the Academy of Miserable Ghosts, Central Park Bicycling Track, New York):* In this brilliant hoax paper, the authors concoct a superbly absurdist scheme that is designed to pass any peer review by promising to generate sustainable and renewable energy through the eco-friendly method of pushing millions of gallons of fresh, clean Snowy River bottled sparkling mineral water back uphill so it can perpetually create clean and renewable eco-energy as it gurgles and gushes back down the pristine mountainside. In order to overcome the fairly self-evident Newtonian and Einsteinian laws of physics that this theory would normally challenge, the authors have suggested a gigantic pipeline be constructed directly from an underground bunker in Canberra to the Upper Dam itself, where a constant flow of billions of so-called 'taxpayer dollars' will ensure the eco-friendly sustainability of the entire project for all eternity.

'*V-for-Victory, V-for-Victa. Securing Our Naval-Gazing Future' by Professor Kristina Pyne, Batchelor of Mardi Gras Studies (postponed), University of Winning Circles, Cherry Bar, South Australia:* In this laughable paper, already peer-reviewed and eagerly accepted for publication in the highly respected French scientific journal 'Le Grand Rip-Off', the author suggests that through the simple expedient of buying a dozen or so highly advanced nuclear submarines that can silently prowl the waters undetected for months on end and swapping their engines with

Advanced South Australian built and designed 2-stroke Victa Lawnmower Engines Australia's naval supremacy and national security will be ensured for decades to come—namely, those decades that begin in about four decades time.

'Brainwashing Begins at Three' by Professor William Shortpants, A.W.U., C.F.M.M.E.U., Batchelor of Mushroom Workers Salary Thresholds (wiv Hons), University of Albanese: Wiv vis paper I want to make sure vat we get every little boy and girl, er, sorry, I mean every little ze and hir and uvver, er, transfluid persons into Kindy so vey can start learning about the Trade Union Movement and Catastrophic Climate Change and Gender Fairies, er, I mean, Gender Fairness wiv teachers who value Fairness etc. etc. until the next election.

'Getting Energy Prices Down, Down, Deeper and Down, Down, Down, Prices Are Down' by Professor Scott Morrison, BSco. Mo., University of Happy Clappers, Pentecostal Avenue, Cantor, Paris: Despite an extensive process of garnering peer-reviewed approvals (45 in favour, 40 against) the jury is still out as to whether or not this is a genuine paper or a deviously clever hoax. Supporters of the paper point to a favourable review and citation from renowned realist and pragmatist and Rhodes scholar Professor Angus Beef-Taylor, whereas critics point to the last-minute intervention by an obscure left-wing academic writing under the improbable pseudonym of Marise Pain who claims from New York that the entire scheme rests on the full implementation of the Paris Accord. Clearly a hoax, then.

Red shoes

30 November 2018

The world of empowering bright young women to enter the toxic world of masculine politics was turbo-charged this week following the inspirational gesture by our former Foreign Minister to donate her red satin 'resignation shoes' to Canberra's famous National Female Grievance Museum.

Fighting back the tears as the cameras flashed and a bevy of empowered young news floozies, er, sorry, highly-skilled journalists and diverse and inclusive television reporters tripped over TV cables and each others' red stilettos desperate to get a shot of the one female politician who so successfully overcame the dark forces of misogyny, sexism, toxic masculinity and men in blue ties (wasn't that the whiny redhead?—ed), the former Foreign Minister proudly announced the reason for her extremely generous and thought-provoking donation: 'Finally young girls and women seeking empowerment and inspiration will get to come to this museum and ponder what Australia's most successful, talented and let's face it, appallingly treated first female Foreign Minister actually stood for, er, I mean stood in.'

Opening the brand new taxpayer-funded wing of the museum dedicated to celebrating her extraordinary personal popularity and amazing political skills—to be called the Scott Morrison Hall of Perpetual Shame and Infamy Wing—the former Foreign Minister announced that her red shoes were only the beginning of what promises to be a magnificent collection of various items of fashionable clothing and personal belongings that commemorate the key moments of her glittering career. They include:

The Empowering Silk Shawl of Female Emancipation: worn to world-wide acclaim on her highly-praised diplomatic trip to visit the fragrant, peace-loving and benevolent ayatollahs of Iran in 2015, this long rectangular shayla, or headscarf, which can for added allure be tucked or pinned at the shoulders, was woven from the finest Persian silk by a team of highly experienced and dedicated Iranian boys with very small fingers who worked tirelessly night and day in their empowering Isfahan orphanage to handcraft this emblem of female emancipation from tyrannical white colonial oppression especially for this historic visit, the first of its kind by an Australian female fashion affairs, er, sorry, foreign affairs minister.

A closer examination of the intricate stitch work reveals hidden delights, barely visible to the naked eye, including elegantly scripted local customary greetings which translate loosely as 'Give us our Nukes' and 'Death to Israel, Death to the Great Satan'.

Smashed China set: A potent reminder of the exceptionally gifted manner in which our first female foreign minister so skilfully handled the delicate relationship with our most important neighbour and potential aggressor China, this extremely expensive porcelain china tea-set in its quaint 'Fragile. Handle With Extreme Care' DFAT packaging somehow or other ended up smashed to smithereens. Students and visitors to the museum are encouraged to work out how to put the pieces back together again, although this may prove a fruitless task.

Original, signed copy of Yassmin's Story by Yassmin Abdel-Magied: a collector's delight, this un-opened copy of the riveting story of the author's personal journey from top-of-the-class Christian schoolgirl to hard-working engineer to ABC Islamo-luvvy is in mint condition as if it had never even been opened! Accompanying this prized first edition book are a number of handwritten notes by the author herself, comprising of boarding passes, hotel receipts, restaurant bills and other empowering book-tour expenses from across the Middle East all of which have been signed off and stamped by the DFAT accounts department.

Original, un-opened invitation in pristine, sealed envelope: absolutely mint condition invitation circa early 2016 for the former Foreign Minister to meet and build a personal relationship with Republican candidate for the US presidency, D. J. Trump esq.

Red satin 'clutch' purse containing various loose items: deserving of a special wing all to itself, girls and young women will be amazed and inspired by the number of deadly self-advancement implements that can be concealed within one such tiny and innocent-looking personal fashion accessory. These include a razor sharp and carefully concealed dagger which can easily be slipped into the palm of a delicate female hand and wielded with alarming efficiency and deadly accuracy in the dead of night; a fold-up calendar with a bright red circle around the mysterious date of 14 September 2015; and a pocket torch and map showing the location of a garden shed in Queanbeyan complete with encrypted WhatsApp notes detailing MPs attending the meeting.

Also known by fans of the former foreign minister as her 'Loyalty Kit', this much-loved clutch purse is immediately recognisable as being a perfect match for the red satin shoes also on display, although fashion experts note that the clutch originally came in pure white, but somehow or other became stained bright red over the years through constant handling and contact with some unidentified sticky substance on the owner's hands.

2019—the Year of Miracles

Safely ensconced in his own harbourside mansion in Kirribilli as well as in the Lodge, Scott Morrison, or ScoMo as he has now been universally nicknamed, is faced with losing the forthcoming election to the unlikely pair of Bill Shorten and Chris Bowen.

Proving that only those with a healthy sense of humour should be entitled to predict the outcome of Australian elections, this author is one of the very few commentators who accurately predicts that Scott Morrison will indeed pull off a miracle win.

Naturally, such a victory would not have been even remotely possible without the brilliant contributions of Labor MP Chris Bowen's sensible advice to disgruntled retirees: 'if you don't like Labor's policies, don't vote for us.'

Cracks appear in a Sydney tower.

Faulty Liberal Towers

11 January 2019

In shocking news this week, the developer of Sydney's troubled Liberal Tower is demanding an explanation on what's gone wrong with the disaster-plagued building, telling conservatives who were forced to flee their natural home that it could be years, if not decades, before they dare return.

Irate conservatives have been forced into temporary accommodation for over 36 months since fleeing on 14 September 2015—as specialists carry out investigations to determine what caused the once-proud Liberal Tower to subside so dramatically.

Although a spokesperson for the troubled Tower claims it is 'basically sound', experts disagree; pointing the finger of blame at the pre-fabricated Turnbull Tiles that proved completely unsuited to the job.

'They'd been boasting about how slick and modern these Turnbull Tiles looked and how easy they were to install, but it turns out they were all just for show and had no substance to them whatsoever. Immediately we put them in, the entire edifice started wobbling. You could see large cracks opening up right before your eyes.'

Horrifying photos have emerged of leaky pipes stuffed with waffle-baffles and ceilings collapsing under the sheer weight of excessive verbiage.

Angry conservatives claim that last year a new team of interior decorators from the Shire were brought in to paper over the problems with a fresh veneer of locally-sourced ScoMo cladding, but already fracture lines are starting to appear.

'They told us every unit could have cheap energy prices AND lower carbon emissions, but of course that was all just marketing blurb. From the day we moved in our bills have gone through the roof and our popularity has gone through the floor,' said one desperate former resident.

Another pointed to the base of the building, which is currently deserted. 'I've no idea where we stand any more,' she complained. 'We asked Mr Texta from the PR firm but he just laughed and said we have nowhere else to go.'

One distraught resident believes that the Tower should never have been built on such an ideological swampland in the first place—but engineers say that that shouldn't have been a problem thanks to the sturdy '90s-era Howard foundations, which have held up remarkably well.

Indeed, local real estate experts recall the enormous popularity of the development when it first came on the market in 2013. 'The original Warringah designs sold off the plan like hotcakes. People were so excited that here was somewhere that everyday mainstream conservative families could finally feel relaxed and comfortable in, without being harassed by prancing inner-city latte-sipping bicyclists with avocado-stained beards.'

Said another homeless victim of the Tower: 'Little did we realise, but there were these black ants, sorry I mean Black Hands, white-anting the entire joint before we'd even moved in. It was a disaster waiting to happen.'

Critics are adamant that the main fault actually lies with the flashy Sydney development group Photyos, Zymmerman & Co, who poured squillions into their glitzy Green Lobby with its transgender solar panels and renewable rainbow-powered windmills but in doing so undermined the entire structural integrity of the Tower.

Union officials promise the Tower is due for demolition in May of this year.

Revenge thriller

9 February 2019

The world of Hollywood heart-throbs was rocked to its core this week following the shock admission by a leading male superstar that he used to harbour dark revenge fantasies and would roam the streets at night, sometimes for weeks on end, looking for someone to violently extract vengeance upon.

Liam Turnbull made the shocking announcement during a run-of-the-mill press conference last week in which he was asked to explain his 'motivation' for playing the lead role in his latest blockbuster, 'Cold Pursuit'; a dark film about an ordinary, everyday prime minister who calls a spill on himself, loses, then sets about extracting vicious and bloody revenge on all those colleagues who dared to vote against him.

The theme is similar to a long line of revenge thrillers Liam Turnbull has starred in in the past, all of which involve a psychopathic narcissist of one sort or another convinced he's the smartest person in the room but who in fact turns out to be a surprisingly hopeless politician who keeps getting dumped but then mysteriously refuses to disappear into oblivion.

The firebrand actor first came to the public's attention when he starred in the tear-jerker 'Swindler's List', the true story written by Thomas Keneally about a wealthy merchant banker who draws up a list of his favourite luvvies to become the first-ever President of Australia after he leads them to a magnificent and historic victory in the 1999 republican referendum. However, the film ends badly when the public won't have a bar of it. There isn't a dry eye in Point Piper as the villainous John Howard 'breaks the nation's heart' in the closing, tragic 'ballot count' scene.

But it was in the blockbuster thriller Turncoat (Dec 2009) and its terrifying sequels Turncoat 2 (Sept 2015), Turncoat 3 (July 2016) and Turncoat 4 (Aug 2018) that Liam Turnbull created the extraordinary revenge character known as 'The Waffler' a pitiful everyday millionaire Dad who hides away in his harbourside mansion whenever he can't bring himself to face the public and then uses his only son to act out his unquenchable desire for violent and bloodthirsty revenge.

Critics, however, complain that the series has long since failed to achieve any genuine suspension of disbelief, relying on the same contrived plot line in each new film, as The Waffler tries to convince everybody around him that he can save the planet from catastrophic climate change by pushing water uphill and getting people to invest in hopelessly unreliable renewables but invariably each film ends in the same predictable disaster. In particular, the script-writers clearly lack imagination in finding new 'villains' to have wronged the innocent martyr The Waffler, relying on trite stereotypes such as a bloke in a pair of red speedos. Worse, the so-called 'heroes' of each script, all based on the sinister Dr Felps-Steggles of the original 'Turncoat Disappears in Wentworth' smash hit and described in the marketing blurb as being 'your typical independent sensible-centre former Liberals' are horribly miscast and desperately unconvincing in the role.

In one of the most memorable and oft-quoted scenes, The Waffler wanders the leafy streets of Double Bay promising revenge for having had his prized National Energy Guarantee ripped from his grasp. During a passionate and intimate conversation with his two female stars Lucy and Julie he delivers one of his most chilling performances: 'I will find them all. I will destroy them all. I will hunt them down, one by one. I will tear down the entire Liberal party if I have to.'

A tearful Christopher Pyne explains in an interview that
'Malcolm is Aslan to me', bizarrely comparing Malcolm Turnbull to
C.S. Lewis's character Aslan in the children's novel The Lion,
the Witch & the Wardrobe.

Aslan

16 February 2019

The world of Narnia was rocked to its core this week following the shock discovery of a 'secret chapter' of C. S. Lewis's famous chronicles. Deemed too explosive to ever be released, the terrifying denouement has now been revealed exclusively to Fairfax by Narnia scholar and expert Mr. C. Pyne of Adelaide.

Far from being a wonderful, omnipotent, messianic Christ-like figure, it now appears that the lion king Aslan was in fact a psychopathic narcissist millionaire banker who lived in a harbourside palace with his Queen plotting to seize power from the rightful Lord of Narnia, Prince Tony:

'This must be an enormous wardrobe,' muttered young Christopher as he took another step forwards, arms outstretched. He was a snotty-nosed, smirking boy, the sort that the popular boys would steal lunch money from. But Christopher was also a fantasist who saw himself as a 'fixer' who would build the world's greatest naval fleet and had even designed a boat that could sail underwater driven by lawnmower engines and powered by the wind! He had, of course, heard stories from his uncles Peter and Edmund about a magical land, that could only be entered into through

Aunt Susan's wardrobe, where dreams came true so long as you believed in Aslan!

As his aunt's garments brushed gently against his face, Christopher took another step. He could feel something crunching beneath his feet, like broken glass. And then he saw there was a bright light, like a disco ball, not a few inches away where the back of the wardrobe should have been but in the distance. Suddenly he felt a clammy hand on his shoulder and spun around. To his surprise, it was a half man, and a half goat. 'Welcome to the Cherry Bar,' hissed the pointy-faced Faun, handing him a large glass of bubbling Turkish Martini. 'My name is Mr Trent.' 'Am I in the magical land?' said Christopher, breathlessly. So the stories his uncles had told him were true! 'You are in the winner's circle,' giggled the Faun, 'where all dreams come true if you want them to!' Christopher took a sip, and glanced back over his shoulder. He could just make out Aunt Susan's dresses and the open door of the wardrobe and the light coming from his empty electoral office. But there was no going back now.

'Count me in,' he smirked. 'What do I have to do?' But the Faun had already skipped away, twirling with his friend the Satyr to the pounding music and flashing lights.

'Would you like to meet Aslan?' whispered a seductive voice in his ear. 'He's waiting for you.' Christopher spun around again. She was smiling at him, her bright eyes sparkling, her blonde fringe teasing him. Her diamond earrings twinkled in the lights! Christopher swore he had never seen anyone more glamorous or powerful-looking or awe-inspiring. 'You must be… Queen Lucy,' he stammered, awkwardly. But to his surprise the woman's smile turned into a nasty snarl. 'Ignorant fool! Lucy is his wife. I am his Empress! Empress of All Lands over the Sea, you snivelling brat.' With that she stomped away, and Christopher's face went as bright red as her shiny stilettos.

Normally, of course, Christopher would have blubbed at such a put-down, but now he felt emboldened by the scent of power. He was in the winner's circle, after all, just like his friend Mr Trent had told him. That meant anything could happen!

And just at that moment the most extraordinary thing did happen. Aslan came sauntering into the Cherry Bar, and everybody instantly fell to their knees and a hush fell over the room. Even Mr Trent and the Satyr let go of each other. 'Oh Aslan, we worship you, Oh Aslan the Innovator,' they all started wailing in unison. 'Oh Aslan, you who will stop the seas from rising and who can push water uphill even in the Mountains of Snow, we praise you! Oh Aslan, you who will give us weddings so marshwiggles can marry dufflepuds, we adore you! Oh Aslan, you who will defeat Tony at the Battle of Onion's Breath and banish him forever to the land of War in Gah!'

Christopher felt giddy, and in his excitement he didn't notice what you or I would have noticed. And that, of course, was that this wasn't the real Aslan at all! It was just a cunning, grinning harbourside alley cat dressed up to look like a genuine lion! But nobody cared, because the fake Aslan had told all the dwarves and hobgoblins of Narnia that they could have whatever they wanted so long as they gave their undying loyalty to him – and not to the rightful ruler.

The magical land and its forgotten people would never be the same again…

Former foreign minister, failed leadership candidate and Turnbull's biggest fan Julie Bishop announces she is quitting politics and is 'confidant the government will be returned to office'.

Lady Macbeth

23 February 2019

In a bombshell announcement this week, Lady Macbeth said that she would quit the stage before the opening night of Shakespeare's most famous tragedy. Appearing in her trademark blood-stained shoes at a packed press conference in Stratford-upon-Avon, Lady Macbeth was seen vigorously washing her hands backstage before announcing she was satisfied Shakespeare would win the Golden Globes in May.

'I have reconsidered my position as the leading female star,' she sobbed, fighting back the tears and dabbing at her eyes with a concealed brown onion that, mysteriously, somebody had taken a bite out of.

'I've been contacted by a number of talented actors, including one who plays a Christian porter, who have indicated to me in the strongest possible terms that this is my final Curtin.'

Lady Macbeth was surrounded by her closest colleagues - three witches from the cross-bench and Turnbull's ghost.

Lady Macbeth served four consecutive kings of Scotland, but was most famous for sleepwalking outside Peter Hendy's Queanbeyan lair one night in September 1615 whilst a motley group of bit-part actors including her own chief of staff were busy plotting the bloody slaying of the king they had sworn to loyally serve.

In other bombshell news this week, Lucrezia Borgia announced that she would quit playing politics before the next papal bull due in May because she was satisfied the Borgias would retain the Holy See. Said a tearful Lucrezia, speaking at a packed press orgy: 'I have reconsidered my position as the leading female politician of the Renaissance. I've been contacted by a number of talented, indeed extraordinary noblemen, including my very own brother Cesare Porter, who have indicated to me in the strongest possible terms that my poisoning days are well and truly over.'

Lucrezia Borgia loyally served four consecutive popes, none of whom were available for comment because they're all dead.

In other bombshell news this week, Mata Hari announced that her double-crossing days are over and that she would resign from the Deuxieme Bureau before the end of war as she was satisfied the Prussians would win it. Said a defiant Mata, photographed in front of a pre-selection firing squad wearing nothing but her trademark pearl tiara and exotic dancing shoes: 'A politician? Yes. But a traitoress? Never!'

In other bombshell news this week, Cruella de Vil announced she was resigning from the fur coat trade because she was satisfied the puppies had escaped and would win first prize at May's 'Best in Show'. Cruella made the shock announcement as she raced away to the airport in her chauffeur-driven Commonwealth car wearing her trademark fur coat, pearl earrings and red high-heeled shoes. Ms de Vil came to international prominence in her starring role in the animated cartoon '101 Parliamentarians', in which a bumbling group of 54 hopeless MPs meet in a dark Queanbeyan backyard shed and plot to skin the PM alive and replace him with a psychopathic narcissist. Her most famous line was: 'If you want a loyal deputy in politics, get a puppy.'

In other bombshell news this week, Mrs Danvers announced that she was resigning as head housekeeper at Manderley because she knew it would burn to the ground sometime in May. Mrs Danvers was best known for jealously keeping alive the flame of her dearly departed Malcolm, a charismatic leader whom she believed ScoMo could never hope to emulate.

In other bombshell news this week, Jezebel announced that she was quitting her royal duties because she knew she would be thrown out of her window at the next election. The bejewelled princess became a household name when she convinced her party to switch their allegiance from the rightful PM and start worshipping the false gods of Malcolm and climate change instead.

In other bombshell news this week, Carrie announced she would quit practicing telekinesis and hurling knives through the air without even touching them because she now accepts she hasn't a hope in hell of ever being crowned Prom Queen. Best known for her terrifying 'death-stare', Carrie was frequently spotted wandering around Canberra in the middle of the night with her hands covered in blood and leaving the Liberal party room a blazing wreck behind her.

In other bombshell news this week, Nurse Ratched announced that she would resign before her next shift because the lunatics were threatening to take over the entire asylum. Said the unrepentant Head Nurse: 'Just because I lobotomised the Liberal party, helped install as Chief a grinning narcissist with a borderline psychopathic personality disorder, ratified the bonkers Paris Agreement and paved the way for all the Labor loonies to take over the cuckoo's nest in May doesn't mean I shouldn't be rewarded with a cushy job at taxpayer expense somewhere like Washington or Geneva'.

In late February 2019 it is announced that Cardinal George Pell has been found guilty of child sex offences. It would be another fourteen months before the verdict would later be overturned by the High Court. In a piece that never gets published, I have a crack at what is widely acknowledged to be the lowest form of humour, a bunch of dodgy puns.

If I pell

Unpublished

Taking of Pellham 123

Classic 1970s thriller movie in which a gang of defrocked priests takes a group of drunken choirboys hostage in a runaway pope-mobile. When the police try to interview them, one of the choirboys pulls the dead-man's switch but even though the first trial goes completely off the rails the second one gets the green light and goes careering ahead. One of the priests ends up in jail.

William Pell

Famous legend in which a prominent member of the Pontifical Swiss Guards who happens to be an expert swordsman, William Pell, is forced to take aim at a young drunken choirboy conveniently tied up to a tree in the grounds of the Apostolic Palace and, er, shoot an apple off his head. For centuries experts have debated the metaphorical and subliminal messages in the tale and its warning to young choirboys. In the end William Pell manages to jump off a boat on appeal and escapes into the Holy See.

Pell's Bells

Opening track on the best-selling hard rock 'Back in the Sacristy' album by Australia's most famous heavy metal band. The song begins with a bell slowly tolling before the lead guitarist dramatically enters the vestry on the shoulders of a drunken young choirboy and to the delight of the audience starts peeling off his sacramental robes. The song builds to a thundering crescendo which lasts for five or six minutes which is, some musicians argue, only at the vanilla scale of hard rock climaxes.

For whom the Pell tolls

Classic novel by Ernest Hemingway set in the turbulence and chaos of the Spanish Culture Wars. As the lefties fight the Catholics, a group of guerrillas are sent to dynamite a cardinal's reputation. As the deadly fascist planes sweep down out of the sky, the guerrillas, led by El Sordid, take refuge in an abandoned Catholic church, only to stumble upon a priest mucking around with two drunken choirboys in the sacristy. Critics have long argued over whether Hemingway's lurid description of the priest's state of undress was even remotely physically possible given the cumbersome garments of the day.

If a tree pell in the sacristy, would anybody see?

An age-old philosophical conundrum, first mooted by George Berkeley in 1710 when he pondered whether a tree falling on a deserted island actually made a sound. Can something exist without being perceived by consciousness, is a question that has plagued scientists and philosophers ever since. Even Albert Einstein struggled to prove that the moon exists when nobody is looking at it, and modern philosophers have wrestled with the equally tricky question of whether an archbishop can interact physically with a choirboy in a room with an open door if nobody walks past?

Pell me why

Classic Neil Young song from his folksy 'After the Rush to Judgment' album, famous for its melancholic and introspective observations that it's 'hard to make arrangements with yourself'. Fans have long argued over the precise physical contortions required to 'make arrangements with yourself' if one hand is already occupied doing something else, such as struggling to get the alb, the stole, the chasuble, the dalmatic and all the other ceremonial tunics over your head.

If I pell

Classic early Beatles ballad which tells the story of a love gone awry as John Lennon plaintively sings that 'I've been in love before/ And I found that love was more/ Than just holding hands.' The song featured prominently in the band's first movie, in which the Fab Four try to escape from their wild and adoring female fans by taking refuge in a church, where they stumble upon a group of choirboys singing 'help!'. The film ends just as 'Father Mackenzie' discovers them in the sacristy 'biding their time, drinking his wine.'

Pelly's Heroes

Classic '70s cult movie in which a group of US soldiers during World War II decide to sneak behind enemy lines in order to rob a bank. The plan goes awry when they encounter a Panzer division and are forced to take refuge in a local Catholic church, where they hope to disguise themselves as priests in order to escape detection. The film's final scene, when they break open the door into the sacristy, was mysteriously left on the cutting room floor.

In an interview with legendary (and incredulous) BBC interviewer Andrew Neil, deposed leader Malcolm Turnbull puts forward the theory that he was dumped by his colleagues because they thought he was going to win, describing the vote against him as 'a peculiar Australian form of madness'.

Mad Mal

9 March 2019

In a world exclusive, *The Fin*'s in-house historian Prof Rowena Blainey-Windshuttle reveals that a cache of papers discovered down the back of a sofa in an obscure Point Piper harbourside mansion is in fact the transcript of a secret diary in which Napoleon Bonaparte explains his defeat at Waterloo. The notes were smuggled off Elba by veteran pamphleteer Monsignor Andre de Neil, following a bizarre interview in which the deposed Emperor explained the real story behind what should have been his most famous victory:

'Mais oui, if you look at eet objectively, monsieur, eet is clear what really 'appened. Let us look at ze facts, non? Eet is well-known zat my Grande Armee was level-pegging wiz ze Duc of Wellington and ze Prussian army and in fact I had ze secret polling zat showed my cavalry was at least four points ahead of zem in ze marginal village of Hougoumont when tout a coup mes generals zey decided to pull me off my 'orse! You could argue zat zere concern was not so much zat I was going to LOSE at Waterloo but zat I was going to WIN! Eet was a peculiarly Belgian form of madness.'

In other shocking revelations, the mysterious reason behind the hitherto-unexplained failure of Apollo 13 to land on the moon has been dramatically exposed in a surprise interview between Flight Commander James A. Lovell Junior and veteran astronautics reporter Andy F. Neil. In the interview, the commander of the only Apollo mission that ever failed to complete its mission spells out the reasons for the disaster:

'What's clear, Mr Neil, if you look at the facts from an objective and rational point of view is that I was well on the way to reaching the moon as per schedule and my craft was level-pegging with the orbital trajectory of the lunar surface and indeed some of my instrumentation indicated that I was at least four light years ahead in a marginal astrophysical plane when all of a sudden my co-pilots decided to abort the mission! You could argue that their concern was not so much that we'd miss the moon altogether and go hurtling off into outer space but rather that we would actually land on the moon and I would become an international hero! And that of course infuriated them. It was a peculiarly lunar form of madness.'

In other shocking revelations, a last-minute log-entry found hastily scribbled on a paper napkin in an encrusted bottle on the sea bed off the Azores Islands by veteran marine explorer Andrew Kneel reveals the true story of what happened to the abandoned brigantine, the Mary Celeste:

'We are sailing along beautifully and making good time towards our destination and indeed level-pegging with the Portuguese coast and in fact by my secret calculations at least four nautical points ahead of the marginal outer reefs, but suddenly the crew have decided to toss me overboard! You could argue that their concern is not so much that we are becalmed but rather that they don't want me to safely get them to shore! It's a peculiarly Portuguese form of madness.'

In other stunning revelations, a hitherto undiscovered parchment believed to be a lost chapter from the writings of media slave Andreas Neilius Cicero reveals the untold story of how the Roman commander and the world's richest renewables investor (is this right?—ed) Marcus Licinius Crassus came to lose the Battle of Carrhae in ancient Turkey. Cicero is clearly incredulous as he quotes Crassus's own words:

'At the time of our approach across Mesopotamia we were level-pegging with the horse archers and we were four points ahead of the foot-soldiers in the marginal court of King Artavasdes II. Then suddenly 65 of my legates stab me in the back! You could argue that their concern was not that I would lose the battle, but rather that I would win it and become the greatest, wealthiest, most powerful and most loved person in the ancient world. It was a peculiarly Parthian form of madness.'

Aslan 2

6 April 2019

A hush fell over the large crowd of hobgoblins, dwarves, satyrs and
dufflepuds, as Prince Christopher rose to his feet. His face was flushed
from the heat of battle. 'My fellow Narnians,' he declared, brandishing
his sword in the air, 'to those of you who have betrayed me, and to those
of you—far too many I'm afraid—whom I have betrayed, I am standing
before you today to declare that it is time for me to hop back into the
Closet, er, the Wardrobe.' A chorus of loud groans and guffaws and
ghoulish gibbering echoed across the giant stone hall of Cair Paravel,
once the hallowed throne room of Aslan himself but now a hideous and
treacherous swamp of intrigue and embittered enmities. 'But before
I return to my own land,' exclaimed Christopher, 'I would pray ask
your indulgence, friend and foe alike, to reflect upon the many great
achievements of my time as a reigning Prince of Narnia.'

The grunting and groaning quietened down, and you could hear an
awkward shuffling of hooves and sense the nervous sideways glances.
'Achievements?' muttered Tony, the Lord of War-in-Gah and Master of
the Brown Onions, looking puzzled. 'Were there any?' 'Don't be such
a meanie!' hissed Mr Trent, the half man-half goat, who was looking
resplendent in his new royal feather boa and rainbow tiara. 'Thanks to
Prince Christopher every Narnian kiddy now learns at school than he

can grow up to be a boy or a girl or a mugglepod or a rumblebuffin or whatever other creature ze wants to be! Even a King can be a Queen now!'

'It's twue,' lisped Mr Timnis, the moderate fawning faun, who had once been a fierce warrior for the free speech of all the animals in Narnia until he fell in love with another faun and promptly forgot all about such silly principles. He turned and to the delight of his close circle of friends, raised a gin and tonic and loudly pronounced: 'Here's to Pwince Fixer and his Winner's Circle! Now even a Beaver can marry a Beaver! Fweedom of weligious expwession be damned!'

'My dear, dear friends,' shouted Prince Christopher, brandishing his sword in the direction of the beach below, 'Behold the mightiest of my many triumphs! Look upon the Narnian Navy that I alone am responsible for, the finest fighting fleet ever assembled!'

Now, it's true that if you or I were standing there we would have been slightly perplexed. For what Christopher was pointing at was certainly not the finest fleet Narnia had ever seen. The wooden shells of a dozen or so ships were scattered across the beach. Christopher had purchased them from the Frog and Snail Eaters across the Seas for the somewhat extravagant sum of fifty billion gold doubloons. But for reasons best known to himself, Christopher had decided to 'adapt' the vessels to his own design by chopping down their magnificent masts and ripping down all their resplendent sails and replacing them with small wooden paddles. Of course, the local Narnian ship-builders and craftsmen were not only far too polite to point out that the boats were now hopelessly un-seaworthy, they were also rather keen to keep their well-paid jobs, not to mention their heads.

With a sorrowful shake of his own head, Christopher wiped away a single tear from his cheek, and gazed forlornly out to sea. 'Were Aslan still here, He would be so proud of me!'

At the mention of Aslan's name, a strange unsettled feeling crept over the crowd. For nobody had yet dared to tell Prince Christopher that the Aslan he had so slavishly served and fought so many battles for and stabbed so many other Narnians in the back for wasn't in fact the real Aslan at all. It was a fake Aslan, a cunning trickster called Mr Trumble who dressed up as a Lion and lived in the Great Mansion Upon the Harbourside with his wife Queen Lucy and the Red-Shoed Witch.

Thanks to them, the once-mighty and wealthy Kingdom of Narnia had turned into an impoverished, backward industrial wasteland littered with gigantic windmills that never turned, rusted solar panels even though there had been no sunshine for years and magic electric cars that didn't work. A land that foolishly believed you could make water flow uphill in the Mountains of Snow.

But everybody in Narnia knew that when the real Aslan finally returned, his wrath would be mighty indeed.

As Christopher disappeared forever back into the Closet, everybody got back to noisily bickering. But then there was a sudden commotion from the crowd. A new pretender was strutting arrogantly towards the empty throne. 'Oh no,' cried Mr Timnis. 'What have we done?!?!' Mr Trent fainted. 'We're doomed! It's King Shorty the Dwarf!'

In preparation for the election everyone else says he is bound to win, the Labor leader announces his grandiose plans for mandatory electric cars.

EV

5 April 2019

Marjorie had only been dozing for a few minutes when the alarm went off. She never got much sleep when she knew the grandkids were coming for the weekend. She glanced across at the time; 3.47. Hauling back the covers she shivered as she quickly pulled on some clothes. The retirement village units had Optional Heating but most of the residents chose not to sign up for it. She scurried downstairs and drove round to the Recharging Bay. She smiled warmly at her elderly neighbour, but he merely scowled back at her as he waited to the very last minute to unplug before driving his car back to its spot. The village only had six rechargers for over thirty units, so everyone worked to a strict three-hour roster. Marjorie had the Tuesday and Friday 4 am to 7am slot. With any luck, that would get her car close to three-quarters charged for the weekend.

Or so she'd hoped. But at six on the dot the power went down as an ELM kicked in— typically just as Marjorie was hopping into the shower. She swore under her breath. Labor's (upgraded) Electricity Load Management Suburb Selection Schedule 'blackouts' as she called them, although her son always snapped at her for using such politically-incorrect language in front of his kids—was even tougher than last year, in keeping with PART 2, the recently-ratified second Paris Agreement

Revisionary Targets. The government said the ELMSSS was random, but Marjorie and many others couldn't help noticing that it seemed to happen far more in blue ribbon suburbs than in Labor ones.

Her son and the kids arrived bang on time, as always. Although the traffic was a nightmare at the start of the Indigenous Day long weekend, fortunately, because of his position as an Environmental Brigade Union official, her son got to use the Green-Lane reserved exclusively for government employees.

Marjorie was keen to take them down to the beach for the day, and had phoned up and booked a table for three at the kiosk there, including one hour's worth of recharging. Like everybody who didn't work for the government, the constant stress of ensuring you had adequate charge was just an irritating fact of life.

But the trip took a lot longer than planned. There was an FBVI—a flat battery vehicle incident—in the Spit Tunnel and all the traffic piled up. As always, one FBVI led to several more along the way. The NRMA's fleet of mobile diesel turbo-chargers were flat out and had to be given right of way by all other traffic. Crawling through the tunnel Marjorie was forced to play over and over her grandchildren's favourite pop star Jaylye. Marjorie had no idea if Jaylye was a boy or a girl, or a bit of both, as was all the rage these days, but when she'd complained to her son about the lyrics ('Can I keep the fun bits of me to play with later?') her son had snapped at her for being genderphobic. Marjorie sighed as she watched her charge slipping away. She turned off the music and heating and let the kids shiver in sullen silence.

Finally they cleared the tunnel. But by the time they got to the beach, she knew, she would have missed her booked hour of charging at the kiosk, so she had no choice other than to take her chance at the Customer-Only Chargers at what used to be McDonalds. It was now a Medicare Inclusive Healthy Living Outlet, which served subsidised halal vegan takeaway food. Her luck was in – there was one free charger available, but just as she pulled up a young man shot in front of her and took it, giving her a rude gesture.

Eventually she managed to grab eight minutes of battery turbo-charging (a 'Shorten', everybody called it), even though she knew from bitter experience that turbo-charging ruins a battery's life—only last year she'd had to put in a new one at a cost of $2,500. The kids didn't believe her when she told them that she used to fill up her beloved Corolla in less than five minutes. And all this effort, she muttered to herself, for nought. Her friend at the retirement village, Zang, had seen a report on the dark web about how China still emitted more CO_2 every month than Australia saved in a year. The kids finally got to the beach at 4.30 and had a quick swim. But the water was freezing, and they sat shivering on the sand in their wet towels. On the drive back home Marjorie switched on the radio, where the weatherman was explaining that the Antarctic Vortex, for the third summer in a row, was conclusive proof of global warming.

A mysterious fire sees the roof of Notre Dame burn to the ground as Labor leader Bill Shorten struggles to explain the cost of his policies.

Notre Bill

18 April 2019

The world of crumbling edifices was rocked to its core this week as one of civilisation's greatest landmarks was engulfed in a firestorm and came crashing down in front of shocked onlookers. Experts fear that the damage is so extensive that the famous structure, Notre Bill, could collapse at any minute. Built up over many years and containing rare and invaluable artefacts, Notre Bill is the soul and beating heart of Labor's electoral prospects and Australia's most revered place of worship for climate believers. Panicked experts fear that it could take decades—if not longer—to restore Notre Bill to its former glory; and that the cost to the grieving public could be in the many billions. (347, to be precise—ed.)

The inferno that ripped through the leafy outdoor press conference in Boothby on Tuesday is believed to have been sparked when an itinerant TV journalist, Channel Ten's Jonathan Lea, asked Mr Shorten about his emissions reduction target and what the cost to the economy would be. Alarm bells started ringing when Mr Shorten tried to avoid the question altogether, and within minutes the PR disaster was out of control. Despite the valiant efforts of over 500 emergency spin doctors and ABC luvvies who rushed immediately to the scene to try and extinguish the lethal blaze, horrified voters watched as Notre Bill was engulfed in a humiliating inability to answer even one simple question.

Despite the extensive damage, experts say Labor's most precious artefacts have nonetheless been saved from the flames. 'A small piece of the original Crown of Thorns, worn by Saint Julia the Persecuted herself when she was crucified alive by an apostate in a blue tie, has survived intact,' declared one elated passer-by. The prized Tunic of St. Albo-the-Patient is also completely unscathed, and it is believed that most of the gargoyles, including Penny, Chris, Tony, Tanya and Kristina, are largely untouched by the disaster.

Onlookers were astonished to learn that Notre Bill's spectacular rose-tinted windows, through which visitors can gaze back fondly on the impressive economic works of St. Paul the Treasurer, escaped without significant damage.

As well as being a popular cultural monument, Notre Bill is a fine example of classic gothic horror politics, propped up entirely by its famous lying buttresses. Built largely on fanatical religious fervour, blind faith and apocalyptic visions of rising sea levels, Notre Bill inspires the most devoted climate believers to don a hair-shirt and pay indulgences of exorbitant electricity bills in order to avoid the end of the world in twelve years' time. Notre Bill is also famous for its numerous reported miracles, with worshippers claiming that if they park their electric vehicles within the shadow of its towers they are miraculously fully recharged within as little as eight minutes.

For decades, non-believers have wondered how such a medieval belief structure could actually survive proper journalistic scrutiny. There were reports that within minutes of the tragedy, vast swathes of Labor's economic manifesto had been wiped clean from its website.

Notre Bill is also the stunning backdrop for the classic novel by Victor Hugo, The Hunchback of Notre Bill, about a hideously deformed climate change believer known only as Quasimalcolm who lives in the ivory towers of his harbourside mansion pulling the strings behind the scenes and slowly going insane as he mutters to himself 'The Libs! The Libs!'

Many concerned citizens have long foreseen the demise of Notre Bill, relying as it did on a complex structure of interwoven new and old taxes, franking credits, super grabs, renewables subsidies, negative gearing, capital gains changes and rolling blackouts. All it took was one intrepid journalist to actually light the spark, and the whole edifice quickly collapsed in spectacular fashion.

In other news this week, the notorious 'journalist' Barrie Assange was finally dragged kicking and screaming and frothing at the mouth out of the Ultimo Embassy where he has spent the last decade holed up inside a tiny cramped studio seeking refuge from the real world.

Barrie Assange, known to his bosses at the ABC as 'the host', spent most of his time irritating everybody by sitting on a couch reading from a notepad and chatting aimlessly to like-minded journalists before smearing conservative politicians all over the studio walls.

'It just got too much,' complained one irate viewer, 'and it was quite frankly disgusting to watch. His personal manners were unbelievable, interrupting Coalition politicians even when they were doing him a favour by appearing on his show.'

Despite his decade long stint as an 'Insider' living entirely indoors without access to sunlight, doctors were concerned that Barrie Assange had an unnaturally healthy-looking perma-tanned pallor. 'We had to get him out of there,' confessed one panellist, 'so we could take over the show ourselves.'

As the election campaign gets underway, a Melbourne comedy festival finds legendary comedienne Barry Humphries is transphobic, or something like that.

Stand-up comedy

27 April 2019

The world of stand-up comedy was shocked by the announcement that the Melbourne International Comedy Festival has stripped Barry Humphries' name from its most famous awards, The Barry's.

To replace The Barry's, *The Fin*'s own transgender comedy correspondent Rowena Leslie-Patterson has revealed that the upcoming Canberra Comedy Federal Festival has decided to name its most prestigious new award The Bill's.

Says Rowena: 'The Bill's are designed to be an entirely new type of comedy award that reflect the modern preference for comedians who make us laugh simply by being true to themselves and performing their routine with a completely straight face. All our comedians take themselves extremely seriously because comedy should never be a laughing matter.'

This year's nominees for The Bill's go to the following outstanding comedy acts:

Chris Bowen: geeky, stand-up performer from Sydney's western suburbs, Chris looks and sounds like your drab suburban accountant but you'll be clutching your sides as he tosses hundred-dollar bills at kids in the crowd whilst cunningly nicking it straight back out of the pockets of all the oldies! Chris's catchphrase always gets a terrific response, when he finishes up by challenging the audience: 'If you don't think I'm funny then don't vote for me.' Irresistible advice!

Rob Oakeshott: a blast from the past! Who can forget Rob's classic 17-minute monologue in which he gets his own two kids to decide who'll be the next Prime Minister!? Rob promises his new act is even crazier, as he dresses himself up as a 'deep Greenie' who will save Port Macquarie from rising sea levels by closing down all its businesses and factories by 2030. As Rob always quips, 'it'll be beautiful in its ugliness!'

Zali Steggles: donning her famous chicken suit and strutting her famous chicken-wings dance, Zali's silent mime routine is a must-see for all lovers of non-verbal forms of communication. You'll be astonished how deftly Zali avoids any live debates or interviews! Zali also mimes being a small-l Liberal before stripping off to reveal a hardcore lefty under all the glam and glitter! More of a get-up comedian than a stand-up one.

Alex Trumble: son of the famous Clown of Vaucluse, Alex writes hilarious gags on Twitter before promptly deleting them the next morning.

Bill Shorten: you'll be rolling in the aisles as Bill performs his brilliant 'doorstop interview' routine where members of the audience are invited to ask him joke questions such as 'what will your emissions targets cost?' and 'do you have any plans to tax super?' The highlight comes when Bill promises to 'look into' tax cuts for millionaires. An accomplished ventriloquist's dummy, Bill can say he's against Adani out of one side of his mouth whilst saying he's in favour of it out of the other.

Bill Shorten turns to McDonalds for oratorical inspiration on the hustings.

Maccas

4 May 2019

The world of spell-binding oratory was rocked to its core this week by the rhetorical device of explaining complex economic and political issues via the simple example of a Big Mac.

But is this really the first time such erudite eloquence has been used to change the course of history? In this world exclusive, *The Fin*'s very own rhetorician Rowena Upsized-Bunns explores the long history of the Big Mac in political speech-making.

Winston Shortchill, 1940: whatever the cost may be, we shall eat burgers on the beaches, we shall eat fries on the landing grounds, we shall eat nuggets in the fields and in the streets, we shall slurp Coke in the hills; we shall never stop upsizing, and even if, which I do not for a moment believe, this Island or a large part of it were starving, then we'll go back and order some more.

Abraham Shorton, 1858: a Ronald McDonald House divided against itself cannot stand. I believe this franchise cannot endure, permanently, with both a Brekkie menu and an All-Day menu. I do not expect the Sausage McMuffin to be discontinued—I do not expect the Classic Angus to fail—but I do expect they will cease to be available at different times. It will become all one thing or all the other.

John Fitzshorten Kennedy, 1963: ich bin ein Hamburger.

Winston Shortchill, 1940: the Battle of the Bulge is about to begin. Let us therefore brace ourselves to our duties, and so bear ourselves that if the Macca's empire with its yellow arches lasts for a thousand years, men will still say, 'This was their finest burger.'

Shortcrates, 483 BC: he is richest who is content with the cheeseburger, for contentment is the wealth of nature.

Margaret Shortcher, 1980: you flip if you want to. The lady's not for flipping.

Shakespeare's Mark Shortony, 1607: friends, Romans, countrymen, lend me your ears. I come to order a Chicken Caesar, not to wrap it.

Shortcrates, 461 BC: the unexamined burger is not worth eating.

Nelson Shorndela, 1964: it is a McDeal I hope to live for and to enjoy, but if need be, it is a McDeal for which I am prepared to pay.

Ronald Shorgan, 1987: Mr Gorbachev... tear down this Wendy's!

John Fitzshorten Kennedy, 1961: ask not what a Triple Cheeseburger will do to you—ask what you will do for a Triple Cheeseburger.

Marcus Billius Shortero, 63 BC: a Drive-Thru without Big Macs is like a body without a soul.

Arishortle, 342 BC: the Big Mac is more than the sum of its parts.

Martin Luther Short, 1963: I have a dream that one day under the yellow arches of Georgia the sons of former slaves and the sons of former slave owners will be able to sit down together with a Family Size McValue Box.

Franklin Delano Shoortevelt, 1933: the only thing we have to fear is Burger King itself.

Queen Elizabeth the Shortest (addressing her troops), 1588: I know I have the body but of a weak and feeble woman; but I have the appetite and stomach of a king, and of a king of England too, and think foul scorn of Hungry Jack's and KFC.

Alexander the Short, 326 BC: I have asked you to meet me here at

Macca's so that we may come to a decision together: are we, upon my advice, to go forward, or, upon yours, to stick around for the McFlurry's?

Marcus Billius Shortero, 68 BC: if you have a garden and a library, you have everything you need, so long as you remembered to stop at Macca's.

Arishortle, 354 BC: we must no more ask whether the soul and body are one than ask whether the beef patty and the gherkin impressed on it are one.

Mahatma Shorti, 1942: ours is not a Drive-Thru for power, but purely a non-violent fight for an independent Indian franchise.

Shakespeare's Shortlet, 1601: to beef or not to beef, that is the question. Whether 'tis nobler in the end to suffer the slings and arrows of outraged vegetarians, or to go a Double Quarter Pounder Wagyu and by opposing infuriate them?

Margaret Shortcher, 1979: the problem with socialism is that you soon run out of other peoples' nuggets.

Neil Shortstrong, 1969: one small step to upsize, one giant obesity problem for mankind.

Marcus Shaurtelius, 152 AD: very little is needed to make a Happy Meal; it is all within yourself, in your way of thinking.

Bill Shorten, future Prime Minister of Australia, 2019: but if you had a friend who was perhaps on the large side, the chubby side, and they had 10 Big Macs a day… there's a cost to not eating the Big Macs. But in the long term it's an investment isn't it?

Election day looms and all the pundits predict an easy victory for Bill Shorten. All the pundits? Not quite…

Bill's family tree

11 May 2019

The world of family histories was rocked to its core this week following newspaper allegations that the Leader of the Opposition, Bill Shorten, had omitted key elements of his own family's history and his posh upbringing during his appearance on the ABC's *Q&A*. In this exclusive scoop, *The Fin*'s genealogy investigator Ms Rowena Trace-Roots tracks down the lesser-known members of the expansive Shorten family tree.

Professor Bill Shorten-Wivvers (circa 1965): famous elocutionist who specialised in teaching privileged schoolboys and wealthy toffs how to downplay their aristocratic roots by learning to speak as if they were working class Cockney yobbos. Shorten-Wivvers, whose students included the Rolling Stones, various aristocratic playboys, photographers, Michael Caine and many others, sorry, uvvers, was famous for having patented the use of the word 'wiv' in a political context (meaning 'accompanied by') and adding a non-silent 'K' as a suffix to words like 'something' and 'nothing' in order to help disguise a private school background.

Viscount Sir William Shorton-Funds the Third. (circa 1750): famous English landowner and tax collector best known for imposing punitive levies on his hapless serfs to pay for his lavish spending habits. After his crippling Window Tax failed to raise sufficient revenue, Shorton-Funds imposed a Door Tax, followed by a Roof Tax, then a Lavatory Tax and finally his notorious Air Tax which he claimed was necessary to tackle 'imminent catastrophic miasma', a form of noxious fog that he claimed would lead to the end of his estates in twelve-years' time.

'Dopey' Short'un (circa 1905): popular vaudeville comedy act featuring a midget in a yellow vest who would run around the stage pulling silly faces, rolling his eyes heavenwards, sighing heavily, putting a finger on his chin and generally acting the buffoon while a member of the audience had to try and pin him down and ask him a serious question. When finally caught out, Dopey would scratch the top of his head, pull a cheeky grimace, and then use his catchphrase 'that's a dumb question!' to wild applause from the hand-picked audience.

Edgar B. Shorten (circa 1925): well-known ventriloquist and vocal acrobat capable of projecting complex phrases such as 'I promise to stop the Adani coal mine if I win the election' without moving his own lips.

Arthur Shorgill (circa 1980): famous firebrand Yorkshire union boss who as soon as he heard that a bunch of miners were trapped down a Welsh coal mine immediately called up his billionaire mate and got him to fly him there in his private jet with a well-stocked mini-bar so he could be there in time for the TV cameras when they got rescued.

Bill the Ripper (circa 1888): although the actual identity of this famous knife-wielder is often disputed, the body count alone makes Bill the Ripper one of the most notorious and bloodthirsty politicians of his day, with at least two grisly political corpses found (one a nerdy blond, the other a redhead) lying in their parliamentary offices with multiple stab wounds to the back.

Nostrashortus (circa 1520): French apothecary, psychic, clairvoyant, seer and oracle who was able to read peoples' minds even when they weren't in the same room. Famously commented about the legendary

Joan of Arc: 'I have no idea what she is prophesising, but I agree wiv every word she foresees.'

Gretel Shornburg (circa 2019): famous Swedish 16-year old girl who galvanised the world's leaders into declaring a 'global climate emergency' after her mother revealed she can not only 'see' the invisible gas carbon dioxide, but she can also 'see' huge invisible piles of money being generated by renewable energy subsidies and targets.

Enzo Shorrari (circa 1964): famous automobile designer and Formula 1 racing aficionado who designed the world's fastest re-charging electric car, which could fully recharge from scratch in a record 36 hours and 53 minutes.

ScoMo pulls off his miracle win.

Bill's jobs

25 May 2019

The world of federal politics was rocked to its core this week (literally!) following Bill Shorten's astonishing, poll-defying, Hewson-esque, uncanny ability to pull off a reverse-Bradbury with a double pike by coming from miles and miles in front and at the very last moment losing the unlosable election. So what now for Mr Shorten? As a grateful nation weeps tears of relief, the offers are surely pouring in. In this unique Insight Special, our careers correspondent Rowena Jobs picks out some of the tantalising employment opportunities that now await Bill Shorten.

Electric Used-Car salesman: with his solid grasp of the economics and viability of the electric vehicle industry in rural and remote Australia, what better job for a former Labor leader and union boss than that of a used-car salesman? With his chirpy manner and common touch (his missus is the daughter of a fair dinkum Aussie sheila governor-general, you can't get more down-to-earth than that!) 'Honest Bill' would be a real hit with a balloon-strewn yard out in the western suburbs of Sydney or Melbourne. What better person to reassure angry buyers when they come back several hours later that the recharging time for their new purchase is normally only 8 to 10 minutes? And when the buyer asks the price of the vehicle? A simple 'that's a dumb question' will reassure even the most dubious tyre-kicker.

Progressive pastor: with his unique ability to determine who does and doesn't get admission to whichever type of after-life, who better to convince nervous individuals of a religious bent that thousands of years of scriptures or Koranic verses don't actually apply to them? No doubt Reverend 'Purgatory' Bill will have them queueing outside his Confessional, as he blithely reassures drunks, adulterers, liars, fornicators, thieves, atheists, idolaters, apostates and anyone else that they've nothing to fear from a modern, progressive, diverse, inclusive and, er, vengeful God.

Elocution teacher: wiv—er, sorry—with his sublime mastery of the syntax, eloquence and structure of the English language, it is hard to imagine sumfink—er, sorry—something more suitable for Bill Shorten to do than to teach posh, privileged, private schoolboys how to annunciate complex words and phrases in a postmodern, brutalist manner so as to give the impression of an illiterate and disadvantaged working-class background in order to gain entry to the highest echelons of a hardcore left-wing political party.

Marathon runner: having mesmerised athletics fans with his individualistic and unorthodox running style, visually reminiscent of a hobbled galley-slave having spent years in chains finally being allowed the chance to escape, what could be better for our international reputation as a great sporting nation than for Mr Shorten to take up long-distance running? And for the bookies, the exquisite knowledge that no matter how far in fronter 'Shiftyer—' sorry, I mean er 'Swifty' Shorten may be for the duration of the race, he'll always finish last.

Body language trainer: these days, personal success and career development may come down to who has the best inter-personal relationship skills. Do you stand too close to people in conversation? Are you a classic space invader? Does your breath smell? Do you tend to grin awkwardly when others are talking to you? Does stroking your chin make you look more—or less—intelligent? With his instinctive feel for how to communicate via body language, a lucrative career clearly awaits Mr Shorten in training others how to be successful in life by feeling awkward—sorry, comfortable—in their own skin.

Suburban accountant: these days, too many people get confused by all that silly stuff like franking credits and negative gearing and capital gains tax. Who cares? Just hand over all your dosh and Bill & Chris will take care of the lot.

City tour guide: with his experience in not only hobnobbing with, but also demonising, the top end of town, who better than Mr Shorten to sit in an open-top bus travelling through the CBD pointing an accusatory finger at all the rich folk?

Mobile knife sharpener: if all else fails, Bill can always fall back on his most successful talent, his ability to sharpen a knife. Bill's Blades would be a big hit travelling around the shopping malls employing the skills he honed not only on two prime ministers but on an Opposition leader as well (himself).

A journalist has her undies drawer raided by the police.

Undies drawer

8 June 2019

The world of espionage and covert surveillance was rocked to its core this week following the shock raids by the Australian Federal Police on the underwear drawer of a highly respected Canberra journalist. In this world exclusive, leaked to our own political intelligence investigative reporter Ms Regina Grundies by a highly placed and anonymous informant deep within the Department of Defence who goes by the name of (hang on, aren't we supposed to leave that bit out?—ed.), we can now reveal that the AFP has a long and distinguished track record of unearthing secret information simply by rifling through the intimate apparel drawers of some of Canberra's most suspicious and dubious characters. Seized items include:

ScoMo's undies drawer: large signed photograph of former Prime Minister Malcolm Turnbull screwed up and hidden within frayed and well-worn 'Go the Sharks' Men's XXL Y-fronts / ancient shredded copy of 'Where the bloody hell are you?' storyboard confidential focus group results / well-thumbed and heavily underscored copy of 'How Popular is Malcolm in the Shire?' confidential focus group results / Lonely Planet 'Guide to Destinations As Far Away From Canberra As Is Humanly Possible', bookmarked with complementary first class one-way ticket in the name of A. Sinodinos.

Albo's undies drawer: coded documents cunningly disguised as the transcripts of Michael Douglas Hollywood movies with entire paragraphs suspiciously highlighted and underscored in bright fluro yellow / hastily-shredded signed photograph of individual standing outside Westminster with arms around a scruffy man with a grizzly grey beard signed 'All the best Albo, I'll always be your soulmate and your mentor, love and best wishes comrade Jeremy' / ripped leaflet in green red and black 'Free Palestine Now' / crumpled complimentary pass to Green Socialist Left Alliance student Initiation Shindig

Kristina's lingerie drawer: ratings notification and cancellation of TV show (2015), ratings notification and cancellation of TV show (2016), ratings notification and cancellation of TV show (2017), ratings notification and cancellation of TV show (2018) / crumpled 'Vote 1 Labor Keneally How-to-Vote card' (March 2011), crumpled 'Vote 1 Labor Keneally How-to-Vote card' (Nov 2017), crumpled 'Vote 1 Labor How-to-Vote card' (May 2019) / unopened bus map of central Queensland / well-thumbed brand new copy of 'How to Turn Back Boats—the Successful Border Protection Policies of Peter Dutton'

Bill's undies drawer: well-thumbed dog-eared copy of 'Elocution Tips—the Aural Difference between Wiv and With' / two large and well-used butcher's knives (dried blood and DNA samples indicative of repeated usage upon a blond middle aged man and a red-headed woman) / large stack of 55 Newspolls heavily underlined with suspiciously torn out section headlined Preferred PM / well-thumbed dog-eared government document entitled 'Interior Decor, Curtain Measurements & Other Essentials—Preparing for Life in the Lodge' / battery-powered hand-held massage device (recharge time 8–10 mins) / well-thumbed copy of 'That's a Dumb Question! & Other Sneaky Ways To Avoid Serious Scrutiny' / well-thumbed copy of 'Do Gays Go To Hell? & Other Tricky Progressive Theological Conundrums' / Interflora receipt for extremely large bouquet of flowers, champagne and chocolates with accompanying message 'Sorry hun, Stuffed up Big Time Wil U Eva Forgive me? luv Bill' / recently purchased shiny brand new butcher's knife still in packaging

Tony's undies drawer: bulk-purchase discount pack of man-size red Speedos / more red Speedos (loose) / collection of individually wrapped red Speedos (gift pack) / recipe book: 101 tasty varieties of onion

Malcolm's undies drawer: twelve pairs neatly folded and individually pressed breathable anti-odour men's slim-fit boxers medium size 100% cashmere embroidered with 24-karat gold thread monogrammed with hand-crafted blue and yellow Team Turnbull circular logo

Tanya's lingerie drawer: recently purchased set of sharp stainless steel carving knives / recently purchased Sun Tzu novelette / recently purchased Niccolo Machiavelli memoir / recently purchased DVD box set of 29-part series 'The Borgias' / assortment of unusual and exotic-looking herbs and plant extracts

Josh's undies drawer: shredded copy of 'The Climate Sceptics Handbook – Gaia is Crap!' (2013) / shredded copy of 'The Climate Believers Handbook—Save the Planet!' (2016) / new copy of 'The Climate Fence-Sitters Handbook' (2019)

Chris's undies drawer: indecipherable scribbles on aggressively torn scraps of paper including incomplete phrases 'if you don't like…' and 'don't vote for…'

A doco looks at the vile coup that brought down a visionary and noble Prime Minister.

The Dismal

29 June 2019

The world of explosive documentary-style mini-series about constitutional crises was rocked to its core this week following revelations that Malcolm Turnbull's downfall was every bit as dramatic as that of Gough Whitlam's, as seen in the classic mini-series 'The Dismissal'.

Echoing those events, the new mini-series, directed and narrated by *The Fin*'s own Rowena Savva-Speers, is simply called 'The Dismal'.

Says Rowena: 'My film 'The Dismal' clearly pays homage to 'The Dismissal'. I make no pretence otherwise. I couldn't help but notice the extraordinary similarities between the despicable tearing down of Australia's two most significant Prime Ministers, Gough Whitlam and Malcolm Turnbull. Both mesmerising, charismatic, visionary leaders; both supreme masters of oratory with outstanding political judgment and of course both sophisticated, progressive geniuses of the Enlightened Left whose indomitable spirits illuminated the darker recesses of our national soul but who were torn down by sinister forces of the Hard-Extreme Far-Alt Right. It's hardly surprising that in scripting the downfall of Malcom Turnbull, I drew inspiration from the equally treacherous treatment meted out to Gough Whitlam all those years ago.'

Critics have praised 'The Dismal' for drawing out these similarities, as viewers are left in no doubt that as evil as Sir John Kerr may have been

2019—THE YEAR OF MIRACLES

in 'The Dismissal', his role was nothing compared to the villainy and chicanery of Attorney-General Christian Porter in 'The Dismal'. Indeed, director Rowena prides herself on having taken great care to accurately re-construct the truth of events as they unfolded in those dark days of August last year; relying solely on 'highly accurate anonymous sources from the Point Piper district.'

In one poignant and carefully recreated scene, the noble Prime Minister Malcolm Turnbull (played brilliantly by Chris Hemsworth) is confronted in a filthy underground Canberra carpark by a crippled, hunch-backed and scar-faced Christian Porter (played by Geoffrey Rush) who hisses at him through yellowed, rotting teeth, 'you can't just phone up the G-G like that, that would be unconstitutional', before skulking off into the festering shadows.

In another dramatic confrontation, Hemsworth/Turnbull walks into a meeting to put the finishing touches to his extraordinary masterpiece, his Renewable Energy Target, and accidentally bumps into a barely recognisable Russell Crowe who through the wonders of superb prosthetic make-up and sinister harsh overhead lighting looks uncannily like Peter Dutton. As Russell Crowe fumbles to conceal behind his back a large, bloodied butcher's knife, director Rowena, with the deft touch that fans of her work have come to love, subtly cuts to a close-up of a toy Mr Potato Head nodding away on Christopher Pyne's desk.

Indeed, former Defence Minister Pyne (played with a delicate, whimsical touch by Hugh Jackman in the performance of his career) comes across as one of the most sympathetic and likeable characters in the entire drama, with his pithy one-liners and acute sense of the historic importance of events. 'Why are they being such meanies to Malcom?!?' he screeches hysterically at the climax of Part 1, as a naked Jackman visually recreates the raw emotion and suspense of the scene by curling himself up into the foetal position in the spa of his Canberra penthouse.

Again, deploying her unique directorial skills, Rowena's camera lingers on a forlorn plastic model French submarine as it slowly sinks beneath the bubbling waves.

Part 2 opens with a romantic encounter between the two most powerful protagonists, Hemsworth and Nicole Kidman (playing the prime minister's wife Lucy) in an Italianate-style bedroom overlooking the harbour. In one of those tender symbolic scenes that help define character and bring such momentous historic events to life, Hemsworth spots a seagull with its foot caught in a bit of old fishing line out on his jetty and rushes to save its life. Wiping a tear from her eye, the beautiful Kidman, propping herself up on silk pillows, whispers wistfully to the camera: '… and this is the man they seek to destroy.'

Events unfold rapidly as a veritable Shakespearean cast of rogues and villains (including Matthias Cormann played effortlessly by Arnold Schwarzenegger) betray and lie to the Prime Minister as he gallantly fights to save his party and the nation from the chaos and electoral oblivion that awaits should the treacherous plotters succeed in unconstitutionally bringing him down. But Rowena treats some of these rumoured events with the contempt such untruths deserve, preferring to allow the facts to speak for themselves. No mention in the film, of course, of the silly notion that Turnbull stupidly called the spill on himself, but rather, the film devotes a great deal of screen-time to the heroic roles of Craig Laundy (played by Eric Bana) and Arthur Sinodinos (played by Hugo Weaving) who through sound reason and logic seek to divert their crazed colleagues from their suicidal course of action. All to no avail.

The banks are told to self-assess on where they went so wrong.
And the PM says no to a third chamber in parliament for
Indigenous Australians.

Self-assessment

13 July 2019

The world of damning banking self-assessment reports was rocked to
its core this week following a brutal Self-Assessment Report Summary
(SARS) released by one of Australia's leading banks in which the
entire board heaped criticism upon 'nobody but themselves' for their
'unacceptable but entirely excusable practices of blame-shifting and
scapegoating' when it comes to 'challenging self-assessment procedures'
such as 'effusive OROOA (over-reliance on obscure acronyms)' and
'turning a blind eye to and walking away from the repeated use of verbal
clichés' which inadvertently fostered an 'opaque, impenetrable, oblique
and evasive climate of fuliginous corporate jargon'.

Said a spokesperson for the bank's highly-regarded Self-Assessment
Sub-Committee, Ms Rowena Hartzer-Elliott: 'Clearly we have
inadvertently been responsible for a low-performance culture when it
comes to self-judgmental, forthright, transparent and customer-friendly
self-assessment reporting. This is something that we are determined
to immediately address at a grassroots level with our new 16-step Self-
Assessment Reporting Protocol Discussion paper which we are planning
to pin up next to our staff Voluntary Self-Assessment Suggestions Box in
the kitchen at some point in the not-too-distant future.'

What's more, the bank's freshly-branded Self-Assessment Customer Service 'We Are Your Friends, Trust Us' Programme will require all bank customers to self-assess their own new fee structures, allowing account holders and pensioners numerous options of self-assessment including which level of new fee structures they are eligible to compulsorily participate in, ranging from 'Slightly Increased But Spread Across All My Accounts So I Hardly Notice' to 'Barely Noticeable At All But With Lots of Hidden Extras Buried in the Fine Print.'

On top of which, as part of the desire to better engage with the lifestyles of rural and regional account holders, a team of highly-qualified inner-city digital engagement experts led by the multi-awarded Smashed Ads interactive brand agency have developed a special app. According to Head of Corporate Inclusivity, Ayliss Gaia-Rainb*w, 'We call it the 'e-selfie assessment app'! It's so awesome coz like now we get all the bogan farm kids to take loads of selfies standing in front of all their tractors and machinery and cool stuff in the shed and post them on Instagram so the moment their Olds go like into the red we can repossess the lot simply by sticking it straight onto e-bay.'

But the bank's self-assessment processes have been designed to not only radically transform the culture within the bank, but to promote inclusivity and diversity in order to help cut down on wasteful plastic carbon emissions in order to save the planet. 'We ask the staff to self-assess on how much voluntary carbon reduction donations they would like us to remove each month from their paycheque,' explained the bank's Head of Payroll. 'And then we double it.'

'But it's not just at the grassroots level that we want to affect change,' said Ms Harzer-Elliott. 'In order to encourage a far more robust and sustainable self-assessment process at the highest echelons of the bank, the Board has unanimously voted to implement an attractive new Dollar-Plus Director's Leveraged Bonus Self-Assessment Rewards Scheme available exclusively to all current, former and future board members who fill in an online self-assessment form (non-compulsory), effective immediately.'

In other encouraging banking self-assessment news, the highly-respected Governor of the Reserve Bank of Australia, Mr Philip Alltime-Lowe, called an urgent press conference to release his own highly anticipated RBA Self-Assessment Report which had just been handed to him at gunpoint by a Mr J. Frydenberg of Kooyong Heights, Victoria. Said a pale-faced Mr Alltime-Lowe through chattering teeth: 'Basically the Australian economy is going absolutely gang-busters!! Woo-hoo! You beeewdy! Jumpin' Jesus on a pogo stick!!! Hoo-waah!!! Happy days are here again!! Ken oath!! Christmas on a cracker!! Hot diggety! Fo shizzle my nizzle!! Holy moly! Go you good thing!! Yessirreee!! I'll have what's she's having!!! Yippee-kay yay!!... which is why, er, I have to keep on slashing interest rates to zero.'

Meanwhile, in medical news this week, the federal Indigenous minister Mr Ken Wyatt admitted to a packed newsroom that he had unfortunately lost his Voice. Sucking on a Soothers and sipping from a steaming mug of hot lemon tea with a scarf wrapped tightly around his throat, Mr Wyatt croaked to reporters that his vocal chords had been in perfect shape until only a few minutes earlier when he had been asked to pop in for a 'frank and friendly chat' with the Prime Minister.

'Mr Morrison started yelling and screaming at me until he was blue in the face and then booted me out with a string of foul expletives. I never got to utter a single word but somehow or other when I walked out of the PM's office I had mysteriously lost my Voice. And to tell you the truth, it did nothing for my Constitution either.'

Re-imagining a woke Moon landing on the anniversary of Apollo 11.

Woke moon landing

20 July 2019

As the world celebrates the extraordinary achievement of landing a man on the moon fifty years ago today, our in-house behavioural science and organisational cultural psychologist, Ms Rowena Boardroom-Shrinq, reveals that rather than being lauded as a glorious moment in Western civilisation, the Apollo 11 moon landing should be condemned as a seething hotbed of misogyny, sexism, white male privilege, toxic masculinity, Islamophobia and racism.

'Accordingly,' says Ms Shrinq, 'in order for modern corporations to more fully engage with an inclusive historical narrative, I have re-written the account of the moon landing to better reflect the values of today.'

The story of Artemis 11

Addressing Congress in 1961, American president John F Kennedy, a notorious sexual abuser, launched the #MoonToo campaign as a way of diverting attention from his and his brothers appalling treatment of wom*n, many of whom were forced into traditional submissive female stereotypical roles (the seductress, the singing movie starlet, the party girl and so on) in order to prevent them from fulfilling their undoubted potential to design a rocket program.

Much of the desire to reach the moon was driven by the so-called 'space race' between the Russians and the Americans, a clearly racist programme built around the superiority of one race over another.

With their exploitative capitalist system of privilege and oppression, the Americans were determined to humiliate the compassionate, caring, enlightened Soviet socialist community with its proud record of human rights and equality by getting there first.

The Artemis Project, named after the appallingly-treated sister of the god Apollo, saw the most inclusive and diverse range of over 400,000 people ever assembled to work within sensible hours negotiated by union boss Sally McMoonus with three weeks domestic violence leave and Recognition Day holiday in order to complete the project by the end of the decade.

The date for the landing was chosen by consulting Islamic scholars about the precise phases of the moon so as not to clash with Ramadan.

The first lunar invasion occurred on 20 July 1969, when Nell Armstrong-Cortes, an unemployed transgender Hispanic mother of three and Ilhan 'Buzz' Al-drin, a transgender Muslim rap artist made their way carefully down the disabled ramp to take their first tentative steps on the lunar surface, with Nell proudly proclaiming 'one small step for the sisterhood, one giant leap for the trans community.'

During that first fateful trip, Nell noticed that not only was it over 260 degrees Fahrenheit on the surface of the moon, but she also detected sinister traces of carbon dioxide and methane. Worse, the whole joint looked like a giant lump of coal! Looking back at the pristine blue planet behind them, 'Buzz' pointed to the swirling patterns which she immediately recognised as extreme weather events on Earth. 'It was one of those lightbulb moments, except we didn't have a lightbulb, just a torch', said an agitated Nell recalling the event several decades later. 'Buzz burst into tears and said that Earth would become so hot it would be just like the Moon within twelve years unless we stopped mining coal.'

'That's when we realised there was no time to waste and we had to hop back in the solar-panelled landing module and get back to earth as fast as we could to save the planet.'

Meanwhile, back in drought-stricken, cyclone-ravaged, racist, homophobic, sexist Australia, a group of stale, pale old men were tracking the lunar mission on their Dish. Says an irate Rowena: 'To even think of calling something a Dish, with all its connotations of oppressed housewives having to 'do the dishes' and gawking, groping men calling innocent young girls 'dishy' shows just how out-of-touch Australia was back then and indeed still is. And then they go and build this gigantic metal statue to the Dish in Parkes! How insensitive can you get?'

In other moon landing news this week, a spokesperson for MAIDUP Week revealed that astrophysicist and cultural psychologist Rowena Whattawoppa believes that the first Australians had travelled to the moon long before the Apollo expedition. Said an excited Rowena: 'If you go back to the old stories there is clear and unequivocal descriptions of the round shape of the moon and the dark bits on the surface. How could they have been so accurate? There is so much that we are now only beginning to understand about the cultural, scientific and astrological knowledge of the First Peoples as handed down through the millennia.'

Asked to give her thoughts on the anniversary of men walking on the Moon, a clearly agitated Rowena confirmed that given its spiritual, cultural and religious significance to Indigenous peoples, 'it's hard to think of anything more disrespectful than walking all over it leaving dirty great footprints,' she said. 'It's not just this great big rock in the sky, you know.'

Boris Johnson replaces Theresa May as British PM, with a mandate 'to get Brexit done'.

BoJo

27 July 2019

The world of maverick conservative leaders was rocked to its core this week with the stunning elevation of Boris Johnson to the prime ministership of Great Britain. Known affectionately as BoJo, Alexander Boris de Pfeffel Johnson is one of the most flamboyant, charismatic and colourful characters yet to take up residence (alone) in the big double bed on the top floor of Number 10 Downing Street.

But for how long will his bed remain empty? And who are the mystery women who have shaped the life of this most remarkable man?

In this world exclusive, former 'good friend', 'intimate confidante' and 'journalist colleague' Rowena Jolliet de Spiffing Rogers, known to her large cohort of bachelor friends as Jolly Rogers, lists the long line of women who have exerted such a powerful influence on the man she affectionately calls Swinging Boris after she left him dangling over the Thames waving his Union Jacks at her.

Maggie: Boris's late adolescence was dominated by his infatuation for this well-known 1980s Westminster dominatrix 'with the lips of Marilyn Monroe and the eyes of Caligula', also known in top London political echelons simply as 'She Who Must Be Obeyed'. Such was her mesmerising influence over many a hot-blooded young Etonian schoolboy that Boris was rumoured to have kept a large poster of 'Mrs. T' pinned up over his bed on his dormitory wall above the 'I Heart Maggie' doona he would scramble under whenever his fag-master Little Lord Davy Cameron came looking for him.

Nigella Farage: sexy Nigella is the hot tip for who Boris will be jumping into bed with next for a little post-electoral rumpity-pumpity!! Rumours of their love-hate relationship go back all the way to the hot, lusty summer of 2016 when Nigella insisted that Boris immediately 'Leave' with her and cut all ties to Nanny Europe. But like a true Eton cad, Boris blinked at the last moment, bolted indoors and refused to come out to play, leaving Nigella to storm off in a huff. Nigella has only recently re-appeared, throwing her own new party and attracting all the lonely hearts on the Brexit swingers' scene with her Eurotrash-talk and boozy no-nonsense working class appeal.

Michaelia Gove: good-time party girl, also known to her suppliers, sorry, close friends, as 'GoGo', 'Charlie', 'Candy Girl', 'Snowflake', 'Crystal', 'Tootsie', 'Powderpuff' and 'Jellybeans', Michaelia has long had her eyes on the toilet seat at Number Ten. A keen lover of sado-masochistic psycho-sexual parlour games, GoGo has a fondness for exerting equal amounts of pleasure and pain through her exquisite timing of when to offer you her love and affection and when to hastily withdraw it. Also handy with a sharp stiletto and a chief whip.

Trumpie (also known as 'PoTus', 'DoTru' or 'Mr. President, Sir'): to see these two love-birds with their identikit blonde bouffant hairdos and 'shambo-chic' fashion styles playing tootsies under the table with each other you'd think they've been lifelong lovers, but in fact BoJo was desperately unimpressed with DoTru when she first appeared on the international leadership scene, rudely calling her 'unfit' to be Prez! Not anymore! The hot gossip is that Trumpie wants a menage a trois with Nigella, BoJo and herself!

ScoMo (also known as 'who?', 'never heard of him', 'doesn't ring a bell' and 'whatever happened to that prat Malcolm?'): BoJo has always had a soft spot for the Aussie chicks ever since his gap year out here and one of his first plans as PM is to introduce an 'Aussie-style points scheme' for rating his future bed partners. Whether ScoMo, the bodacious bikini model and Sutherlandshire miracle worker famous for her catchphrase 'Where the bloody hell am I?' makes the grade remains to be seen, but a fling later this year or next isn't out of the question. Perhaps they'll even strike up a new trade partnership together!

Jezza Corbynovich: Stunning ash-grey haired undercover Russian soviet KGB operative and Hamas honeytrap escort girl known for her extraordinary inability to seduce even the most luvvy members of the British voting public. By far Boris's best asset!

Tezza May (also known as 'Darling Buds', 'Dancing Queen', 'Mother Theresa', 'Useful as a Chocolate Teapot', 'Useful as Tits on a Bull' and 'Good Riddance'): former British Prime Minister best known for successfully preparing for and then decisively implementing complex Brexit withdrawal from the EU on the specified date of 29 March 2019 no, er hang on, not sure… well… um, give us a mo, will you, what about the back thingy? er, can we make that April 12, um, no? how about October, or maybe next year, sorry, why not? What about a second referend…?

When her plans for an exciting TV career fail to eventuate, a former Foreign Minister opts for a gig at the ANU.

Red Shoes 2

3 August 2019

The world of higher education was rocked to its core this week following the shock appointment of a former foreign minister to the chancellorship of the Australian National University. The radiant new Chancellor praised the university as one of Australia's great institutions and has promised that under her stewardship the ANU will create 'a better world'. But what sort of a better world? In this better-world exclusive, *The Fin*'s higher education correspondent Professor Rowena Louboutin-Gucci examines some of the courses that the new Chancellor may introduce.

Bachelor of Loyalty in Leadership (BLL): an exciting new course which focuses on the diverse and productive roles a 'deputy leader' can play in ameliorating an unsatisfactory political leadership scenario by re-interpreting outmoded concepts such as 'loyalty', 'integrity' and 'honesty' and re-imagining them in a more progressive context. Highlights of the course include a night-time secret workshop in a backyard shed in nearby Queanbeyan where students get to role-play diverse historical figures such as Wyatt Twerp, Peter Hendy-with-a-knife, Mal Dross and Arthur Iscariot.

Bachelor of Superannuation (BS): a complex yet revealing economics course in which students are placed in a high-pressured situation (such as a talkback radio interview during a federal election) and asked whether they have even the faintest clue what their own superannuation policy is. Honorary degrees are also awarded to those students who are able to immediately identify a 'Gotcha!' moment and run away as fast as they possibly can.

Bachelor of Ratification (B.Rat): in these days of catastrophic climate change and extreme global heating, this popular course encourages students to learn how to 'ratify' important and challenging multilateral emissions reduction target agreements without actually telling anybody, particularly the electorate, what they are up to. The successful student will learn that timing is crucial, with students encouraged to 'ratify' their own agreements on the very day that a climate-sceptic US president and his administration are sworn in.

Incision and Insertion Studies (Honours): one of the more esoteric of the new courses, this unique program teaches the ambitious medical/political student how best to subtly insert a fine blade with exquisite precision into the spinal column of a political adversary and then leave the handle of the blade wiped clean of any tell-tale fingerprints.

Bachelor of Feminist Fashion (BFF): combining exciting third-wave feminism, gender fluidity, diversity and unconscious bias theories with the latest hot tips from the red carpets of the celebrity fashion world, this course is a must for the modern woman who wants to 'have it all'. Now you can be an adorable, giggling, girly, bimbo, airhead clothes horse AND a highly-respected, emancipated, intellectual feminist CEO all at the same time!! OMG!!! Course highlights include, well, highlights mainly. Plus: botox injections, pearl earrings, red stilettos, and how to apply blusher, eyeliner, lippy and push-up bra to make the most awesome impression while you're up on the podium educating the impoverished masses about the Evils of Demeaning Female Stereotypes at the Diversity and Gender Equality Workshop in Geneva (all expenses paid, first-class travel, bubbly and accommodation included).

Bachelor of Iran: tutored in person by exceptionally gifted and highly charismatic, suave, telegenic and sophisticated Iranian Foreign Minister Mohammad Javad Zarif, this course enables diverse, inclusive and compassionate female politicians to sensitively 'don the hijab' in order to show their respect for the ancient and venerated highly progressive feminist sharia law of Iran. Female students are encouraged not to raise their eyes, or indeed their voices, in order to show their solidarity with the 'most feminist of religions'.

Harbour (Masters): set in the magnificent grounds of our luxurious new waterfront ANU Point Piper Campus, the Harbourside-Mansion Masters' Degree teaches you to see yourself as the smartest person in the room and endlessly spout meaningless waffle.

Bachelor of Snowy 2.0 (BScPhys): cutting-edge technology course in which students learn how to defy the basic laws of physics, economics, gravity, energy-production and common sense by creating ludicrously expensive electricity by pushing water uphill and then trying to make a quid by diddling the market on the way back down again.

Statistics and Probabilities Studies: a unique course that uses cutting edge algorithms based around the number 11 to gauge how popular you are with your colleagues and how they would likely vote for you in a secret ballot scenario (course cancelled due to lack of votes).

Multi-media Studies: exciting course in which students get to star in their own celebrity TV chat show to be filmed with 12 cameras in exotic villages such as Positano and Monte Carlo, with your favourite A-lister female guests, such as Amal, Hillary, Meryl, Michelle, Greta, Meaghan, Alexandria, Ilhan, etc., about how evil Donald Trump is and which shoes to wear so as not to clash with the red carpet at (cancelled due to worldwide lack of interest).

*The American conservatives CPAC conference comes to town,
but nobody is really very interested in attending it until a Labor
Senator starts hysterically calling for the conference to be banned.
Meanwhile, Qantas realises that if people ban fossil fuels the airline
will soon be broke.*

Ad guru

10 August 2019

The world of effective advertising campaigns was rocked to its core this
week following the astonishingly successful ad campaign created by
adland's latest trendy hotshop, the brilliantly postmodern agency 'Wong,
Albo, 'Nese, Keneally', popularly known within the industry as WANK.
The boutique agency are now the talk of the town after having managed
to sell out tickets to a boring old conservative conference in a stunning
viral campaign which went, er, viral. In the hugely popular TV ad, the
remarkably talented and versatile actress Kristina Keneally plays (totally
against type, mind you!) the hilarious post-ironic role of a half-witted
blonde bimbo federal Senator who hasn't actually won any form of
election whatsoever in over 12 years and who only got the job because
of female quotas and who is dressed like a Liquorice All-sort when she
rises to her feet in the federal parliament and launches a blistering attack
on the mad racists and far right extremists who will be attending the
aforementioned cavalcade of intolerance known as the CPAC conference
talkfest of hate (is this bit alt-right?—ed. No—Rowena.)

Said advertising guru and former host of the ABC's hit series 'The

Groin Transfer', Ms Rowena Hustle-Rowcroft, as she handed the agency their Most Brilliant and Best-est Gold Plutonium Ad Campaign Ever Gong at the Cannes Festival: 'The genius of this ad campaign is that the hot female creative duo of Kristina and Penny managed to take a rather humdrum and, let's be frank, rather boring and tedious conference concept; i.e. a bunch of conservative nobodies getting together and droning on about free speech (yawn), freedom of religion (double yawn) the free market (mega yawn) and paying off your debts (as if!) yadda yadda yadda snooze snooze zzzzzzz boring boring and somehow against all odds these two creative gurus managed to turn it into the hottest show in town with people literally clambering over each other to get tickets.'

Said a blushing and clearly excited and jubilant third wave feminist Kristina, as she clutched the award tightly to her, er, well, tightly to her low-cut, um, well, the ahem, somewhat protruding middle button of her voluptuous and fetching figure-hugging jacket: 'Thanks yoaawell thass awaoired mayens sooo march to Pinny and moy and...' (I can't understand an effing word she says! It's those weird fake vowels and that fingernails-on-the-blackboard half-Seppo half-Ocker accent! Drives me completely friggin' bonkers!—ed. #MeToo—Rowena.)

The campaign has been lauded as reinvigorating the conservative pro-Trump, capitalist, free-market, libertarian, and otherwise comatose conservative conference market, with tickets to CPAC now being traded for astronomical sums on the black market (surely white market?—ed. No—Rowena).

In other advertising and media news, Qantas CEO Alan Joystick this week announced his new 'climate change is a bunch of old hooey' brand ad campaign in a (somewhat belated) desperate attempt to counter the global hard-left neo-Marxist campaign by climate activists to 'flight shame' people into not flying on his or any other airplanes ever again in order to 'save the planet'.

In the new campaign, a happy group of smiling young Aussie choirboys and choirgirls gently cradle glistening lumps of coal in the palms of their hands as they run in slow motion through the shallow pristine sparkling lapping waters of the Great Barrier Reef which is healthier than it has ever been before and then stand in a line on the ramparts of Fort Denison in Sydney Harbour pointing to the high tide mark which is exactly the same as it was a century ago, singing Peter Allen's famous and poignant climate-sceptic lyrics:

I've been to cities that never will drown
From New York to Rio and Old London Town
But no matter how far or how wide I range
I still don't believe climate change

I'm always travelling
I love being free
And I love the warming of the sun and the sea
But the national grid will always be whole
If I still burn Australian coal

It's the 50th anniversary of Woodstock. The very same weekend a climate shindig is held on Tuvalu. Every satirist loves such happy (or is that hippy?) coincidences.

Tuvalustock

17 August 2019

The world of famous outdoor rock concerts was, er, rocked to its core this week as a remote South Pacific island decided to celebrate the 50th anniversary of Woodstock by holding its very own alternative lifestyle festival—Tuvalustock, billed as three days of free loading, free cash and free luvvy. But who was there? Why, none other than our own peacenik and music lover Ms Rowena Purple-Haze, who was supposed to write a detailed report on the festival but can't actually remember ever having been there.

In keeping with the original festival that changed the world back in 1969, Tuvalustock saw a veritable army of hippies, lefties, free-loaders, addicts, musicians, eco-warriors, doom merchants and peddlers of the most bizarre fantasies descend on the remote island to indulge in three days and nights of an orgy of rolling around in other people's cash and getting high on virtue-signalling. Whilst some may have turned up for the music, critics said most appeared to be unemployable politicians and assorted bureaucrats and hangers-on addicted to the limelight.

Said one excited reveller: 'It was unbelievable. Everyone was wearing these identical tie-dyed shirts with flowers in their hair and we all got to splash around in the shallow waters so the photographers could take pictures of us and send them round the world to make it look like the island is sinking! Far out, man!'

Said another: 'Everyone just let it all hang out, man, like no rules and no clothes and bare-breasted women wandering around and by the end of the festival most of us were just rolling around in a naked grab for cash.'

'It was just so wild, and, like, the smell of hashtags was everywhere.'

Performers at Tuvalustock came from across the South Pacific to entertain the adoring crowds with not only music but passionate pleas for a more caring and progressive world.

Fiji's famous Bananarama were a complete sell-out when they began their set with their number one hit 'The Tide is High' which segued into a solo from Frank Bananarama singing 'I Want to Take You Higher' as he begged Uncle ScoMo to give him the cash to relocate a village foolishly built on a flood plain. Creedence Deepwater Revival wowed the fans with hits from their 'Green River of Cash' album, including 'Gravy Train', 'Who'll Stop The Coal?' and 'Bad Sea Rising', as The Incredible Sinking Band had the audience clapping along to 'The best things in life are free, but you can keep 'em for the birds and the bees, we want money, that's what we want.'

As the sun rose over the glistening tropical atoll, Jefferson Airplane (who have now changed their name to Jefferson Yacht to show their disapproval of evil, disgusting carbon-emitting air travel) sang their smash hit 'Wooden Ships on the water' before hopping into a helicopter to fly back to their luxury private jet waiting with engine running at a nearby airport. Joe Cocker and the Greased-Palm Band then launched into a blistering cover of the Beatles 'With a little help from my friends', adapted especially for Tuvalustock: 'What would you think if I sank out of sight? Would you carry on still burning coal? Lend me your cash and I'll sing you a song, but I'll try not to sink in the seas. Oh, I get by with a little cash from my friends.'

Meanwhile, Crosby, Textor & Nash improvised around their huge flop from 2016, 'Conservatives have nowhere else to go', as former band leader Malcolm Trumble sent the crowds to sleep with a rambling and incoherent monologue about his brilliant climate change policies.

But it wasn't all sweetness and light. Dressed in flowing robes and wrapped in a cloak of sanctimonious smugness kiwi folk singer Jacinda Baez attempted to galvanise the audience with a stirring rendition of her one and only tune 'Kumbaya' but hit a sour note when she turned on fellow antipodean band member Scott Joplin and warned him that he 'must answer to the Pacific'. At that point a roadie leapt onto the stage and instructed the toothy virtue-signaller to put a sock over her microphone.

But critics suggest that although the festival claimed to be a free luvvy-in, behind the scenes hundreds of millions of dollars were exchanging hands, as the festival's promoters demanded up-front payments to stop the island venue from disappearing under a sea of embezzlement and fraud (surely 'rising sea levels'?—ed).

Said one disgusted performer from Country ScoMo and the Josh: 'They forced us to sign this dodgy Paris Agreement even though we had no idea that we were signing away the rights to all our future earnings. They made a fortune out of us and yet the Australian taxpayer walked away empty-handed, as usual.'

The Attorney-General Christian Porter releases draft religious discrimination laws. And all hell breaks loose.

Religious freedom

31 August 2019

The world of religious freedom was rocked to its core this week as Attorney-General Christian Porter released his draft bill to prevent people being discriminated against on the basis of their religion. But just how many religions are out there? *The Fin*'s religious correspondent Ms Rowena Sharria-Laws details some of the many bizarre and unusual religions that clearly deserve legal protection.

Religion of Gaia: rapidly taking over as the most popular religion in the modern world, this religion is built on the premise that Gaia sent her only daughter Greta, who happens to be sixteen and suffering from Aspergers, on a forty day boat trip across the Atlantic to rescue mankind from the sins of electricity, medicine, air travel, food production, economic development, infrastructure, science, lighting, cooking and education by returning to a more simplistic lifestyle of eating cold tinned tuna on a millionaire's ocean-racing yacht whilst encouraging kiddies to wag off school. Disciples include anyone under the age of 21 and grown-ups who should know better. Indulgences and absolution for past and future sins can easily be bought by sticking a heavily subsidised solar panel on the roof of your three-car garage. Holy rites include the ceremonial Slaying of the Farting Cow.

Religion of the God Trans, er sorry, Goddess Trannie, er, um, hang on, well, anyway let's just call him 'Her', er no, her 'Him', ah, anyway how about we just say 'Zir'?: complex religion which requires devotees to undergo a spiritual and physical process of renewal by changing their Victorian birth certificates whenever they feel like it at the stroke of a pen (but no more than once a year!) and discarding the individual material world of, er, materials such as frilly knickers or Y-fronts before embarking on a fulfilling journey of purification which may or may not include an extremely painful out of body experience requiring the surgical and chemical manipulation of one's tackle. Places of worship include non-gender specific public service dunnies.

Religion of Aldi: extremist materialistic cult who worship the accruing of radical socialist-inspired political power through the incessant acquisition of physical manifestations of extreme wealth by all means possible but preferably cash thanks, fifties are easier to get rid of than hundreds. At the famous Temple to Mammon in Sussex street, Sydney, a congregation of mainly Chinese waiters and Chinese bar staff are encouraged to ritually stuff the holy plastic Aldi bag with as much spare dosh as they have on their persons having been given it 10 minutes earlier in the back alley by local Chinese warlord, er, sorry local businessman Huang Chok-Full Moneybags of up to $5,000 each although obviously some of them will pocket a few hundred themselves along the way but why wouldn't you I mean we're only human after all.

Religion of Maal: rapidly disappearing religion based upon the worship of the God Maal whom many believed to be the Saviour when he rose up from a bloody spill in September 2015 surrounded by ululating sycophants and adoring bed-wetters. As one devout disciple, Elizabeth Farrelly, wrote in her newspaper column at the time: 'Already, after only a few weeks, the country feels different. The air itself has a new edge. And that edge has a name. Intelligence.' Maal turned out to be a false prophet who claimed to be able to make electricity by pushing water uphill and speak in tongues until it was revealed that he only spoke Waffle. Nowadays, his dwindling band of disciples have to make do with miserable, ghostly apparitions via his Twitter account.

Religion of the Voice: based upon ancient texts discovered by climbers on top of a large red rock in the middle of the desert that it is now forbidden to climb and known to worshippers as the Sacred Heart of Uluru, the Voice is a mysterious god-like spiritual force that worshippers believe will deliver great harmony, equality, wisdom, peace and prosperity to the warring tribes of the Invasion of the First Peoples of the First Nations of Paradise following the Enlightenment of the '67 Referendum and the Cleansing of the Apology by Saint Kevin and the Troubled Era of Recognition brought about by the blessed Expert Panel although nobody has the faintest idea what exactly the Voice is or what on earth it will do.

Religion of ScoMo: miracle-worker who parted the red armies of socialists and defeated the evil usurper known as The Short One, He Who Wants Us All to Drive Electric Cars, the religion of ScoMo, or ScoMoses as he is rightly proclaimed by his congregation of quiet worshippers, meet regularly in large auditoriums known as 'churches' where they pray, sing songs and wave their hands in the air (where's the satire?—ed.)

As Brexit flounders, Rowena comes to the rescue.

Plans

7 September 2019

The world of Downing Street was rocked to its core this week by the spectacular failure of the British parliament to agree on any plan whatsoever to do anything at all about leaving the EU, leaving the EU with a deal, not getting any deal, getting a very bad deal, holding a general election, holding a second referendum or staying put. However, help is at hand! In this world exclusive, *The Fin* can reveal that Number 10 has now turned to top Australian political adviser and strategist, Lady Rowena Crosby-Nash, who is currently war-gaming a series of radical options designed to bring about a clean Brexit, drawn from her extensive knowledge of Australian political strategic thinking.

The Aldi Plan: in this dramatic plan, members of the British Labour party will be invited to a fundraising dinner at a swanky Chinatown restaurant, Huang Bo-Jo's, where the waiters and bar staff will generously offer them large plastic Aldi bags stuffed with pro-Brexit incentives and sweeteners, such as hundreds of thousands of pounds in non-traceable cash. The MPs will then be invited to attend a corruption hearing at which they are perfectly entitled to burst into tears and claim they knew nothing about it all along.

The ScoMo Plan: a popular proposal whereby Boris Johnson immediately gets reborn in a Hillsong church in the Shire as a radical Pentecostal pastor who performs electoral miracles by speaking in tongues, an obscure and ancient Aramaic language which has the advantage of being far more comprehensible than anything that comes out of Brussels.

The Rudd Plan (1): in order to strengthen the political power and decision-making skills of the European Union, former Australian Prime Minister and world-renowned diplomat Kevin Rudd is parachuted into Brussels as Head Honcho, a job clearly beneath his skills but one which he may deign to accept out of the charitable goodness of his heart. This will have numerous advantages, the most obvious of which is that the EU will disintegrate into a cess-pit of squabbling and incoherent chaos within a breathtakingly short period of time and in spectacular fashion. With no EU left, Britain will have nothing to Leave and nothing to Remain in. Peace, harmony and goodwill will once again return to her green and pleasant lands.

The Turnbull Plan: also known as the 'pushing-water-uphill' strategy, this superb concept has the advantage of being entirely emissions-free and eco-sustainable. Giant pumps will be installed along the Embankment of the Thames to pump a muddy, faecal-like sludge up out of the riverbed during off-peak times and then flooding it throughout the corridors of the Palace of Westminster during peak parliamentary sitting times. Repeat until the swamp has been thoroughly drained.

The Rudd Plan (2): drawn up on the back of a boarding pass at Gatwick Airport by K. Rudd and Stefan Con-Roi, the National Brexit Network (NBN) is designed to strengthen links between Britain and the European continent through a gigantic multi-billion pound high-speed broadband cable under the English channel that connects every single UK household directly to Brussels bureaucrats via fibre-à-la-node. Once installed, this unique patented technology guarantees that Brussels will never be able to communicate with Britain ever again.

The Reverse-Keneally Plan: with an enviable CV chock full of such outstanding successes as the NSW state election of 2011 (worst loss in NSW history), four separate TV shows on Sky News Australia (all axed), the Bennelong by-election (which she lost) and captaining the bus and kissing puppies during Bill Shorten's unlosable 2019 federal election (which he lost), what better plan could there be than putting Kristina in charge of negotiating a deal with Brussels to keep Britain *in* the EU?

The Rudd Plan (3): in order to combat catastrophic climate change and avoid the need for an Irish backstop, rooftops in homes along the border in County Donegal will be installed with subsidised and highly flammable pink brexits (that's enough Rudd gags, thanks—ed.)

Rowena re-imagines a famous encounter between Australia's High Commissioner to Britain and a US intern that allegedly sparked the Donald Trump–Russian collusion hoax.

One night in a Kensington wine bar

5 October 2019

Alexander wiped the sweat from his upper lip as he stepped, or rather stumbled ever so slightly, out of the High Commissioner's car and into the balmy Kensington evening air, feeling momentarily like a character in a John le Carré novel. He loved London at this time of year—the lengthening daylight hours meant you could always slip in a quick snifter, sorry, an 'important diplomatic information-gathering encounter', on the way back to the office. He'd just left lunch with two bearded internet start-up wallies Malcolm had asked him to meet. What were they called? Alsatian Brooks? Atlas Cannon? Something daft like that. Alexander prided himself on being a good judge of character and an even better judge of business acumen and he could confidently predict that these two geeky hippies would be long forgotten and broke within six months. Still, lunch had been tolerable, mainly thanks to the Chateau Margaux.

Alexander pulled up his collar and glanced over his shoulder. He'd been looking forward to this encounter all week. This was where the action was! An intimate clandestine drink with one of the greatest political operatives in American history! A real player! Alexander, too, prided himself on his own political instincts, his own unerring grasp of the nuances of power, his own insights into the strategic plays of the Deep State...

With his keen observational skills it only took Alexander a few minutes to spot the Mediterranean-looking gentleman sitting alone at the bar—although he made a mental note that the man looked a lot younger, more tanned and swarthier in the flesh than on Google. Must be those Mediterranean genes, he told himself. 'George, so glad to meet you!' Alexander gushed, thrusting out his hand. The man looked up. 'You must be Mr...?' 'Oh, just call me Your Excellency!' Alexander chortled, employing his renowned diplomatic skills. He waved for the barman. 'What can I get you to drink, George? I'm going for a large Russian Mule myself!' His guest shrugged. 'Maybe a glass of Chianti?' Alexander nodded amiably, keen to put the man at ease. 'Chianti? I'm guessing your family originally came from that part of the world?' The man frowned. 'Er, I'm Greek, not Italian.' Alexander felt like kicking himself. 'Of course, 'opoulos', there's a clue right there!' he laughed, trying to cover his embarrassment as he fumbled for the iPhone in his trouser pocket. He liked to secretly record his diplomatic encounters so his assistant could transcribe all the key phrases and send them in the pouch to Canberra each week.

He knew Malcolm would be mightily impressed that he'd scored a private tete-a-tete with the legendary George Stephanopoulos—Bill Clinton's top adviser and a key political player who'd even inspired political best-sellers like *Primary Colors* and TV shows like *House of Cards* and *The West Wing*. Malcolm was of course a huge fan of any kind of Machiavellian political intrigue! But as they chatted, it struck Alexander how unimpressive Stephanopoulos was in person, sounding more like a rookie intern than one of the great practitioners of the dark arts. No doubt a clever ruse. Alexander decided to use his own renowned skills to surreptitiously nudge the conversation towards more fruitful political intrigues. 'I guess a man in your position has seen a few saucy emails in his time,' he teased, casually waving for another vodka. 'Clinton's, for example! I mean, there must have been some pretty fiery ones between Bill and Monica back in the day - you know, the sort of stuff you wouldn't want the Russians to get their hands on!' he winked.

The man shrugged awkwardly. 'Well, I'm not even sure they had email back then, and, er, I'm more of an expert on Donald Trump's foreign…' 'TRUMP!?!' Alexander blurted out, spilling his vodka. 'What a dreadful, uncouth, hopeless buffoon that loser is! As I told Malcolm and Julie, Trump's got Buckley's of ever making it anywhere near the White House!' He leaned forward and tapped his nose conspiratorially. 'That's why Malcolm chose me for this job. Political insights! My antenna's never been sharper! For example, I told Malcolm he'd be a phenomenal leader, and now, thanks to Snowy 2.0 and the NEG, he's never looked stronger! Stroke of genius! He'll be PM for at least a decade, mark my words! Plus, I always said Julie would make a superb Foreign Minister and I always predicted Christopher's French submarine deal was an absolute bargain!' Alexander raised his vodka. 'Here's to the Russians, eh! And what's the bet they've got every one of Clinton's private emails!' he chortled merrily, still enjoying his own little joke.

Shortly afterwards, a baffled George Papadopoulos, a relatively unknown adviser on Trump's campaign team, made his excuses and hurriedly headed out into the cool Kensington night air.

The causes for the crash of a Boeing 737 Max are urgently investigated.

Plane crash

2 November 2019

Five months after the shocking crash of the ALP in the early hours of 19 May 2019, when the entire party inexplicably nosedived shortly after take-off wiping out everyone on board, a report this week will be released by a team of experts who were called in to investigate and identify any obvious flaws in the design of the entire Alboeing fleet.

Analysis of the flight path of the ill-fated Shorten Airbus (pilot; Captain K. Keneally), shows that a secret software programme installed in order to make the Alboeing engine appear more environmentally-friendly meant that in any unfavourable headwinds the nose automatically veers sharply to the left with catastrophic consequences. Those piloting the ALP have repeatedly claimed that despite struggling with the controls they are simply unable to change direction.

One investigator, Next Generation co-pilot Jim Charmers, claims that the problem stems from the fact that the Alboeing has been designed exclusively to cater to the whims of the inner-city flyer. 'We need to start landing in the outer suburbs again,' he said this week.

Others disagree, claiming that the entire design of the Alboeing is far too noisy to appeal to quiet Australians. Indeed, one formerly-unknown ALP air hostess, Ms Clare O'Kneel, astonished investigators when she claimed that the problem stems from the black box of ideas within the ALP itself. 'Anybody who has a different opinion is "obviously wrong, probably stupid and possibly subhuman", she said, moments before a spokesperson for Alboeing quickly refuted her remarks, declaring Ms O'Kneel is 'obviously wrong, probably stupid and possibly subhuman.'

Experts note that massive cracks started to appear in the 737 MARX when it was originally trialled by Russian and Chinese airlines in the early 20th Century yet has continued to remain popular with so-called 'progressive' airlines around the globe. The 737 MARX is now being held responsible for the recent Venezuelan air disaster, when an entire crew found all the in-flight shelves on the plane were empty, forcing starving passengers to eat each other in order to survive. And aviation experts have pointed to the sharp decline in popularity of Corbyn Air, a no-frills budget British airline popular with unwashed undergraduates that specialises in flying anywhere other than Israel and refuses to direct passengers towards the Brexit doors.

Meanwhile, the man once dubbed 'the world's greatest pilot', Captain Wayne 'Blinded by the Right' Springsteen, reassured nervous ALP passengers that the Alboeing is maintaining a steady course and no change in direction is anticipated prior to an expected crash-landing in approximately three years' time.

Bushfire Debate Plan

15 November 2019

As furious debate rages like a wildfire across the nation about precisely who or what is to blame for the severity of the current bushfires, make sure you have prepared a proper Debate Survival Plan. There are five critical steps to preparing your own Bushfire Debate Survival Plan.

1. Don't discuss it over dinner: many families find that it is best to avoid discussing anything to do with the causes of the current bushfires over dinner with the family. This is because this is the only time the kids don't actually have their faces buried in their iPhones so there is a strong risk that they may join in (however briefly) an inter-generational discussion. Whatever you do, avoid fanning the flames with highly incendiary comments such as 'the Black Friday fires were far worse' or 'I told those damn rangers that I needed to do some burning off but the bastards slapped me with a massive fine' because this is likely to ignite a spontaneous combustion of heated debate. The risk is intensified because any members of the younger generation who have been educated (to use the term in its loosest meaning) in our public school system will already have been convinced that these catastrophic bushfires are due entirely to three things: catastrophic climate change, catastrophic white supremacy and catastrophic racism. And any attempt to dissuade them otherwise may well prove futile (not to mention fatal).

2. Prepare for the worst: there are plenty of things you can do around your home to prepare for a fiery debate about the severity of the current bushfires such as memorising the facts and statistics to do with other deadly bushfires going all the way back to 1926, but understand that even these basic steps may not necessarily be enough to protect you if you are engulfed in a full-blown Gen X or Millennial-inspired maelstrom of apocalyptic climate change hyperbole.

3. Know the key words to watch out for: in any debate about the causes of the current bushfires, several key words and phrases may prove highly flammable. Even when you think you are safe, the conversation may suddenly change direction and a poorly chosen word may in fact simply pour more fuel on the fire. Also, be prepared to immediately hose down any strong language or profanities that belong in the gutter. Here are a few key dangerous words to watch out for: 'Arsonist'. This is a word you may think refers to a person caught with a can of petrol, a match and a fondness for pyromania in the middle of a bone-dry national park, but in fact in the hands of an hysterical Greens politician the word 'arsonist' actually refers to members of the Liberal government who recognise that our prosperity depends on mining coal. 'Unprecedented'. This word normally means something that has never happened before but in any debate where climate change may appear the word unprecedented means something that has never ever happened before even though there is plenty of evidence that it has. 'Catastrophic'. In any debate about the causes of the recent bushfires, this word is a ubiquitous adjective that automatically precedes phrases like 'climate change' or 'global warming' or indeed the word 'bushfire' itself. But if you really want to fire up the debate, try blanketing the discussion with comments such as: 'yes, the South Australian blackouts really were catastrophic' or 'shutting down Liddell will be an absolute catastrophe' and watch young minds literally explode in front of your eyes.

4. Do I stay and fight or do I pack up and flee? This is the toughest decision you will face if you are ever unlucky enough to be directly threatened by an imminent discussion with your family about the causes of the current bushfires. Many parents and grandparents understandably choose to run a mile as fast as they possibly can in the opposite direction. But if you are determined to stand your ground and protect your ideological turf, get ready to hose down the discussion if things suddenly turn nasty and get completely out of hand. The most important thing is to protect your own sanity. Remember, in an emergency you can always beat a hasty retreat to the wine cellar and hide down there until it is safe to come out again but ensure you have stocked it with lots to drink because you may be down there for quite some time.

5. Aftermath: a full-blown causes of the bushfires debate can rage for many hours, if not days or even weeks, and will suck the very oxygen out of the room leaving family members gasping in disbelief. Remember, the damage to your sanity can last for years, so try to salvage whatever you can from the wreckage.

The Gospel According to Malcolm

21 December 2019

In recent weeks, Malcolm Turnbull has informed an astonished public that not only would he have won the 2019 election, but also that everybody he knows agrees with him. What's more, he has claimed that the Turnbull government was hugely successful and achieved many great things, not least of which was the crafting of his brilliant National Energy Guarantee.

In this world exclusive, *The Fin*'s fiction correspondent Ms Rowena Luke-Matthews reimagines the nativity story as it might be told by the former PM, tentatively titled The Gospel According to Malcolm.

'In those days, there was a great and wise leader named Herod who was the smartest person in the palace and who ruled wisely and justly and with an abundance of compassion over his innovative and agile kingdom of Judea. It was an exciting time to be alive and everything was on the tablet until it was off the tablet. Lo and behold in the interests of gender diversity and inclusiveness Herod decided to conduct a census of the entire land to be professionally carried out using the latest technology by the Judean Bureau of Statistics, but unfortunately the scrolls crashed on the day and the census wasn't worth the papyrus it was written on.

Meanwhile, Joseph, a humble hedge fund manager and renewables investor from Nazareth and the son of Goldman from the line of Sachs and his partner Mary were fleeing catastrophic bushfires caused by rampant global warming which was the Lord's way of punishing the sinful Philistines and Deniers of the Galilee, just near the Basin. And so it came to pass that Joseph and Mary were forced to return to their hometown in the Surry Hills by riding on a light tram from Circular Quay which was almost as fast as going by donkey. Since transitioning Mary had miraculously become pregnant despite not actually having a womb or any ovaries, but to point this fact out was of course a mortal sin that would get you crucified on the spot by Twitter and rightly booted out of your job and stoned to death by the screeching Sodomites in the land of Clover.

When Joseph and Mary arrived in Darlinghurst they found all the Airbnb's were full so they were forced to take refuge in an organic vegan cafe called The Manger instead where all cattle and farmyard products were banned due to the high methane output of farting oxen.

Joseph and Mary had decided to bring the child up as gender neutral and so asked for visitors to avoid any sexist toys such as carpenters tools for boys or swaddling cloth dolls for girls.

Three wise men arrived bearing gifts of immeasurable wealth. One was a King of the Orient known as Xi who brought an Aldi bag stuffed with cash and demanded nothing in return apart from 5G access, which Herod had decreed must be denied.

Another Magi was the King of Photios, who brought forth from his own land the gift of abundant energy sourced directly from the sun and the wind and abundant power sourced directly from the factions given to him directly by the money-lenders in the Temple of Gaia thanks to their unlimited supply of taxpayer-subsidised gold. And the wise men declared that the baby would grow up and rule the land forever and he or ze depending on his or zir choice of pronouns would be a mighty King even a president of the new Republic as was his pre-ordained destiny. Indeed, even the donkey and the ass and the chicken and the goose and the poodle all bowed their heads down before the newborn child declaring him to be the smartest baby in the manger.

Alas, the boy grew up in extreme and dire poverty after Mary ran off and joined a troupe of passing shepherds and the young man was brought up alone by his hard-working Dad who owned a humble Inn and in fact a whole portfolio of them. But the boy was loved and adored and worshipped by all who met him and knelt before him. And yet it came to pass that when he reached the age of 33 he was forced to spend forty days and forty nights wandering in the wilderness of opposition before returning in triumph to the Capital Hill as the newly crowned Messiah and acknowledged by Julie and Chris and Wyatt and Arthur as the smartest Messiah in the party room. And verily his name was Malcolm.'

2020—the Year of Covid

Licking his wounds after having made the egregious error of thinking he deserved a holiday in Hawaii with his wife and kids without first checking with the ABC and the *Guardian*, Scott Morrison rushes home to literally help put out the raging media inferno (and the bushfires).

As he tosses the cash around and tours bushfire-ravaged parts of the nation, a humbled Prime Minister secretly hopes he will get another go at a national disaster some time before the next election in order to prove to the luvvies that he 'gets it'.

He doesn't have to wait long.

A mystery virus is rumoured to be spreading like wildfire in Wuhan, home to a Chinese bioweapons lab. There is much talk of bowls of baby bat soup.

Corona

1 February 2020

The world of pandemics was rocked to its core this week (as indeed was the world) with news that a deadly new virus threatens civilisation as we know it. In this exclusive, *The Fin*'s medical correspondent Dr Rowena Black-D'Ath examines the symptoms and the likely effects of this and other dangerous modern viruses.

Coronavirus: believed to have originated in the crowded slums of Mexico when an itinerant tourist accidentally squeezed the lemon from his guacamole into his beer, this common virus rapidly spread across the globe chiefly among young male Millennials. Symptoms include incoherent speech, severe pounding headaches, dry mouth, feverish night-sweats and occasional vomiting.

Peronivirus: closely related to the coronavirus, the peronivirus originated in the back streets of Naples before spreading to trendy bars and nightclubs across the globe, but does not require a lemon to be transmitted, thereby making it easier to swallow. Symptoms are identical.

Younghenryvirus: more commonly known by its abbreviated form, the 'harryvirus', this highly infectious and deadly pathogen usually enters the (royal) bloodstream via a foreign agent, such as the parasitic markle genome, before taking control of the host and in extreme cases tampering with its genetic code by kidnapping the baby. Sufferers should immediately be quarantined on a remote Canadian oligarch's island.

Gretavirus: highly infectious among impressionable young teenage girls, the gretavirus is extremely contagious and invariably results in time off school (sometimes for up to a year) with victims suffering severe delusions about economic disruption, mass extinctions and the end of the world in eighteen months' time. There is no known cure.

Scomovirus: believed to have originated on a tropical beach in Hawaii, this highly contagious virus can be fatal if it enters the body politic for any prolonged period of time. Symptoms include a false sense of well-being and harmony as you sneak off to relax with your family on a well-deserved break, only to suddenly wake up in a cold sweat with your phone ringing madly and realising you've been sprung. Exacerbated by extreme heat, such as proximity to a bushfire or at the National Press Club, the best antidote is to aggressively fight back using all political remedies at your disposal.

Palaszczukvirus: symptoms include a pathological desire to 'hook up' with other state premiers in order to spread the blame for the coronavirus onto the host government in Canberra.

Turnbullitis: extremely non-contagious, this hallucinatory virus makes you so self-deluded you believe yourself to be the smartest person in the room, which is only ever likely to be true once you are in an isolation ward. Symptoms include a miserable, ghost-like complexion followed by permanent and irreversible loss of reputation.

Huaweivirus: deadly virus that sprang out of a major Chinese metropolis where it was deliberately being cultivated in a computer lab by Chinese scientists designed to run rampant through the West and infect as many 5G devices as possible until the host countries get entirely taken over. Symptoms include complete loss of independence as well as severely leaking eyes (all five of them) followed by a slow and painful death (of Western democracy).

The former Defence Minister insists his French submarine deal
promises lots of local jobs.

French jobs

15 February 2020

As former defence procurement honcho Christopher Pyne advises the government to 'hold their feet to the fire' to ensure the French manufacturers give some submarine-building jobs to Aussie tradies, *The Fin*'s industrial correspondent Mademoiselle Rowena Métiers-Francais details the many jobs that Aussies could easily fulfil to help in the construction of our magnificent fleet of subs.

Futurologist: with the delivery date of the final subs already a matter of some conjecture, Aussie futurologists will be in hot demand over the coming century to help inform the French designers as to precisely who and what we will be at war with by around the end of this century or the beginning of the next. Will China even exist by then? Will America be the first totalitarian woke nation? Will Britain still be trying to get out of the EU?

Victa lawnmower maintenance engineer: with the classic Aussie 2-stroke lawnmower increasingly a thing of the past, who will still be around and have the requisite skills to maintain Christopher Pyne's diesel lawnmower engine parts that he insisted we replace the French nuclear engines with? How do you fix a broken pull cord? Can you start a submarine engine without one? Where can you get diesel in 2095?

Spin doctors: over the coming decades, there will be a frequent requirement for a specialist team of government public relations experts who on a regular and monotonously predictable basis will be wheeled out to explain why the budget has blown out yet again and why none of the delivery timetables have been met. A school-leaver starting today in the Submarine PR Department can look forward to a long and lucrative career including a slap-up retirement party and gold watch (Cartier, of course) long before a single sub ever gets wet. (Note: successful applicants will be expected to be fluent in French. English optional.)

Choux-pastry chef: Napoleon said that an army runs on its stomach. But what about a navy? As any self-respecting submarine designer knows, a truly functional nautical submersible vessel must be fitted out with the latest high-tech gizmos including a fully-equipped and up-to-date 'grande-cuisinerie' to guarantee submariners enjoy the lightest éclairs, croissants, boeuf en croûte and other such staples of traditional Aussie tucker.

Data expert: with all instruction manuals, computer codes, automated navigational systems and other such malarkey designed and written in French for the northern hemisphere, some kid who knows how to use a sat nav at 2,000 feet underwater could come in handy.

Climate change expert: with climate alarmism and catastrophism a key motivational factor in daily political and military life over the coming decades, every submarine will require at least one on-board climate change expert fully versed in IPCC directives and armed with a complete box set of Sir David Attenborough videos and UN Secretary-General Thunberg speeches who is able to convincingly explain to the hysterical and gullible 'millennial' crew members why whenever they re-surface the sea level is exactly the same as it was back in 2020!

Toilet cubicle designers: lost in the small print of the French translation of the original procurement papers (copyright C. Pyne esq.,

Adelaide, 2016) is a small clause, likely to only be discovered during the actual construction phase of the first submarine unit (circa 2055) detailing that conditional upon the expected success of the marvellous same-sex marriage plebiscite in 2017 all future submarines must replace 'male' and 'female' toilets with a specific cubicle for each and every recognised new gender (currently 100 and climbing).

On-board historian: in order to satisfy the no-doubt endless media and academic interest in and speculation about precisely who originally proposed the procurement of the fabulous Australian submarine fleet all those years ago and the reasons why they specifically chose this design, there will be an abundance of work for those professionals well-versed in the history of the bounteous achievements of the most successful Australian prime minister ever, a towering progressive intellectual known affectionately to his legion of adoring fans as the smartest Ghost in the miserable room (is that bit right?—ed), a man whose powers of communication were legendary, a man who inspired great loyalty and devotion from not only his entire cabinet (apart from the vile, evil, sinister, Machiavellian group of Murdoch-backed climate denying terrorists) but also an adoring public who flocked to the voting booths time after time in gratitude, a man who bequeathed to the nation the magnificent NBN, the enlightened Murray-Darling Water Plan, the most compassionate subsidised renewables energy portfolio on the planet, the majestic literary masterpiece 'A Bigger Waffle' that now adorns every school kids bedside table, the innovative (I think you've made your point, thanks—ed).

A breakaway group of disgruntled Labor MPs forms the Otis Group.

Otis

22 February 2020

The world of Labor factional in-fighting was rocked to its core last week with the stunning revelation that a radical group of rebel right-wing Labor MPs has formed the breakaway Otis group in order to dramatically overturn existing Labor policies in favour of ones that the Australian public might actually consider voting for. In this world exclusive, *The Fin*'s chief Labor factions correspondent Ms Rowena Lighton-Hill reveals that hidden clues about which policies will be ditched lie in the obscure choice of name for the secretive group. But which Otis were the rebels inspired by?

Otis Redding: this renowned climate realist was famous for such sceptical ballads as 'Sitting on the dock of the bay', in which a young man wastes his time waiting for the tide to roll in, suggesting a subtle switch in Labor's climate policies to a more pragmatic 'let's just wait and see what happens' approach to rising sea levels. Otis's other famous lyrics in his hit song 'My Girl' also hint at a more positive approach to carbon dioxide emissions: 'I get sunshine on a rainy day, when it's cold outside I get the month of May', suggesting the rebels believe a warming planet might actually be a good thing.

Milo and Otis: the symbolism is unmistakable in this famous film about a pug called Otis and a cat called Milo who, despite being of different species, become firm friends. Otis bravely comes to the rescue of the struggling kitten—symbolising the Labor party?—by pulling it out of the hole it has fallen into. Can the Otis group pull Labor out of its own deep hole? Certainly. But the moral of the story of Milo and Otis is crystal clear. Despite their cross-species attraction, the cat decides to marry a cat and have lots of kittens and the dog decides to marry a dog and have lots of puppies. End of story. Expect a dramatic shift towards more traditionally-minded and conservative Labor attitudes on gender fluidity, intersex marriage, homosexuality, lesbianism, transgenderism and abortion.

Otis elevators: again, the heavy symbolism is unmistakeable. When eight people were trapped for eight hours in an Otis elevator—the group of eight rebel Labor MPs trapped in last year's marathon post-election caucus, perhaps?—the repair man—Joel Fitzgibbon?—who tried to fix the problem slipped and plunged to his doom. A cautionary tale! Moreover, when an Otis escalator in Beijing changed direction without notice, 30 people took a tumble. Are we about to see a dramatic reversal of Labor policy towards China taking down those right at the top? Even more tellingly, when a one-year-old Otis escalator changed direction from up to a rapid descent, in what officials called a 'free fall', it turned out that the gear boxes had completely rusted. Is Labor ideology in such poor shape after years of neglect that any change in direction will be fatal?

Otis Milburn: were the Otis group inspired by this fictional character in the Netflix series 'Sex Education'? In which case, the signs are not good for Labor. In 2010, Otis famously witnessed his father (the Labor party?) having sex with one of his clients (the Greens?) which traumatised him to such an extent he never fully recovered.

Otis sunglasses: with a logo that famously features rose-tinted glasses and boasts of its 'mineral glass' product, it is likely that the Otis group may well have taken this particular Otis as their inspiration. In which case, expect a return to a more nostalgic Labor party that fondly looks back at its romantic past with the mining industry as a cure to Labor's current political myopia.

Otis B. Driftwood, aka Otis Firefly: fictional serial killer and renowned psychopath who skins his victims alive in the cult horror film 'House of 1000 Corpses'. If this is the inspiration for the group's name, heaven help Albo, Penny and Richard!

Otis Bar and Grill: although some Canberra-bubble journalists have mistakenly claimed that the rebel Labor group is named after a restaurant in Canberra, this was simply a ruse to disguise the real restaurant they met in and the real reason they were there. The Otis Bar & Grill on Old Menangle Road in Campelltown is almost certainly where the rebel group had their first meeting and it is of course in the electorate of and just down the road from the home of a former Labor leader who is now one of New South Wales' and indeed Australia's most popular conservative-minded politicians. Was the Otis group actually formed over clandestine burgers and beers with none other than climate realist, coal-loving, gender pragmatist, immigration reductionist and NSW One Nation leader Mark Latham? If so, there's hope for Labor yet!

Toilet paper sells out as the country plunges into lockdown.

Dunny paper

7 March 2020

Now that Aussies have stripped the shelves bare and stocked up their homes with adequate supplies of toilet paper, what on earth are they going to do with it all? In this week's world exclusive, *The Fin*'s home survivalist expert Dr Wuhena Dunny-Lu offers her handy tips on what to do with all those stacks of bog rolls now you've finally got your hands on them.

Save the planet: no need to install Kevin Rudd's pesky pink batts anymore when you can insulate your entire roof cavity all by yourself with hundreds of rolls of Quilton 3-ply floral print pink and white soft double-length toilet paper! You'll be astonished just how quickly you'll reduce your own carbon footprint and thereby save the planet from mass extinction and species annihilation in twenty years' time (I thought it was twelve?—ed).

Save your ear-drums: fed up with listening to your teenage son's electronic drum-beat, doof-doof, musical creations being crafted and refined at full volume all night long? Stack your bulk discount multipacks of Andrex fully absorbent aloe vera toilet rolls outside his door and the length of the corridor and enjoy the sweet sounds of silence once again.

The Nino Culotta lounge set: remember that great scene in *They're A Weird Mob* where Nino made all his furniture out of old piles of newspapers? Now you can go one better. Amaze your friends and impress your neighbours by designing your very own customised luxury lounge suite out of all those bulk packs of Renova designer ultra-soft 3-ply and you'll never want to leave the lounge room again.

Take good care of your kids: improve your parenting skills by lining even the toughest and ugliest housing estate asphalt backyard with multi-packs of soft and bouncy Coles So Soft double-length toilet tissue. Now your sprogs can run around and enjoy beating the bejesus out of each other without a single bruise or scratch to attract the attention of some busy-body interfering DOCs officer.

Build your own life raft: terrified by rising sea levels and the thought of the waves lapping at your front door within the next twelve years (I thought it was five?—ed) even if you live in Dubbo? Now you can relax, knowing that in a jiffy you can strap all those multi-packs of Quilton King Size together and build your own super comfy, family-sized buoyant life raft. (manufacturer's caution: highly absorbent if comes into contact with water).

Survive a full term as Labor leader: even the most arrogant and self-confidant Labor leader has to recognise the awful truth that if he or she fails to perform in the polls or insists on forcing the party to adopt some madcap emissions scheme or other then sooner or later they'll get knifed in the back. So be prepared! Simply strap an 8-roll discount special Aldi Confidence hypoallergenic quilted softness toilet tissue pack onto your back under your jacket and even the most determined factional warrior will struggle to sink the blade in.

Create a booming economy: desperately trying to balance the books? Frantically trying to stimulate the financial markets in order to deliver the surplus you so foolishly promised twelve months ago? What better way than to turbo-charge the Aussie economy than with a toilet-roll led recovery? Watch shares in Kleenex and Woolies go through the roof as consumers rush to empty those shelves! Guaranteed to get even the most anaemic economy back up off its bottom and wipe away the deficit!

Write your own life story: fed up with being ignored as the smartest person in the room? Eager to set the record straight on all your treacherous former colleagues? Why not write your own best-selling autobiography? Reams and reams of Quilton shea butter-enriched 4-ply toilet tissue is the ideal material on which any self-respecting harbourside-mansion dweller should pen his darkest, most vengeful tales of treachery and demented diatribes about saving the world from the impending catastrophic climate crisis in 18 months' time (I thought it was 12?—ed) or other such innovative subjects. Now instead of cluttering up the remainder bins, your masterpiece can be put to its original use!

Feel-good movie star Tom Hanks gets the coronavirus.

Tom Hanks

14 March 2020

Stuck indoors in self-isolation with the coronavirus depressed and bored out of your mind? Cheer up! You're not alone. Indeed, Hollywood celebrity Tom Hanks is holed up on the Gold Coast with a positive diagnosis twiddling his thumbs, too. But let's be honest, it's hard to think of a more cheerful, optimistic and, er, positive character than those that Mr Hanks has spent a lifetime creating to cheer us all up in these dark days. Indeed, what better way to pass two weeks in quarantine than binge-watching all those wonderfully uplifting Tom Hanks movies. In this world exclusive, *The Fin*'s own well-being guru Ms Rowena Positive-Vibes selects the best Tom Hanks films to help distract you from the lockdown and fear of dying from the virus.

Forrest Gump: a brilliant feel-good movie in which Tom Hanks won Best Actor for his portrayal of a delightfully childlike and innocent character who wanders through America turning up and influencing some of the great events of the day. The film opens and closes with Forrest sitting waiting at the bus stop to meet the love of his life, Jenny, who suddenly dies of a mysterious and unknown virus, and, er, OK maybe this one's not such a great choice.

Cast away: amazingly positive movie in which Tom Hanks was nominated for an Oscar for his portrayal of the lone survivor of an air disaster in the South Pacific who washes up on a desert island where he lives in total self-isolation eking out a lonely and miserable existence until he goes completely bonkers and starts talking to his imaginary friend, a volleyball called Wilson and, er, actually on second thoughts this probably isn't such a great pick either.

Saving Private Ryan: now widely regarded as one the greatest movies ever made and one which earned Tom Hanks an Oscar nomination, this inspirational and uplifting movie begins with a man standing over a graveyard and it turns out his three brothers all died in the war and he had to be rescued by a guy with a fatal disease and, oh, dang, I think we might give this one a bit of a miss, too.

Philadelphia: an incredible movie which earned Tom Hanks an Oscar for Best Actor, this emotionally uplifting tale follows a bloke who is forced to avoid going to work because he has a mysterious virus and everybody is frightened to go anywhere near him and in the end he dies and, er, the Bruce Springsteen and Neil Young songs are pretty good but, er, maybe give this one a miss for the time being.

A Beautiful Day in the Neighbourhood: in this wonderfully inspirational true story about an amazingly optimistic and sunny children's TV presenter which earned Tom Hanks an Oscar nomination, the pivotal scene takes place in a dream sequence about a man in a hospital dying of, ah, crikey forgot that bit was in there, OK, maybe not such a great choice after all.

Sleepless in Seattle: widely regarded as one of the greatest romantic comedies of all time, this warm and uplifting movie is about a bloke who is miserable because his wife has died of a mysterious virus and, er, no sorry, actually it was cancer but anyway he and his kid are bereft without her and there's a woman in Seattle who's all alone and miserable in her apartment all by herself and, bloody hell, forget this one.

Apollo 13: incredibly inspirational story starring Tom Hanks of the crew of Apollo 13 who are stuck together in one tiny, cramped cockpit and everything is going wrong and it pretty much looks like they'll all just die up there in space and, anyway, probably not such a great pick if you're stuck in a cramped room going stir crazy wondering whether you're going to make it out alive or not.

Catch Me If You Can: based on a true story, this hilarious and uplifting movie sees Tom Hanks chasing a fake airline pilot who is flying around the world spreading a mysterious virus which is proving very easy to catch and, ah, hang on, not sure if this one is the go.

Sully: miracle on the Hudson: Amazing true story of an airline pilot who crashes his plane into New York's famous river after several passengers come down with a deadly virus, and, er, come to think of it not quite sure this one's the ticket either.

The Green Mile: a man is on death row and, nup, no way.

Road to Perdition: nope, forget it.

The Terminal: bloody hell.

Now there's a face mask shortage.

Face masks

4 April 2020

As the coronavirus pandemic grips the nation, bewildered Australians are struggling to get their hands on sufficient quantities of potentially life-saving face masks. But forget about trying to track any down—why not use a bit of good old Aussie ingenuity and make your own? In this world exclusive, *The Fin*'s DIY manufacturing correspondent Ms Rowena Handy-Tipps offers up her own suggestions on the best face masks you can make out of everyday household products:

The Malcolm Turnbull face mask: with thousands of unread copies of Malcolm Turnbull's epic tome 'A Bigger Picture' about to hit remainder bins across the nation, you should be able to pick up a copy for next-to-nothing. Within its glossy hardback covers you'll find page after page of hygienic, pristine, untouched-by-human-hands paper. Simply tear out a few pages, fold them together, and attach a couple of rubber bands.

The Stephen Conroy face mask: far-sighted epidemiologist and political hard-head Stephen Conroy anticipated the pandemic many years ago, when he advised a puzzled US audience that he had the power to order people in Australia to wear red underpants on their heads. In fact, Mr Conroy was just preparing the public for the inevitable shortage of masks that would occur in a future Australian police state panicked by a 'red' Chinese virus. Simply turn the red undies upside down, slip over your head and breathe easy! (ed.'s note—shouldn't you wash them first?)

The Kevin Rudd face mask: many households in Australia enjoy the climate protection of large amounts of once-popular pink batts installed in their attics at vast taxpayer expense during the famous 'catastrophic climate pandemic' of 2008 when Prime Minister Rudd came to the rescue of a grateful nation. Simply cut a slim section off the nearest pink batt and gaffer tape it over your nose and mouth before heading outdoors to enjoy a virus-free stroll. (Not advised for smokers or anyone near a naked flame.)

The Julia Gillard face mask: forget COVID-19, the most dangerous epidemics in Australia today are the twin plagues of sexism and misogyny, which have infected the nation since the dark night of 9 October 2012 when in the wet market of the Liberal party room Tony Abbott and a group of batty white men unleashed their contagious Misogyn-12 pathogen upon an unsuspecting world by looking at their watches. As the sainted former Prime Minister noted, simply by wrapping a blue tie across your mouth and nose, the Liberal patriarchy sought complete protection from this deadly virus.

The Tony Abbott plague protection kit: during the Great Plague of 1665–6, it was a common sight to see people with a bouquet of herbs or flowers strapped tightly around their nose and mouth to counter the horrific stench of the rotting corpses that pervaded every corner of London's grisly East End. For similar reasons, during the Great Spill of 2015 former Prime Minister Tony Abbott frequently tied a large brown onion over his mouth and nose in order to counter the horrific stench of his rotting colleagues that pervaded every corner of Canberra's grisly corridors of power.

The Christopher Pyne face mask: also known as the 'two-faced mask', this unique design features two masks tied together and slipped over your head, one at the front and one at the back. Also available in rainbow colours with diamanté edging.

The Julie Bishop face mask: also known as the 'loyalty mask', this popular fashion accessory camouflages all normal facial features so as not to allow any observable signs such as involuntary tics, twitching mouth, avoiding eye contact and so on that indicate you may not be telling the entire truth. A well-used pair of these fashionable face masks now hang on permanent display in the Julie Bishop Wing of Canberra's (now empty and defunct) Museum of Australian Democracy.

The Anthony Albanese face mask: in living up to his popular nickname of 'Each-Way' Albo, the Albanese face mask is cunningly designed to be reversible and to effortlessly flip over to be used on both sides. A novel design feature also allows the wearer to speak out of both sides of his mouth at the same time.

The Kristina Keneally vowel-mangler: manufactured in America, this unique padded face mask has an extraordinary acoustic ability to divert and deflect sound waves to such an extent that when uttered even the most ordinary vowel sounds in the Australian vernacular come out sounding like a baby bat being eaten alive in a Wuhan wet market.

Bob Carr face mask: made in China.

Lockdown grinds on as Malcolm releases his memoir.

Ghost stories

18 April 2020

Settling in for a long, boring winter indoors? Wondering what to read? Why not scare yourself senseless with the latest must-have compendium of Classic Australian Ghost Stories? You won't get a wink of sleep as you lose yourself in these phantasmagorical tales from beyond the political grave. Complied and edited by *The Fin*'s own supernatural correspondent, Ms Rowena Bligh-Hughes, Classic Australian Ghost Stories will haunt you throughout the lonely months ahead. Here are just a few scary snippets:

The Ghost Who Talks: a terrifying story about a group of politicians who believe they are having private conversations in and around the corridors of power leading to Canberra's sinister underground crypt known as the Liberal party room. Yet a ghostly apparition can be sensed silently lurking behind the curtains and preserving their every word using the psychic and magical powers of WhatsApp. Years later, when they least expect it, the Ghost comes back to blab all their darkest secrets to an astonished world, damning them for all eternity with their own ill-begotten words.

Turgid-19: an invisible and ghost-like virus spreads death and chaos among the political careers of anyone it touches as it destroys an entire generation of gullible Liberal party hacks. Believed to have originated in the wet markets of Woollahra, the virus is a weaponised mutation of the deadly Rudd Virus (which originated in pink bats) of a decade ago grafted onto the toxic Turnbull pathogen found lurking in the darkest and dampest corners of old harbourside mansions. This new highly contagious strain attacks and turns into a gluggy mush those parts of the frontal lobe responsible for common sense and a conservative approach to problem-solving. Sufferers complain of being unable to breathe and being suffocated by smug elitist sanctimonious political correctness.

The Wandering Waffler: a wraith-like spectre wanders the twilight zone between hogging the headlines every single day and the nightmare of total media irrelevance. As his desperate and lonely moans echo across the water accompanied by a steady stream of incoherent, ectoplasmic waffle, the Ghost desperately tries to re-discover the lost love of his life who vanished without trace on the night of 24 August 2018: namely, himself.

The Smartest Ghost in the Crypt: terrifying tale from the nether world of a Ghost who turns up one night in September 2015 in an old disused shed in the back garden of a house in Queanbeyan where a secret seance is taking place. Sitting around a circle of sharp knives and brown onions, the plotters are convinced that they have found the One True Leader who will give them unlimited power, only to be betrayed when the Ghost leads them all to eternal damnation at the ballot box.

The Phantom in the Red Shoes: strange and eerie tale of a talented young lawyer from Western Australia who is tipped for greatness but falls under the spell of a miserable Ghost who convinces her to betray her leader to whom she has sworn her undying loyalty. When she does so, her own soul is torn apart and from that moment on she is viewed as pure poison by all her colleagues, all of whom hastily abandon her when she most needs their vote. In the end, all that is left of her is a pair of empty red shoes hanging desolately in the Mausoleum of Australian Democracy (shouldn't that be Museum?—ed).

Ghostly Guardian: left-wing Australian Prime Minister helps set up invisible online newspaper that not a soul reads.

The Spook: old wives' tale about the scion of a wealthy South Australian dynasty who dresses in fishnet tights and is posted to London where he becomes a spook for a sinister crime family from Arkansas and ends up hanging around wine bars plying gullible young Trump supporters with booze hoping to learn their darkest secrets.

The Invisible Seats: necromantic tale of fourteen Liberal party seats that mysteriously disappeared at the precise same moment one dark and lonely night in 2016 from conservative electorates right across Australia. Witnesses claim to have seen a ghostly apparition resembling a wealthy merchant banker from Point Piper hovering over the seats only moments before they evaporated into thin air.

Ghostwriter: creepy tale of a former Australian prime minister who accuses other former Australian prime ministers of hanging around like miserable ghosts while he, er, hangs around like a miserable ghost.

Still in lockdown...

A doctor writes

25 April 2020

Stuck inside terrified to go outdoors in case you catch the Coronavirus? Frantically spraying every surface in order to stop the spread of the lethal contagion? How long does the virus last? Where do I catch it? In this world exclusive, *The Fin*'s hand-satirising expert (surely sanitising?—ed) Dr Wuhena Sars-Covid answers all your questions about the deadly disease.

Dear doctor, can I catch the coronavirus from reading a book?

Dear Worried of Woollahra, you are right to be concerned. As is well known, the virus can survive for different lengths of time on paper surfaces. But not all printed material is the same, so the amount of viral shedding depends on what type of book you are reading. For example, should the printed material in question contain toxic pathogens such as might be disgorged from the highly-contaminated memory banks and mucus spray of a bitter and twisted former prime minister, then you should avoid it at all costs. If you do accidentally read such a book, you'll need to take a long, hot shower straight afterwards.

Dear doctor, Ever since this bloody Coronavirus thing came along I have felt totally isolated, ignored, irrelevant and depressed. Every day I am stuck inside banging my head against a brick wall trying to get some attention and even my colleagues can no longer look me in the eye. Will life ever return to normal?

Dear Mr Albo, yes, it's true that the virus has completely altered the way we now live and unfortunately some jobs have become completely redundant, including, of course, your own.

Dear doctor, is it true that in even the most dire of circumstances, sometimes you can turn a negative situation to your own advantage, or to put it another way, could the virus be my lucky break?

Dear Tanya, it is always worth being prepared to step into the shoes of your superior if he happens to be performing poorly thanks to (a lack of) exposure to COVID-19. In extreme circumstances, surgery may be desirable requiring the simultaneous insertion of several sharp implements into the spinal region of the afflicted individual in order to put him swiftly out of his discomfort and avoid prolonging your own agony.

Dear doctor, Can you please stop calling this thing the Chinese Flu which is of course a completely unacceptable and disgustingly racist and xenophobic term typically employed by the right-wing shock jocks of Sky After Dark. My revered colleagues and indeed my generous employers at the Institute have reliably assured me that there is no credible evidence whatsoever that the Coronavirus was developed as a sinister and highly contagious biological weapon designed to bring down Donald Trump that accidentally wound up in a bowl of bat soup in a Wuhan wet market before being exported across the globe during lunar new year celebrations.

Dear Bob, thanks for that, and in answer to your follow-up question, no, there are no documented cases of people catching the virus from wearing silk pyjamas or eating rolled steel-cut oats.

Dear doctor, can I catch the deadly virus simply from touching a rugby ball?

Dear Raelene, the good news is that this is something you no longer need to worry about.

Dear doctor, I have heard that the virus is commonly found on public transport, such as buses. I spent several unhappy weeks forced to work as the Captain of a large bus back in May 2019. Am I still at risk?

Dear Kristina, it depends how toxic the driver was and how physically close you got to him. Did you, for example, pose for photos together laughing and fondling puppies? In which case you must immediately distance yourself from him and undertake a thorough deep clean of all your media interviews and commentary from that period in order to build up your immunity and quarantine your dangerously-infected reputation.

Dear doctor, can the Coronavirus affect your memory? Apparently, according to a recently-published historical tome now widely available as a free PDF download from the Liberal party it turns out I was the prime minister of Australia for a couple of years and everyone was utterly terrified of me and I ran the entire government, the Cabinet, the economy, the public service and all our international relationships single-handedly but weirdly I have no recollection of ever doing so. How can this be?

Dear Peta, what a shame you weren't!

A year before the rest of the commentary begin to even contemplate the 'lab-leak' theory, I have my own doubts about the official bat soup narrative. Meanwhile, the virus breaks out in an abattoir connected to the Victorian Labor party as a Labor bureaucrat compares Covid to Captain Cook.

Meat works

9 May 2020

The world of abattoirs was rocked to its core this week following the shocking news of a COVID-19 outbreak at a Victorian meat works linked to the Australian Labor Party. But how should the company bounce back? In this world exclusive, *The Fin*'s diverse and inclusive marketing correspondent Ms Rowena Tender-Loins explains how rather than suffering from the adverse publicity, the company should embrace it with a whole new range of progressive meat products:

Stuffed Swan: based on a recipe by former British monarch King Henry VIII, this popular festive dish has been updated to reflect modern Labor values. Requiring extremely careful handling by an expert knife-wielder, the rather messy and bloody preparation requires the carcass of a stool-pigeon to be stuffed inside a galah which is stuffed inside a goose which is then stuffed inside a swan. Also packaged and marketed under the awkward name of a 'Shortruddalboswan', diners should be warned that the dish has been known to cause severe fiscal indigestion and out-of-control budgetary bloating. Takes years to clean up the mess.

Mal's Offal: a handy dish if you happen to be unemployed or permanently on the nose with the electorate, this tired old recipe requires throwing any spare entrails, bleeding gizzards, open wounds or other private internal organs of a butchered animal—in this case the slaughtered remains of the over-cooked Turnbull cabinet—into a cheap throwaway book presented in a glossy cover. The ideal dish for a fancy harbourside dinner party, it is best served cold and raw—or cooked for three hours at 280 degrees using 100% renewable energy, which amounts to the same thing.

Pyne Floater with Pea Soup: an extremely expensive dish based on an obscure French recipe, this sausage-shaped pie is placed in a deep bowl of impenetrable green mushy soup where it immediately sinks to the bottom and is never seen again. Because the dish traditionally can take years if not decades before it is even ready to be served up, by then the seafood components will most likely be long past their use-by-date and might cause numerous bouts of severe vomiting when the bill arrives some time between 2050 and the end of the century. Prior to cooking the books, make sure that the meaty bits of the engine are removed from the carcass and replaced with a drizzle of cold-pressed Aussie diesel oil.

Pangolin Pie: made exclusively from live baby bats, kidnapped koalas and pangolin pups sourced directly from the world-renowned Wuhan Gourmet Wet Market and definitely in no way modified or tampered with or weaponised in the top-secret Xi Jinping World Domination and Wet Viral Bio-Weapons Research Lab right next door, this dish is an absolute must if you want to bring the world's economies to their knees without firing a shot.

KK's Homegrown Red-Blooded Red-Neck Stew: developed exclusively for instant media consumption on board her Celebrity Bus by popular blonde bombshell and Reality TV Chef Kristina Keneally, this locally-grown, locally-sourced, locally-cooked and locally-consumed dish is a real favourite among the, er, locals. Because it contains no foreign ingredients whatsoever KK's Red-Neck Stew is as ridgy-didge, fair dinkum and true blue as vegan meat pies, gender-fluid sausage rolls and eco-conservationist kangaroo steaks.

Van Diemen Knuckle-head: historically-inaccurate dish devised during the long march through the kitchens and popular as a neo-Marxist recipe for undergraduate socialists living in exile in cushy Melbourne inner-city suburbs on massive taxpayer-funded senior public servant salaries. Laced with green dogma, the dish presents as healthy and nutritious but is merely the re-heating of hard left-overs served up on a bed of poisonous social media.

The woke lefty Queensland government decides it wants to buy Virgin.
But what will it mean for the airline?

Virgin

16 May 2020

Bing-bong: This is a special announcement for passengers in rows 1 to 8 waiting to board this morning's early bird Virgin flight VA 9645 from Brisbane to Cooktown… oh ,er, hang on, what's this?…

Bing-bong: This is a special announcement for all passengers waiting to board Virgin flight VA 9645. There has been a slight delay due to an unforeseen problem that our new owners have identified with the, ah, boarding announcement procedures. We hope to get you in the air very soon…

Bing-bong: Er, this is a special announcement for passengers waiting to be welcomed to, er, the Guugu Yimithirr nation, and er, what's that?, wan-ta-tharra nyun-doo, I think that's how you say it, um, whose elders past, present and future may not actually be on this flight but, er, we acknowledge them anyway and have reserved rows 1 to 8 for any, um, gurr-ugu bumma who, er, anyway, we'll be boarding as soon as we possibly can but not quite yet, shit was that OK?…

Bing-bong: This is a special announcement for all passengers waiting to board flight VA 9645 today to apologise that in the previous special announcement at 11.43am we forgot to also acknowledge that this runway and indeed this airport lounge is built upon land that was stolen from the Turrbal nation to whom we owe a deep and eternal and enduring debt of gratitude, no sorry scratch that coz the lawyers will have a field day you know compensation, bloody hell…

Bing-bong: This is a special announcement to update the special announcement of 12.45 for all passengers waiting to board the shiny white aircraft sitting on the tarmac just outside gate 13 with the large red V painted on the side which is going to Cookt… sorry I mean, Guugu whatever, um, ah, due to a recent management decision it has been determined that the word 'virgin' with its overtly sexist overtones which is commonly uttered by patriarchal white males towards female hosties, er, I mean Airline Personal Assistance Staff with suggestive winks and, er, other highly offensive male leering expressions which are likely to trigger deeply distressing memories in young women of a first experience of, er, penetration is entirely inappropriate for a progressive government-owned airline and we would ask all passengers and staff to refrain from using such an inappropriate and unsafe word forthwith…

Bing-bong! BING-BONG!: This is an urgent announcement! Please listen carefully! Following an emergency meeting of the new Airline Ownership Caucus we would like to apologise profusely to all members of our Airline Personal Assistance Union for the deeply offensive and non-inclusive previous announcement earlier today regarding the term 'virgin' and its inappropriate sexual overtones. It has been brought to the Management Team's attention that this announcement caused profound distress to not only female members of the Union but also to all gay and gender diverse employees, including transgender, genderqueer, Two-Spirit and lesbian staff who understandably felt deeply aggrieved by the frankly unacceptable and non-inclusive use of language suggesting loss of virginity is exclusively a binary experience and please rest assured that the privileged white male responsible for holding such disgusting and primitive views has now been arrested and sent off to an intensive Employee's Re-education Program.

Bing-bong: This is a special announcement to update the special announcement that updated, er, anyway, the airline's new Management Team are delighted to announce to all passengers and staff that the large V painted on the side of your aircraft, which hopefully will be departing soon, stands for the word Vegan. From now on, please refer to us as Vegan Airlines.

Bing-bong: This is a special announcement for all passengers travelling on Vegan Airlines VA 9645 to Cookt... sorry, Guugu wotsit, we regret to inform you that the bacon roll and, er, ham sandwich Gourmet In-Flight Snack options are no longer available on this afternoon's flight.

Bing-bong: This is a special announcement for all passengers waiting to fly on VA flight 9645 to the Guugu Yimithirr nation this evening. The current unexpected delay is due to a technical glitch that involves the crew working out how to minimise the flight's unacceptably humongous carbon footprint in order to save the planet from catastrophic global heating. As soon as this matter has been satisfactorily resolved in line with our new owners' unswerving commitment to net zero emissions, we will be in the air as swiftly as possible.

Bing-bong: This is a final announcement to all ticket holders on flight VA9645. Due to its association with our shameful history of white privilege, colonialism, genocide and slavery, Vegan Airlines wouldn't be seen dead going anywhere near a place called Cooktown.

The Dan Andrews Victorian Labor government strikes two secret Belt and Road deals with communist China.

Dan Dynasty

23 May 2020

The Dan Dynasty (Dān wángcháo Chinese: 丹王朝) or the Dan Empire (not to be confused with the Dan Murphy's empire, see separate entry) was an obscure southern outpost of the Imperial Kingdom of China during the Jinping dictatorship of the early 21st century. Historians generally regard the Dan dynasty as a low point in Chinese civilization; a cesspit of self-indulgent cosmopolitan culture and disastrous financial mis-management. Dan territory, acquired by the cunning Emperor Xi without firing a single shot, stretched across the entire swathe of inner-city latte-sipping suburbs surrounding the decadent gwái-lóu capital.

The Dan dynasty reached its despotic peak during the Great Plague of 2020, a pandemic that swept out of a bowl of bat soup in Wuhan and in which an estimated one and a half million people didn't perish.

The Dan capital, known as the Golden City of the One Thousand Shrinking Petals and Quivering Snowflakes (present-day Melbourne), was the most forbidden city in the world at the time thanks to the secrecy surrounding the deals the Dan had signed up to with his Beijing overlords.

When the bungling and woeful Celestial Treasurer to the Dan got down on his knees and swore undying loyalty to the Emperor Xi, it wasn't enough to save him from being garrotted after delivering a disastrous

2021 budget, in which the fiefdom's debt had grown to over 20 billion dollars, all of it discovered in worthless crumpled Yuan notes stuffed into empty cans of baby formula.

But the Dan was able to struggle on for another eighteen months by calling on his loyal armies of ambulance paramedics, firefighters, police, healthcare workers, traffic wardens and an estimated $387,842 worth of taxpayer-funded electoral officers (in red shirts, natch) to intimidate and subdue the populace.

Vassal states such as Queensland and the ACT paid verbal tribute to the Dan court, leaving the mainland Jinping dictatorship free to concentrate on crushing and subduing rebel regions such as Hong Kong in late 2020 and Taiwan in early 2022. Through its powerful 'debt diplomacy' protectorate system, the Jinping dictatorship also gained political hegemony over many neighbouring states in the South Pacific, Sri Lanka and Africa.

Historians record that the Dan dynasty began with a surprising period of progress and stability in the early years of its rule, concentrating on building railway crossings and, er, building railway crossings (is that it?—ed) until the devastating corona plague caused the deaths of at least 18 people across the entire state, including a cluster at the Celestial Abattoir and Cedar Wet Markets. In the ensuing panic, the Dan signed the Imperial Acquiescence to the Belt and Road Initiative, locked down the borders and banned all treasonous activities such as fishing and golf. In late 2020 Emperor Dan adopted the title of Dan of All Heavenly Social Isolations.

Many notable innovations occurred under the Dan, including the development of an anti-bullying scholastic program that encouraged impressionable young girls to blossom into handsome young boys and pony-tailed and bearded young boys to blossom into attractive young ladies and the Dan became a major centre of influence in the kingdom's culture wars, with its academic prowess second only to the Mogul wastelands of Kazakhstan.

However, around this time the scheming eunuch Al-Bo, whom everybody had forgotten even existed, committed political suicide by announcing his plan to reduce the kingdom's net emissions to zero (except in China, of course, which was permitted under the Paris Agreement to carry on increasing its carbon dioxide output until 2030 by whatever its thousands of blossoming celestial coal-fired power plants could possibly manage). The eunuch's insane proclamation sent all economic activity across the land spiralling into a sharp and permanent decline; agrarian riots resulted in visual atrocities such as the Extinction Rebellions of 2019–22 where unwashed devotees glued themselves face-down to the Belt and Silk Road before starving themselves to death on avocado and kale muffins.

Paganism and the worship of religious entities such as the Goddess Gaia and the Sainted Greta flourished under the Dan, with climate cults and Malthusian sects gaining prominence in the halls of power and corporate boardrooms. Traditional religious 'hate-figures' such as Cardinal Hell were relentlessly persecuted by the authorities and thrown into jail for months on end even when they were found to be innocent.

The Dan ruled from 2014 to the 'long night of the incredibly sharp knives' on Saturday 26 November 2022 at roughly around 6pm just after the polling booths shut when it was wiped clean from the pages of history. The Dan dynasty was preceded by the eminently forgettable and weak Napthine rule and followed by the prosperous era of rebuilding the economy now known as the Tim Smith Golden Age.

Queensland and the Labor states maintain the siege.

Siege mentality

30 May 2020

As the federal government pleads with recalcitrant states to open their borders, *The Fin*'s history expert, Ms Rowena Herodotus-Bede, seeks out any historical precedents to the current predicament.

The Siege of Annastacia: the Siege of Annastacia occurred at the height of the Puny Wars of the early 21st century when a motley group of second-rate premiers, union officials and chief medical officers decided to lay siege to their own economies in defiance of the decree to open their borders from Pope Scott Miraculus the First at the Wholly National Cabinet of May 2020. Throughout the long winter of that year, terrified by fear of the plague, impoverished citizens were forced to endure the cruellest deprivations, as rations of decent-paying jobs quickly dwindled and fresh supplies of tourist dollars were cut off at the source and starving tour-operators and cafe owners were locked down in their tropical homes even though none of them had even the faintest chance of actually catching the dreaded virus. Attempting to build a bridge across the Tweed in order to break open the southern border, the Berejiklian forces led by the Dominican Perrottet sought to overwhelm their stubborn northern neighbour with an angry army of cashed-up Grey Nomads, but were repelled at the river's edge by fanatical public health officials, bloated bureaucrats and power-crazed traffic wardens. In a blind panic, elderly cruise-line passengers were dragged out of the otherwise empty intensive care units and thrown over the walls into local nursing homes and left to suffer whatever fate befell them. As famine and fear gripped the once-sunny state through a long gruelling July and August, women were forced to cut off their hair to make catapults with which to repel the southern invaders, with nothing but the carcasses of dead cane toads and rotting pineapples for ammunition.

The Siege of Daningrad: at the same time that Pope Miraculus was attempting to open up the borders to the north, an audacious attack was launched upon his southern flank by the Mogul hordes of Emperor Xi who sent a seductive and exotic princess to distract the local warlord, Genghis Dhan, with the glittering promise of eternal power thanks to a golden belt and silken road initiative. Entranced by the offer of wealth and riches beyond his wildest budget estimates, the premier ignored all his advisers and threw open the doors of the city, lowered the drawbridge, laid out a red (natch!) carpet and invited the plunderers to march on in and help themselves to whatever they wanted, including snapping up all the local dairy farms, vineyards, Toorak mansions and struggling businesses at bargain basement prices. As the streets turned red (literally) with armies of red tee-shirted electoral officers (estimated cost to taxpayers $387,842), the traumatised citizenry found themselves blocked by an elaborate network of railway crossings that came crashing down with loud bells and flashing lights for at least three or four minutes at a time while huge, lumbering freight-trains trundled past, each loaded with all the looted goodies on their way back to the Celestial Kingdom from the bustling Port of Melbourne—which the invaders didn't need to lay siege to because they already owned it, having snapped it up for a lazy $9.7 billion back in 2016.

The Siege of Albo: in preparation for a long-anticipated campaign against the Scomos Empire in 22BC, the Albanian general Albo 'the Unsteady' found himself 'suffering from conflict fatigue', besieged by his own irrelevance and in desperate need of favourable media attention. As enemy forces circled, even within his own caucus, Albo sought divine guidance from the entrails of a white chicken which he carefully cradled in his arms for a by-election photo opportunity on the first anniversary of his leadership victory. As the JobKeeper Wars raged all around him, Albo realised it was his own job he had to try and keep and in desperation poisoned the well of goodwill with the entire business community. The ploy was a spectacular failure and Albo met a grisly fate after being publicly humiliated and dismembered by the Concubine Empress Kristina.

The Siege of Trumble: deposed Emperor Malcolm the Miserable, besieged in his harbourside citadel surrounded by mountainous piles of pristine copies of his philosophical musings, 'Maior Exspiravit' (A Bigger Ghost), ordered an army of 'renewables' engineers and tax-slaves to push vast amounts of water uphill in order to harness energy from windmills and the sun gods with which he planned to power a fleet of sub-marinal vessels in order to escape his own empty legacy. History records Trumble (and his subs) sank without a trace.

Yet again, I cast doubt on the credibility of the official Wuhan bat soup script. But that's not the only weird thing that doesn't make any sense.

You just can't make this stuff up

5 June 2020

'Hey, come on in Rowan, sit down, great to meet ya, kid.'

'Thanks, er, sir, it's an honour.'

'Like a snort?'

'Um, no, ah, I'm fine thanks…

(loud sniffing sound)

'… actually I'm more of a, er, beer and wine kinda guy, sir.'

'Sure, sure, each to their own, kid. No need to call me sir by the way. We're all first names here. Anyway, I wanted to talk to you about the script. Great script, by the way, great script!'

'Thank you sir. As you know, it's my first big budget action thriller. And having Tom and Liam and Natalie…'

'Precisely! And that's my point. We've got this bad-ass all-star Hollywood cast. Highly talented and frankly over-paid actors, kid. Think they know everything! To you and me this movie is just lots of explosions and special effects and fear and mayhem strung together with your script getting us from one adrenalin-busting scene to the next but to them, you know, the plot has to be watertight. The storyline's gotta be credible, Otherwise all their Stanislavsky method acting training crap goes out the window. Know what I mean?'

'Er, I'm not sure...'

'Take the virus scene. Bat soup? Really? I mean two pages later there's a goddam Bio-tech-warfare Virology Lab right next to the fish market! Who's gonna believe the virus came from bats? That's just crazy!'

'But...'

'And anyway, it doesn't make any sense. It says they close down all the domestic flights out of this Woo place but on the next page everyone's flying all over the place on international flights! Bit of a logic gap there!'

'Um...'

'And who's gonna believe that this highly contagious and deadly virus only kills old people in nursing homes but doesn't even touch anyone else? Come on...'

'Well...'

'You haven't thought it through properly, kid. They bankrupt every single nation on earth for a couple of old farts who'd've kicked the bucket anyway? Nobody's gonna buy that!'

'It's just that I thought...'

'That's my point! You *didn't* think! it's called the 'suspension of disbelief'. Don't forget, these audiences have paid good money and they're trusting you to tell them a credible story but instead you're feeding 'em up total illogical BS. Like the cop chase scene. Who's gonna believe half a dozen police cars with flashing lights go screeching across this harbourside park just to hassle a guy who's sunbathing? Really? Or this scene here when six armed officers with guns drawn arrest some little old lady coz she's walking along a beach? C'mon, kid, you can do better than that!'

'I guess I could change that bit...'

'Damn right you will. And what about this scene? They close all the borders coz some 30- year-old guy dies of the virus but in the very next scene the coroner says there's no sign of the virus on him! That's just sloppy script-writing, kid. And it's not just that! In the scene after that you've got the government handing out free cash to all these people to go and get their renovations done! In the middle of a goddam pandemic? In one page we've gone from epic disaster movie to an episode of *The Block*! Are you kidding me?'

'Um, it's because they need to stimulate…'

'Nah, nobody'll buy this crap. And even though everybody's locked down because of your mystery virus that weirdly only kills old people who've been on cruise ships then suddenly in the very next scene everybody's running around in surgical masks looting the joint! That doesn't even make any sense! It's all disjointed. What happened to the lockdown and the deadly virus??'

'I, er…'

'It gets worse. On page 55 you've got the mass demonstration scene. Sure, I like it visually coz there's lots of violence and bloodshed. Nice. But it doesn't make any narrative sense. Why are they protesting in Melbourne and Sydney about some guy who died ten days earlier in Minnesota? What's the connection? But even if we swallow that which is a bit of a stretch, you've then gone and broken your own internal logic - on the one hand the cops don't bat an eyelid while 30,000 total strangers are brawling in the streets but two pages later the very same cops arrest everyone at the wedding scene—why?—because there are more than twenty people gathered together! Huh? I don't get it!'

'Well, I…'

'And what about this scene, which is just plain dopey. The Australian Prime Minister signs a deal with the United Nations that lets some human rights delegation from—as if anyone's gonna believe this!—Afghanistan, Sudan, Libya and—wait for it!—Burkina Faso investigate Australia— for torture! As if! That's just plain silly. You're insulting the audience's intelligence, kid.'

'Um.'

Gone with the Wind gets cancelled.

Gone with the Woke

13 June 2020

As the cancel-culture of the furious mobs devours our favourite books, films and comedy skits, *The Fin*'s literary editor Ms Rowena Georgina-Belle hastily re-writes critical scenes in the classic now known as 'Gone with the Woke'.

*

Scarlett was not pretty, but men, women and genderqueer folk seldom realised it when caught by her Tinder profile as the Tarleton twins were. In her face were too sharply blended the delicate features of her mother, a Coast w*min of white privilege, and the heavy ones of her abusive Irish birth-parent. But it was an arresting face, meaning it frequently got her arrested; pointed of chin, square of jaw, with magnolia-white skin. Not quite the fashion these days. Her eyes were pale green starred with bristly, er, black, hang on can't say that, anyway bristly lashes and slightly tilted at the ends. Above them, her thick, oh crikey here we go again, well anyway her thick brows slant upward, cutting a startling oblique line in her pale and over-privileged complexion.

Seated with Stuart and Brent Tarleton in the cool shade of the porch of Tara, her father's concentration camp, that bright April afternoon of 1861, she made a pretty picture of colonialism, exploitation and white supremacy rolled into one. Her new green flowered-muslim (surely muslin?—ed) dress spread its twelve yards of billowing material over her hoops and exactly matched the flat-heeled green morocco slippers her father had recently threatened to beat the maid senseless with unless she performed degrading favours for him. The dress set off to perfection Scarlett's boyish waist and the tightly-fitting basque showed breasts well matured since the hormone therapy had kicked in. But for all the modesty and demureness of her spreading skirts, her true self was poorly concealed, although 'poorly' is probably a poor choice of words seeing as how she and her family were stinking rich based on the exploitation of black lives, which to them clearly did not matter one jot (this bit's really good!—ed).

Stuart bellowed:'Jeems!' And after an interval a tall, strapping, um, lad of their own age ran breathlessly around the house and towards the tethered horses. Jeems was their, um, anyway, he accompanied them everywhere they went and had been gifted, er, anyway, whatever, for their tenth birthday. Brent turned to him. 'You heard what we were talking to Miss Scarlett about?' 'Nawsuh,' Jeems replied, 'Ah din no teese y'all say anyting ter mek her mad! Look ter me lak she sho cheep long happy as a bird Miss Melly gettin' mah'ied.'

'You can't talk like that, Jeems,' shouted Scarlett from the porch, 'that's cultural appropriation!'

*

The flames licked the Minnesota skyline and the streets seethed with the activity of an anthill just destroyed. Oppressed demonstrators were running up and down the boulevard, their shopping trolleys loaded with jewellery, Nike shoes, Gucci clothing and other such basic essentials; and on porches privileged shopkeepers sat crying untended. The ruins of the mall were crowded with TV news crews and ambulances filled with the noble cries of the wounded warriors for social justice. Defunded police officers on horseback tried to flee pell-mell down Peachtree towards McDonalds. In front of his burned-out liquor store, old Amos greeted Scarlett with rolling eyes. 'Ain' you gwine yit, Miss Scarlett? We is gwine now.'

'Going? Where?'

'Gawd knows, Miss! De Anne-tee-fahs they is comin'!'

She saw an officer on horseback and gathered up her skirts and ran towards him. 'Is it true? Are the Antifas really coming?' There were harsh lines of fatigue in his face, but his tattered grey hat was off with a sweep. 'Madam. They've already torn down the statue of Robert E. Lee and spray-pained Abraham Lincoln. We are pulling out.'

'And leaving us to Black Lives Matter?'

'I'm afraid so,' he yelled, and was gone.

*

'Oh my darling,' she cried, 'if you go, what shall I do?'

For a moment Rhett hesitated as if debating whether a kind lie were kinder in the long run than the truth. 'Scarlett, what is broken is broken. I wish I could care what you do or where you go, but I can't.' He hesitated. 'Frankly, my dear, I don't give a…' Her green eyes blazed with fury. 'How dare you use such misogynistic language! "Frankly" is a patriarchal word derived from "Frank" and don't you dare call me "my dear". I am not your fawn. I am an independent, progressive self-identifying woman who will not be lectured to by a racist, white supremacist, climate-denying, homophobic, transphobic, sexist, cis-gender, heteronormative right-wing nut job!'

'OK,' he said as he turned to walk away. 'How about this?… Comrade, I couldn't give a rat's arse.'

Scott Morrison compares the international political environment to the 1930s.

The times they are a-changin'

4 July 2020

Scott Morrison this week compared the current fraught global political environment to that of the 1930s. But is he right? In a world exclusive, *The Fin*'s historical comparisons intern Professor Rowena Chamberlain-Weimar debunks the prime minister's crackpot claims.

In the lead up to World War 2, Germany built up a massive industrial and military complex whilst pretending to be interested in peaceful relations with its many neighbours. To compare such despicable behaviour to that of the People's Republic of China—an open, free and tolerant society with nothing but harmonious wishes for cordial and mutually beneficial relations with its many neighbours, including their long overdue, environmentally-friendly and tasteful eco-rehabilitation of long-neglected coral reefs and sandy cays throughout the South China Sea and the Spratly Islands—is frankly insulting.

During the '30s, enlightened activists and academics demonised an entire race as perfidious money-grabbing oppressors responsible for all the ills in the world who deserved whatever punishment they got; which led to six million of them being marched off to death camps. Fortunately today, anti-racist activists and academics are enlightening the world about the evils of white people; a perfidious race of money-grabbing and oppressive capitalists who deserve whatever punishment is coming their way.

Chamberlain signed the Munich Agreement which of course merely allowed the Germans time to build up their military might. Turnbull ratified the Paris Agreement, which of course merely allows China all the time it needs to develop its, er, um… OK maybe forget that one.

Once he had seized power, Hitler used the media and an elaborate propaganda campaign to build up a strong personality cult with himself as the central figure of national life. To compare such a campaign with the factual, open and honest reporting of the vibrant, independent and typically self-critical Chinese media outlets is preposterous. Hitler was a lunatic determined to conquer the entire planet with himself as Fuhrer-for-Life, whereas Mr Jinping is nothing but a humble party bureaucrat sorry, typo, I mean President Jinping is nothing but a servant of the peop… sorry, my mistake, they've upgraded his title to, er, President-for-Life Xi Jin… er, sorry, apparently the correct translation from the original Court Mandarin is Emperor of All the Celestial Bodies of the Imperial and Ancient Royal Kingdom of China (including those Stinking Treacherous Rat-Holes Taiwan and Hong Kong) Xi Jinping.

Hitler's government embarked on a massive road-building project known as the Autobahn network, which was supposedly designed to give German motorists the freedom to quickly travel anywhere around the Reich, but was of course merely a front to allow the rapid deployment of troops and tanks to any particular battle front at any given point in time. To compare this with the benign intentions of the Chinese government's laudable and charitable Belt and Road Initiative, which offers cheap loans and assists in the building of much-needed infrastructure such as ports and runways in far-flung impoverished nations is fanciful nonsense.

The 'brownshirts' were violent criminals, anarchists and arsonists that the Nazis used to terrorise the public and vandalise public institutions; torching buildings, burning books and smashing up Jewish shopfronts. Fortunately, today we have the fragrant and benign forces of Antifa to keep such fascists in check.

The rise of fascism would not have occurred had much of the world not been traumatised by the devastating effects of the Spanish Flu, a deadly virus with no known cure that seemingly appeared out of nowhere and killed untold numbers of people and left devastated communities hiding indoors behind their masks suspicious and fearful of their fellow citizens and terrified of all foreigners. Clearly, no such comparison exists today. (Are you sure?—ed.)

The Nazis were a bunch of thin-skinned bullies who would react aggressively to even the slightest hint of dissenting opinion by hauling those who displeased them off to concentration camps or simply by cancelling them out of public life altogether in a secret and hitherto undisclosed program known as Das Kancel Kultur. Obviously, no such program exists today.

The Nazis simply marched into small neighbouring countries like Austria, Czechoslovakia and Poland on the belief that they were inferior vassal states. There can be no comparison with China, which has been highly respectful of its own inferior vassal states such as Hong Kong which should be a doddle now they've ditched the British legal system and, of course, er, Wotsitsname that island off the coast that is 100 per cent a part of the motherland you betcha and which the United Nations, the World Health Organisation and even Qantas dare not call by its proper name.

In the '30s people were forced to queue up at the Hungry Mile. Nowadays you just queue up for JobKeeper.

An entire group of tower blocks is suddenly locked down in Melbourne.

Ivan Danandruvich

11 July 2020

Melbourne, July 2020

ONE DAY IN THE LIFE OF IVAN DANANDRUVICH by Rowena
Soldier-Nitsyn

At five o'clock that morning reveille was sounded, as usual, by the
pounding of the 'doof doof' music coming from the meth lab on the
thirteenth floor of Van Diemen Tower in the People's Seventh Public
Housing Commission on Racecourse Road. The intermittent sounds
barely penetrated the windowpanes on which were taped hastily
scrawled notices forlornly pleading for food parcels hoping to attract the
attention of the ABC TV cameras far below. Ivan Danandruvich coughed
loudly and got up to go to the bucket. The plumbing this high up in the
Tower was notoriously unreliable, in keeping with the overall design of
Melbourne's Soviet-inspired public housing commission buildings, where
the lifts left you dangling precariously between floors and the fragrant
smell of cooking methamphetamine which infused the thirteenth floor,
an odour often described as a mixture of rotten eggs and nail polish
remover, thankfully was stronger than the stench of excrement and vomit
permanently wafting up from the graffitied concrete stairwells. Ivan
usually slept in, but not today, for he had an important meeting with The

Tartar. The Tartar had helped him get his last part-time job at the meat works, heaving the bloody carcasses in and out of the freezers or stuffing the offal into sausage skins. But they'd closed that place down and in the meantime he'd done a week as a handyman at the local school as well as a few days filling in as an orderly at the old people's home. But they'd also shut that place down due to an inexplicably high number of deaths. Of course, what Ivan desperately wished for was some security work like his cousin Kuziomin had recently done, boasting to Ivan, 'it's the coolest job, bro. A quick five-minute training session and then we just sit around all day or take the girls shopping and maybe play a game of cards, coz these women, they get real lonely after a week of quarantine! I got paid and I got laid, bro!' Ivan was so jealous.

There was a loud dry rasping cough and the sound of a match being struck in the next room followed by the familiar smell of cannabis and Ivan knew that his flatmate, Tsezar, was getting out of bed. Ivan quickly pulled a dry Weet-a-Bix from the government rations packet and chewed it with little enthusiasm. No milk. Ivan switched on the television and sure enough there was Old Jug Ears himself explaining why all the Towers still needed to stay in confinement, because there weren't enough public health officials. Last time they had been locked down, the residents had wept when Old Jug Ears had finally said they would be allowed to go out and they'd all hugged each other and danced together to celebrate, but of course it was just another trick. The very next day when Ivan and his friend Tiurin had gone fishing with an old piece of fishing line and a hook Tiurin had hidden in a small hole in the side of his mattress with his other worldly belongings such as the passport papers he had pretended to lose in the crossing from Indonesia, the Police had arrested them on the Pier and fined them over a thousand dollars each for breaking Covid restrictions, the common charge they used these days to justify house arrest.

The door creaked open and Ivan could see Tsezar was smoking, and smoking a joint, not a bong. That meant he might be able to cadge a puff. From across the room, Fetiukov, the jackal, had crawled out from under a pile of beer cans on the sofa. Fetiukov had offered to stand in line for Tsezar at Centre-Linkski in order to get a small share of his weekly JobTzeeker and JobKheeper packages. From next door came a high-pitched wailing sound through the paper thin wall that Ivan knew was Alyoshka's early morning prayers. For Alyoshka, the lockdown was a blessing from above which the Almighty had bestowed upon him in order to allow him to reflect upon His generosity in bringing them all safely to this land of plenty where everything was free and nobody had to do any work. Paradise Towers, Alyoshka called their new home, although Ivan couldn't help thinking that it reminded him more of the 'Socialist Way of Life' settlement camp he had narrowly escaped being sent to in Kazakhstan. The gulag. Ivan coughed, and headed out the door. Today he would get a decent job. He had a meeting with his friend The Tartar who would introduce him to Pavlo the local union boss who had promised him a steady job as one of those new Victorian hotel quarantine guards.

A secret cache of letters to the Queen's Private Secretary are unearthed.

Dismissals

18 July 2020

In shock news, a cache of hitherto secret correspondence from the Governor-General to Buckingham Palace has been discovered stuffed in an old cardboard box labelled 'Probably Best to Chuck This Lot in the Incinerator' in a Yarralumla garden shed. In this world exclusive, *The Fin*'s royal correspondent Lady Rowena Kerrs-Cur reveals their explosive content:

My dear Private Secretary, It is with great sadness that I must inform you that the current individual serving in the role of Her Majesty's Prime Minister is in fact a complete dolt, a vainglorious narcissist with a psychopathic and indeed sociopathic personality disorder who is hell-bent on bankrupting the nation and driving us all into penury and socialism. To wit, this lunatic has made all our hospitals free so every scrounger with a dicky knee can get whatever rolled gold treatment he fancies, made all our universities free so any bludger can rock up and do a meaningless B.A. in gender and the environment, given half the country back to the natives, pulled us out of Vietnam, gone grovelling to the commies and spent a motza on some ghastly painting that looks like someone expunged a perfectly good meal all over the canvas after a night on the Grange. Time to give this clown the flick. What do I do? Your dutiful etc.

My dear Governor-General, Thank you for your recent report which the Queen has read with great interest and asked me to convey to you her clear and unequivocal advice that you need to trim his fur at least every four weeks otherwise corgis, oops, sorry, wrong letter, I mean, ah yes, she advises that she is watching events with great interest and is relying upon you to exercise your duties with constitutional propriety. Of course, if it were down to me old bean I'd get that bloke with the Easter Island jaw to take over, but what would I know?

My dear Private Secretary, It is with great sadness that I must inform you that the current individual serving in the role of Her Majesty's Prime Minister is in fact a complete dolt, a vainglorious narcissist with a psychopathic and indeed sociopathic personality disorder who is hell-bent on bankrupting the nation and driving us all into penury and socialism. To wit, this lunatic has already caused a recession which he claims 'we had to have', given what remains of Crown land back to the natives, declared we should be a Republic (God help us!) and driven interest rates through the roof! Time to give this clown the flick. What do I do? Your dutiful etc.

My dear Governor-General, Thank you for your recent report which the Queen has read with great interest and suggests you place a few bob on Balmoral Jingle in the 3.45 at Epsom on, oops, sorry, wrong letter, I mean, she advises that she is watching events with great interest and is relying upon you to exercise your duties with due constitutional propriety. Of course, if it were down to me old bean I'd get that fellow with the bushy eyebrows to take over, but what would I know?

My dear Private Secretary, It is with great sadness that I must inform you that the current Prime Minister is a complete dolt, a vainglorious narcissist with a psychopathic and indeed sociopathic personality disorder who is hell-bent on bankrupting the nation and driving us all into penury and socialism. To wit, this lunatic has already been caught sending $900 cheques to dead people, torched half the rooftops in Queensland in order to save the planet and apologised to the natives for giving them our own land back or some such. Time to give this clown the flick. What do I do? Your dutiful etc.

My dear Governor-General, Thank you for your recent report which the Queen has read with great interest and asked me to send you two tickets to the Chelsea, oops, sorry, wrong letter, I mean, she advises that she is watching events with great interest. Of course, if it were down to me old bean I'd get that fellow in the speedos to take over, but what would I know?

My dear Private Secretary, It is with great sadness that I must inform you that the current individual serving in the role of Her Majesty's Prime Minister is a complete dolt, a vainglorious narcissist with a psychopathic and indeed sociopathic personality disorder who is hell-bent on bankrupting the nation and driving us all into penury and socialism. To wit, this lunatic is secretly funding the Guardian and trying to push water uphill. What do I do? Your dutiful etc.

My dear Governor-General, How about the guy who used to work in marketing?

Australia's TV ratings are hacked. But by who?

Guangdong Gogglebox

25 July 2020

The world of TV ratings was thrown into chaos this week as it was revealed that the entire Australian TV ratings system had been hacked into in what is being called 'a massive cyber attack'. The secretive ratings system is used by television executives to determine which shows are worth financing. Although the motivation for the cyber attack remains unclear, sources have revealed that they believe the culprit was a powerful state actor with unrivalled cyber warfare capabilities. (Er, China?—ed.)

In other media news this week, the major television networks have just announced a surprising new line-up of imaginative new shows going into immediate production for 2021.

Selling Houses in Hubei: new hosts Chang, Shanyuan and Ah Lim travel across China's most populous (and popular!) province to do what they do best: sprucing up dodgy old knockdowns so they can be sold for a fortune! This season sees the team face a range of challenging abodes to fix up. Highlights include a tiny Viral Lab that's in need of a real 'deep clean' and a delightful cottage overlooking Xinjiang province that needs some imaginative screening to cleverly disguise the irritating sights and sounds of a nearby re-education camp.

MasterChef Season 13: unlucky for some, but not for the 13th exciting new season of MasterChef which promises to serve up a gastronomic feast (and a ratings bonanza!) as the contest moves to its new home in Wuhan,

China. 24 new contestants (in masks!) descend on Wuhan's famous wet markets and bat caves with only one mission: who can make the tastiest three course meal using nothing but live baby bats! Spoiler alert: the Bat Short Ribs and Deep-fried Wing Tips baked on charcoal with bat-digested Figs is not to be missed!

Hainan and Away: in a shock move, the long-running popular Aussie soapie defies quarantining rules and up stumps and moves the entire cast (and action!) to picturesque Hainan island in the South China Sea. Sea, surf and sand and lots of the usual excitement, but how does Marilyn cope with the move? Can Amber forgive Cody for falling in love with the stunningly exotic, beautiful and sexy new cast member the gorgeous Lijuan? And what's that mysterious fully equipped military runway that's just popped up on a nearby coral reef?

Have You Been Paying Attention? Now under the exciting new production team at Running Dog Productions, the new updated formula will have even more fans flocking to this quirky game show, with exciting new segments such as 'Uighur or Not?' in which contestants get to watch unverified snippets of drone footage from some undisclosed train station in China and decide whether they are looking at a) ordinary everyday holiday makers playing a friendly game of Blindman's Bluff with a group of fun-loving railway guards? b) ordinary everyday religious men and women kneeling in prayer waiting to hop on a comfortable high-speed train to an exciting mysterious holiday retreat? or c) Muslims about to be executed.

Extreme Railway Journeys: see above.

Border Patrol: exciting new version of the popular reality TV show in which a crack team of Chinese naval officers patrol the waters around the Australian continent probing for any weaknesses.

Millionaire Hot Seat: now hosted by a popular former Labor Senator, the new format sees contestants having to explain how on earth they became so fabulously wealthy simply by sitting on a board or running a university faculty.

8 out of 10 Bats: re-vamped version of the classic comedy panel show, where contestants are presented with an array of statistics and opinion polls and must decide whether or not they are factually true—such as '99.95 per cent of people believe the Coronavirus originated in a CIA bio-weapons laboratory in order to wipe out China' or 'the Port of Darwin has been purchased for entirely peaceful purposes'.

Embarrassing Bodies: you'll be squirming in your seat watching Dr Tedros and his team at the WHO explain how the Wuhan virus isn't contagious.

Big Brother: moving from its current home at a disused military base on Sydney's North Head to a very much in-use military base in Xinjiang province, the new Big Brother sees a group of contestants living in a house under the watchful eye of, er, Big Brother. Sponsored by Huawei, the new format sees contestants get evicted if they happen to do, say or even think anything remotely negative about the Motherland or make any jokes or sarcastic comments about the prosperous, harmonious, benevolent leadership of President-for-Life Xi Jinp… oops, damn, just got evicted.

Marine physicist Peter Ridd vows to challenge in the High Court his sacking by James Cook University for his supposed failure to be 'collegiate'.

Galileo Ridd

1 August 2020

University of Pisa, 1592.

'Ah Professor Galileo, come in, please.'

'It's Galilei, but never mind. Galileo is my...'

'Yes, of course. A common mistake, I'm sure. But what we are here to discuss is of a somewhat graver disposition.'

'I'm sorry?'

'It would appear you've ruffled a few feathers, to put it mildly.'

'Feathers? You mean my study on speed, velocity, gravity, free fall, hydrostatic balances, geocentrism and the principle of relativity, inertia and projectile motion? I've not yet completed...'

'As I say, you've ruffled a few feathers.'

'But I didn't actually use any feathers. That's just malicious gossip from the idiots in the staff room. Obviously a feather would encounter excessive air resistance, which would defeat the purpose of the experiment. Mind you, this would not apply in a vacuum, for example, as one might find, I suspect, outside of the Earth's gravitational pull. Imagine a scenario one day where a man might walk upon the surface of the Moon and such an individual, assuming he had conquered the not insignificant problem of what I imagine to be a severe lack of oxygen, imagine he were to drop a hammer and a feather… it is clear to me that they would indeed hit the ground at the precise same moment. But I digress. My own more humble experiment used a cannonball and a pellet. You see, Aristotle claims that the one must fall faster than the other, given their different mass, but I have developed an opposing theory I am calling 'kinematic law', until I think of something a little catchier, which explains that for the distance travelled during a uniform acceleration starting from a resting point, then the distance is proportional to the square of the elapsed time of the fall, or $d \propto t^2$. I can prove it! I was fortunate to be able to take advantage of the ungainly lean of the campanile in the square which allowed me to determine whether the heavier shot would hit the ground first, being larger in mass, by connecting the two objects with a piece of string and of course If we assume heavier objects do indeed fall faster than lighter ones and if we also assume the converse that lighter objects do indeed fall slower than heavier ones it only follows that the string will soon pull taut as the lighter object retards the fall of the heavier object and over a distance this would be clearly visible to the naked eye, a process I call observable evidence, which, by the by, I am currently using as the cornerstone of my new theory about the rules of scientific evidence which I am calling the 'scientific method', until I think of something a little catchier, which explains what I have repeatedly demonstrated these twelve years past that such an assumption can be debunked simply by…'

'Well, I'm afraid you're wrong.'

'I'm sorry?'

'You're wrong.'

'I'm wrong? About what?'

'About everything.'

'Um, could you be a tad more specific, learned Vice Chancellor?'

'You are wrong about everything! Well, most of it at any rate. Men walking on the moon dropping hammers and feathers and gadding about on the leaning tower like some snotty schoolboy showering innocent pedestrians in the square below with lead pellets and cannonballs. It's preposterous and your colleagues and the university administrators and I have all had a gutful of it.'

'My colleagues?'

'Yes. Your colleagues are extremely upset.'

'What about?'

'About everything. About you. And your rudeness.'

'My rudeness?'

'Indeed! I am told you did an interview with the Pisa Express in which you commented that all your colleagues' scientific endeavours are, hang on, I've got it here, 'claptrap and hogwash'. Claptrap and hogwash! Hardly collegiate.'

'But it's true. They're idiots. And their theories are fraudulent and untrustworthy.'

'Well, hang on, that's a bit harsh!'

'Harsh but true. One of them claims that the Earth in fact sits at the centre of the universe like the plug-hole in a giant bathtub and every time it rains the oceans keep rising and soon all our cities will go down the gurgler. He calls it "catastophic global sinking".'

'Precisely! St Mark's Square flooded only last Christmas! What more proof do you need?'

'Venice is sinking because some idiot built it on a swamp. Gravity...'

'That's quite enough, thank you, Professor. I must ask you to take your leave now.'

'Leave?'

'Yes, I have consulted our lawyers and you are clearly in breach of the University's Code of Conduct as outlined in our Enterprise Agreement clause 14.3 which demands you respect the opinions of your colleagues. You're sacked.'

'But you can't do that! You're infringing upon my intellectual freedom!'

'We shall see about that, Professor, and if needs be we'll take it all the way to the Federal Inquisition.'

Victorian Premier Daniel Andrews baffles the nation with his endless daily news conferences, draconian lockdowns and disastrous hotel quarantining.

Andrews family tree

8 August 2020

As Victoria leads the way in defeating the spread of the Coronavirus, through the brilliant implementation of its quarantine, contact tracing, social distancing, compulsory mask-wearing and lockdown policies, the eyes of the world have naturally turned to this utopian nirvana for political inspiration. Across the globe, jealous leaders are asking: 'Who is Dan Andrews? Where did he come from?' In this *Fin* exclusive, genealogist Ms Rowena Andrews explores the fascinating family tree of the extraordinary Andrews clan, and traces their story from the remote Scottish highlands to treading the spotlights on the world stage.

Wee Danny Andrews: famous Caithness leech-collector turned plague-burier who briefly came to prominence in the late 16th century when he insisted on protecting the elderly and most vulnerable peasants in the bog from the ravages of the Black Death by quarantining them all in a mud hovel together guarded by a strange group of out-of-towners distinguished only by the unusual black spots on their fingers and noses.

Julie Andrews: world-famous diva who starred in blockbuster musicals such as *The Sound of Masks*, where she plays a nanny-state who has to teach the entire Von Trapped family who are stuck indoors hiding from a tyrannical despot who refuses to allow anyone to go fishing or even play golf. But in the end she wins him over by singing beautiful ditties such as: 'Boys in red tee-shirts with white cotton sashes/ Snowflakes with lattes and painted eyelashes/ Belt and Road deals tied up with strings/ These are a few of my favourite things.'

Andrews also starred in the classic fantasy movie *Mary Poppins*, in which she again played a nanny-state, this time flying in on an umbrella over the rooftops and tower blocks of Flemington during a pandemic because there were no airlines anymore. The plot revolves around a run on the banks and a hopeless politician who insists on 'Feeding the Birds' at press conferences every day where he blames everybody else for his own incompetence. In the end he dances off into a cartoon-like fantasy world of renewable energy but he's brought back down to earth when he blows up the local coal-fired power station chimney stacks and ends up with soot all over his face.

The Andrews sisters: three famous American singing sisters (LaVerne, Maxene and Danny) of the swinging voters era who were adored despite their consistent disharmonies. Best known for huge hits such as 'Pork Barrel Polka (Roll Out The Barrel)' and less popular ditties such as 'Don't sit under the apple tree (with anyone else at all or you'll get slapped with a $1,000 fine).'

Brittany Andrews: famous American 'exotic dancer' and adult movies actress who starred in the classic cult porn film 'Lockdown Quarantine' about a group of randy young nightclub bouncers locked down in a tower block in north Melbourne who are offered the dream job of a lifetime, to guard a group of sex-starved airline hostesses who are locked down on the top floor of a swanky Melbourne hotel. In the sequel, the plot moves to a swanky aged-care centre in Toorak where the same bouncers now get to be healthcare workers instead.

Archie Andrews: nerdy comic book character and star of *The Archies*, famous for his jug ears and glasses and passion for building toy railway crossings who has an on-again, off-again love affair with the sultry and mysterious Victoria. In the end, of course, Victoria dumps the hopeless Andrews altogether when along comes the dashing, roguish and infinitely more appealing Tim Smith to steal her heart instead.

Anthony Andrews: famous posh English heartthrob best known for his starring role in the 13-part mini-series *Brunswick Revisited* about two young men (there are rumours they are heterosexual, but that has always been denied) who return to lockdown in the family estate in Brunswick with nothing but sixteen crates of booze and a teddy bear called Dan.

Del Andrews: famous American film director and screenwriter responsible for *The Racket*, in which a despotic politician denies knowing anything about the plethora of local branch-stacking scandals and forces everybody else to resign instead, and the classic *All Quiet on the Western Front (and the North, South and Eastern fronts too)*, about the eerie silence, isolation, misery, despair and financial devastation caused by the horrors of the Culture War. (Don't you mean the pandemic?—ed.)

Dan Andrews: famously inept and incompetent Australian politician best known for Australia's ongoing coronavirus nightmare.

Unemployment numbers soar. In Victoria hotel quarantine security staff are caught sleeping with people in quarantine. The CovidApp is a flop. And I correctly predict that JobKeeper will be rorted by companies.

My virulent career

15 August 2020

With a million Australians now out of work thanks to the Coronavirus, and estimates that it will take many years before a return to normality, it's time to start planning your new career. In this world exclusive, *The Fin*'s recently-fired employment specialist, Ms Rowena Nomoor-Jobs, checks out the plethora of exciting new job opportunities and career paths that have sprung up thanks to the pandemic.

JobForm Creative Consultant: there are so many lucrative government jobs packages to choose from, but where do you start? How do you tell your JobSeeker from your JobKeeper from your JobTrainer? Why not get the lot?!? And what happens when somebody actually offers you a REAL job? Heaven forbid! We'll tell you the most inventive ways to say 'bugger off!'. And for the professional CEO, how do you prove your company's profits are down when in fact you're coining it in like never before thanks to JobKeeper? What's the easiest way to tell your landlord to get knotted and that you refuse to pay rent anymore? For these and a thousand other Critical Covid Questions there's only one solution: hire your very own JobForm Creative Consultant to help you navigate your way through that tantalising array of stimulus packages on offer. Our motto? We know how to tick all the right boxes!

JobCreatorCreator: with the federal government committed to providing a perpetual welfare programme to ensure Australians never need go to work again, there are plenty of jobs going in Canberra for imaginative individuals with a flair for coming up with creative titles for good old-fashioned sit-down-money. JobDreamer? JobDisguiser? JobKiller? To apply, send your suggestions quick smart to the JobCreatorCreator programme, Treasury, Canberra.

Quarantine Social Planner: stuck inside some grotty Melbourne hotel going out of your mind with boredom through no fault of your own? Feeling a little horny lying all by yourself in between those starched hotel sheets? Why not call in your very own Quarantine Social Planner to help you transform the sheer tedium of the next two weeks into the party time of your life? Take your pick from: fondue parties with all your floor mates; dirty dancing sessions with our exotic Turkish bodyguards; boogie-ing the night away in a groovy downtown Melbourne private house party on one of our special Smuggled-Out Tours for a night you'll never forget; or we can even organise your very own personal in-house lover. And of course we guarantee that our Quarantine Social Planners live up to our company motto: All the Contacts, None of the Tracing!

Dan Dissembler: with Dan Andrews destined to be Premier for several more terms at least despite being caught red-handed telling massive porkies, it's clear that there will be a growing need for highly-skilled linguistics experts and communications gurus to find a way to convert the meaning of what Mr Andrews says into their complete opposite. With Dan Dissembling classes available at all Melbourne university humanities courses, why not turn this unique skill into a lucrative career move?

COVIDSafeApp (re-)Designer: always dreamed of designing your own App and becoming an overnight squillionaire?!? Here's your chance! Our team of highly-paid and, er, highly-skilled COVIDSafeApp Designers are desperately looking for any number of talented Millennials to come on board and join our exciting enterprise!!! Successful applicants will be generously rewarded so long as they can demonstrate that they a) know what an App actually is, b) know precisely what they do and how they work, and c) show us.

Border crossing guards: with state governments increasingly relying on closed borders to combat the Coronavirus, it won't be long before local councils get in on the act. Brush up now on your interpersonal skills (issuing fines, harassing ordinary citizens, performing chokeholds on non-mask wearing individuals, handcuffing dog walkers etc.) and you too could soon be a Local Government Border Patrol Enforcer rugby-tackling those little old ladies walking in the park.

Victorian Aged-Care Patient Hospital Delivery Driver: know the streets of Melbourne and the surrounding suburbs like the back of your hand? Fed up with passengers who only want to go two blocks down the street? Missing all those great fares to the airport and back? Have we got the job for you! Now you can drive all day (and night!) for hours and hours taking your aged-care patients to the nearest hospital safe in the knowledge that they'll be turned away and you'll have to go and find another one! Just switch on the metre and with any luck you'll be driving round and round in circles for days until either your patience or more likely your patient expires!

A famous Australian con-man gets arrested.

Catch us if you can

22 August 2020

As a famous con man is yet again nabbed by police just as he is about to flee the country, *The Fin*'s confidence trickster correspondent Ms Rowena Ponzi-Madoff reports on the long and colourful list of notorious Australian con artists who have successfully been duping the public for years:

Dan Foster: with his jug ears and nerdy glasses, this popular rogue began his crime spree with a daring scam whereby he managed to defraud taxpayers of around $380,000 which he splurged on red tee-shirts for his gang of teenage campaign organisers. Once he had a taste for helping himself to other people's money, he moved on to bigger targets, with his notorious Railway-Crossing Gang holding up construction of the East West Link which netted the developers over a billion dollars in cancellation fees. But Dan's most outrageous scam was when he managed to fool the entire state of Victoria that there was a deadly pandemic sweeping across the land and that everybody had to shut down their businesses and lock themselves indoors until they lost all their money.

Brett Foster: handsome and charismatic former medical student who played on people's fears by announcing meaningless statistics about the number of new 'cases' of a mystery virus that very few people actually had in an elaborate con designed to shut down Victoria's economy until a miracle 'vaccine' came along.

Annastacia Foster: notorious con-woman who shut down all the borders of the Sunshine State and drove the entire tourism industry to the wall while her partner-in-crime Jackie Foster secretly bought up all the prime real estate closest to the railway lines.

'Albo' Foster: breathtakingly inept con merchant who talked his way into the top job in the Australian Labor Party but then had no idea what to do when he got there. Perpetuated numerous failed scams, such as his 'Net Zero Emissions' scheme whereby he tried to convince punters that he could create enough electricity to power an entire country by using rusty old Chinese windmills and rooftop solar panels at night.

Kristina Foster: cunning American con artist who had her 'dumb blonde' act down to perfection. Repeatedly tried to pass herself off as an Australian politician by strangling her vowels.

Kevin Foster: adept disguise-artist who successfully managed to pass himself off as a 'fiscal conservative' by pretending he was John Howard. Victims of his scams, which included installing flammable pink batts into unsuspecting people's homes and building empty school halls, were defrauded of over $42 billion. But by far his most successful rip-off was drawn up on the back of a beer coaster with his buddy Stephen 'Con' Roy: a massive multi-billion dollar scam which looted an entire nation out of billions of dollars for one of the world's slowest and least reliable internet networks.

Malcolm and Lulu Foster: immensely talented scam merchant and his wife who managed to trick everybody they met into believing that he was the smartest person in the room. Wearing many disguises, he brazenly managed to pass himself off as a Liberal for many years despite being an avowed socialist. But behind the charming smile lay a highly manipulative and destructive narcissistic ego that in the end proved his undoing. Most famous among his many con jobs were the 'National Energy Guarantee' (basically just a straight rip-off of 'Albo' Foster's equally fraudulent 'Net

Zero Emissions' scam, see above) and his disgraceful attempt to steal the superannuation savings of millions of old-age pensioners. But his most ridiculous swindle, which managed to fool huge numbers of investors, was his elaborate scheme to make electricity by pushing water uphill.

'ScoFo' Foster: ex-marketing boss and scheming political operative who would disguise himself simply by putting on a baseball cap and pretending to be a daggy dad who liked to watch the footy. Was famously caught out holidaying at a luxury resort in Hawaii during the bushfires. Most audacious scam was his 'National Cabinet' rort which was nothing more than a gang of petty thieving premiers pretending to act in the national interest whilst emptying the nation's coffers.

Josh Foster: in one of the most imaginative and preposterous swindles of all time, this colourful Melbourne identity posed as a federal Treasurer touting an imaginative scheme nicknamed JobKeeper whereby punters were convinced they would be paid $1,500 a week by the government to do bugger all. As one victim of the scheme admitted, 'It sounded too good to be true. All I had to do was quit my job and the taxpayers would pay me more than I was earning in the first place. I couldn't believe my luck!' The elaborate con unravelled when the nation went belly up in mid-2021and everybody really did lose their jobs. Josh included.

How to write a woke horror movie.

Monster mash-up

12 September 2020

As Hollywood decrees that from now on you can only win an Oscar for Best Picture if you include a sufficient number of minority identity groups in your cast and incorporate a sufficient number of woke themes in your storyline, *The Fin*'s film critic and aspiring script-writer Ms Rowena Scorcese de Mille hastily revises the final draft of her highly-anticipated, Oscar-tipped blockbuster 'Zombie Lockdown'.

Scene 1.

Dramatic music. A diverse and inclusive wet market in Wuhan. An old Chinese woman, er, sorry, scratch that a young African-American gay man is cooking up a vat of Bat Soup using squealing live baby bats (actually, sorry, better make that a bowl of vegan black-eyed peas instead) when a little old, um, legless Iraqi man approaches her. The man, clearly a victim of Trump's aggression in the Middle East, starts coughing and wheezing. 'Are you from the Virology Lab down the street?' asks the bat-vendor, wiping the sweat off her, sorry, his brow. 'How did you guess… AH-CHOO!?!' the Iraqi replies, sneezing into his sleeve. The vendor eyes him suspiciously: 'Did you just call me Ah Choo? That's a racist micro-aggression!' The disabled man immediately 'takes a knee' and begs forgiveness for his unacceptable act of unconscious bias and racial profiling, oh hang on, he doesn't have any knees, er, anyway…

Scene 2.

Dramatic music. A diverse and inclusive remote yet sustainable and environmentally-friendly forest deep in Xianjing province. Camera pans over a field of shimmering solar panels which are clearly solving climate change to reveal a diverse and inclusive group of Uighurs, including an Hispanic Uighur, a UOC (Uighur of colour) and an LGBTIQU (Lesbian, Gay, Bi-sexual, Trans, Intersex or Queer Uighur) with all their heads shaved being forced into the windowless box-cars of a train by heavily armed Red Army soldiers. Quick cuts of terrified prisoners screaming in fear. A guard shoves a young native Inuit Uighur woman, and says: 'This train will take you to your new home where you will work on an assembly line putting together iPhones. You will be very happy except you might accidentally lose your kidneys or other vital organs.' He leers menacingly at her. Cut to close up her proud expression of female empowerment and self-esteem as she snaps back at him, 'How dare you bodily objectify me, you vile misogynist!' The guard apologises profusely and promises to be a better person in future and to respect her lifestyle choices (before shooting her in the head).

Scene 3.

Dramatic Chinese music (go easy on the chimes and stuff). Chinatown, Sydney. A diverse and inclusive group of Chinese tourists are joining in a Lion Dance to celebrate the Lunar New Year. A Serbian-Chinese man turns and shouts excitedly to his companion, a gay Latino. 'Lucky we got out of Wuhan before they welded everybody into their apartments! There's a new killer virus on the loose and it was created by Donald Trump.'

Scene 4.

Dramatic music. A diverse and inclusive meeting of the newly-formed Australian National Cabinet. The Prime Minister, a Nigerian woman called Skwo-Mo bangs her fist on the table. Next to her is the Mufti of Victoria, Dhan Andrews. 'This is a national emergency and we must speak with one voice!' says the PM. 'Yes, mine!' exclaims Dhan Andrews leaping to his feet. 'I have the latest modelling on my super-computer and it says everybody's going to die unless...' There is a deathly hush. '...unless I bring in an 8pm curfew and lock everything down except for essential services such as heroin injecting rooms and abortion clinics.' The rest of the room nod in feverish agreement.

Scene 5.

Dramatic Aboriginal music (go easy on the didgeridoos). A remote community in the Outback. A group of wise Aboriginal elders are sitting around stoking a smouldering fire discussing the melting ice caps. One of the elders, a diabetic lesbian, lifts a half-burned newspaper out of the flames and gasps. Camera zooms in on the headline: MYSTERY COLONIAL VIRUS INVADES AUSTRALIA! The other elders, an albino transvestite, a Palestinian freedom fighter and a white man with a beard called Bruce all look at each other and nod wisely.

Scene 6 (finale).

In the eerie dawn light a crowd of zombie business-owners is shuffling down the empty streets of Ballarat, drawn irresistibly to a sinister large building. Camera zooms in on the sign: 'CentreLink: JobSeeker and JobKeeper queue here. Observe social distancing.' A sobbing handcuffed woman in her pink pyjamas is being dragged away by masked police officers. The camera pans across the boarded-up shopfronts, smashed windows and graffitied doorways of what was once a thriving happy town.

Title: THE END (LITERALLY)

Cornelius family tree

19 September 2020

Victoria's Assistant Commissioner Luke Cornelius recently described constantly having to arrest anti-lockdown protesters and free speech advocates as being 'a bit like a dog returning to eat its own vomit.' In this world exclusive, *The Fin*'s totalitarian enforcement correspondent Fraulein Rowena Lavrentiy von Beria reveals there is a long line of famous authoritarian Cornelius's stretching right back through history who have likewise had to swallow their distaste for personal liberties in order to maintain strict law and order.

Puke (*Homo Cornelius*): Troglodyte primate believed to have briefly existed in the era of Victorian Man (around one million BC). Puke maintained social discipline with a large club and a heavy rock before dying out from malnutrition due mainly to his habit of eating his own vomit as well as that of his fellow cave-dwellers.

Puceus Cornelius: Roman patrician who rose to the rank of Assistant Quaestor in the time of Emperor Danus Andreus the Insane. It was Puceus who cleverly adapted the Roman concept of the 'vomitorium' and put it to good use maintaining strict law and order during the Justinianic Plague. Slaves and other anti-gladiator protesters who dared to stray further than 5 kilometres from the Colosseum or refused to wear their obligatory iron masks were forced to keep gorging themselves on oysters and other delicacies until they vomited. Those who failed to do so were fed to the lions, many of whom also vomited.

Duke of Cornelius: notorious medieval Duke in the court of King Andrew the Tyrant at the time of the Black Plague. The Duke of Cornelius endured public ignominy when one of his foot-servants was caught driving his carriage straight over an unarmed peasant who was wandering the streets. Another foot-servant then leapt out of the carriage and stomped on the man's head, which required the peasant to be put into an induced coma. The Duke was also infamous for 'taking a knee' in order to express his personal solidarity with the Black Plagues Matter movement.

Lucrezia Cornelius: infamous Spanish-Italian noblewoman who rose to the rank of Assistant Poisoner to Pope Daniel the Mad. Rumours have abounded for years that Lucrezia was responsible for poisoning the well of goodwill towards the police force of the entire state of Victoria by using sinister and ruthless methods to impose her brutal lockdown. Lucrezia was also rumoured to have been in an incestuous relationship with the Labor party.

Jean-Luc Cornelius: manservant to the Marquis de Dan, the sadistic French nobleman most famous for his tortuous press conferences and barbaric business closures. Jean-Luc was responsible for ensuring the Marquis' many victims stayed within 5 kilometres of the chateau and for ensuring strict compliance among those who were locked down in the cellar. The Marquis de Dan had a perverted fetish for ensuring that masks were worn at all times and was known to derive unnatural pleasures from handcuffing pregnant women in their pyjamas and accusing them of thinking unthinkable thoughts and posting them on Facebook. The Marquis always ensured strict social hygiene measures were enforced, especially the sanitising and washing of hands after touching (or being impaled by) any iron-tipped implements that happened to be lying around.

'Il Duce' Cornelius: feared and loathed Commissario Assistante of the dreaded Blackshirts who were the private army to the Italian leader Benito Andrussolini during the time of the Second and Third Waves. 'Il Duce' decreed that to maintain law and order in the fascist state he needed to enforce an 8pm–5am curfew and shut down all profitable businesses including any local delis and restaurants, except for doing takeaway which meant most of them went bankrupt and never re-opened, a process which led to the Great Depression of 2021. 'Il Duce' also disgracefully instructed his officers to 'take a knee' to the Blackshirts Matter movement.

Luciano 'Lucky' Cornelius: colourful American Teamster and hired union muscle who rose to be Assistant Consigliere to Don Andrews of the notorious Victorian Ndrangdrews crime family. 'Lucky' earned his nickname after avoiding being held responsible for the draconian measures imposed by his boss upon the entire state, including an 8pm to 5am curfew and permanent Stage 4 Lockdown. When Don Andrews was given a 25-year jail sentence under his own industrial manslaughter laws for refusing to supply the drug hydroxychloroquine to people suffering from a mystery Chinese virus, 'Lucky' pleaded that he was just following orders and escaped with his reputation in tatters. 'Lucky' was last heard of running a Melbourne soup kitchen for retired police officers where he famously served up a stew that was described by one diner as 'a bit like eating your own vomit'.

Lord Lucan-Cornelius: famous English aristocrat who mysteriously vanished one night and has never been heard of again after committing the appalling and horrific crime of bludgeoning the nanny state of Victoria to death with enforced business closures, unnecessary curfews and never-ending lockdowns.

The first Presidential debate is criticised for its lack of oratorical flair.

Shakespearean debate

3 October 2020

The world of presidential debates was rocked to its core this week following the bruising encounter between Donald Trump, Joe Biden and moderator Chris Wallace. But in a world exclusive, *The Fin*'s public speaking correspondent Ms Rowena Cicero de Lincoln claims that rather than being a 'train wreck' the debate was in fact a masterpiece of Shakespearean oratory.

Wallace: Friends, luvvies and rednecks, we are gathered here this evening to determine who is most fit to be leader of this our proud nation through the friendly but robust exchange of ideas and principles, with questioning as confounded by myself only this day gone.

Biden: How fare thee, good fellow?

Trump: You are well met, sire.

(polite applause)

Wallace: Gentlemen, without much ado let us hasten forth to debate whether 'tis nobler for the fair lady the gracious Amy Coney Barrett to be welcomed verily into the court, be it the highest court in the land?

Trump: Some are born huge, some achieve hugeness, and others have hugeness thrust upon them. Elections have consequences. The Constitution looks not with the eyes, but with the mind; and therefore is sweet Amy painted blind.

Biden: To wait or not to wait, that is the more pertinent question. Tens of thousands of our countrymen have to this day already cast their votes. I say hold onto our horses until February at the earliest. For what perchance if this frail woman of thine own choosing cruelly strikes down the natural justice of this land whereby all womenfolk, as it is written, can stand proud and cry aloud 'my body, my choice'?

Trump: Verily I say it is no choice for a child from its mother's womb untimely to be ripped! I am King for four score years, not three score, Joe, as you would falsely have it. I wear the heavy Crown and doth control the entire Senate! Besides, how do you presume to know what is in fair Amy's mind on Roe v Wade?

Biden: Hark, what I propose is to expand the care of the frail and the elderly as did the great Ruler himself Obama…

Trump: You mean the Moor.

Biden: You let slip the dogs of war upon Obamacare…

Trump: I call it Moorcare.

Wallace: Sire, I beg you with all due respect to desist with these petty insults, nay even these interruptions and falsehoods.

Trump: All I'm saying is he was a Moor. I've seen his birth certificate!

Wallace: Yet you have no plan! This much I know to be true.

Trump: Well, first of all, I guess I'm debating you, not him. But that's OK. Verily I am not surprised.

Biden: Lest we forget, sire, it was through thine own kingly interventions that the plague did cast itself upon these benighted shores! Not even all great Neptune's oceans can wash the blood from thine hands!

Trump: Truly, I am a man more sinned against than sinning! I protest that it was I who did forsake all pilgrimage from the East so that the Cathayan plague full swift should pass us by. There are more things in heaven and earth, Joe, than are dreamt of in your socialist identity philosophies…

Biden: Travelers never did lie, though fools at home unmask them…

Trump: Uneasy lies the head that wears the mask! Sometimes I wear it, sometimes I don't.

Biden: Thou art a boil, a knave, an embossed carbuncle!

Trump: There is no darkness but ignorance, Joe, which is why you agreed with Bernie Sanders on his misbegotten manifesto!

Biden: The fact of the matter is I defeated the ignominious coxcomb Sanders...

Trump: Not by much!

Wallace: You say, Master Biden, that the public can put their faith in the apothecaries but not in Mr Trump. Your liege, Kamala Harris, says the physicians 'will be muzzled, will be suppressed.' What say you to this mischief-making?

Trump: It's all fake news...

Biden: The blessed gods purge all infection from our air whilst you do carry on interrupting me thus!

Trump: A fever she reigns in my blood and will remember'd be...

Biden: A fever in your blood! Why, then injection of a bleach would let her out in saucers, sweet inspiration!

Trump: I was being sarcastic, you know that. This is a tale told by an idiot, full of sound and fury, signifying nothing...

Wallace: Will you please stop interrupting, Mr President! Master Biden, you were saying...?

Biden: I like this place Washington and I could willingly waste my time in it...

Wallace: Agreed, but Vice President Biden, you are holding much smaller events...

Trump: That's because nobody turns up! All the world's a stage, except at Joe's rallies! Where are all the men and women?

Biden: What light through yonder teleprompter breaks??

Viewers chorus: We have seen better days.

Curtain.

JobKeeper spreads the money all round.

Take the money and run

10 October 2020

The world of FM radio music stations was rocked (literally) to its core this week following the shock announcement that the owner of 98 rock 'n' roll FM stations is set to pocket $28 million in JobKeeper payments over the course of the pandemic. However, according to *The Fin*'s rock 'n' roll expert Ms Rowena Fender-Stratt, it is unlikely that this government largesse will in any way influence the radio stations' normal summer playlist of favourite rock standards. These are tipped to include:

Take the Money and Run: classic bar-room blues from the Steve Miller Band, in which 'Billy Joe and Bobby Sue, two young lovers with nothin' better to do' wake up one day and realise that instead of trying to get rich robbing banks 'down in old El Paso', all they have to do is sign up to JobKeeper and earn way more than they have ever earned before! 'Hoo, hoo, hoo, take the money and run!'.

Money (That's What I Want): a crowd favourite in the Beatles Cavern days with its thumping riff and Lennon's snarling vocals, the lyrics now sound embarrassingly out-dated, with the ridiculous suggestion that 'money isn't free'. Hadn't John ever heard of JobKeeper?

Money, Money, Money: frenetic song from Abba that postulates that it must be 'funny in a rich man's world'. Despite the inherent sexism (why no rich wimmin's world??) of this song, most contemporary listeners struggle to comprehend the meaning of the opening lines 'I work all night, I work all day, to pay the bills I have to pay.' Says Alyssia from Bondi: 'who on earth would waste their time doing that? Thanks to Dominic Perrottet we don't even have to pay our rent anymore!'

You Never Give Me Your Money: bitter Paul McCartney song about a mysterious dole recipient who applies for the government's latest JobSacker subsidy after coming out of college with a massive HECS fee, no money and an honours degree in Sexism, Transphobia and Racism in Climate Denialism Studies and is then insultingly offered a part-time job driving a 'yellow lorry' but refuses to show up to such a demeaning interview.

Money for Nothing (and your cheques for free): timely Dire Straits song about the easy road to wealth beyond your wildest dreams by running the federal debt up to over a trillion dollars in order to encourage a nation drowning in debt to simply go on splurging on 'refrigerators, microwaves and colour TVs' with a little help from the $25k HomeBuilder grants.

Money's Too Tight to Mention: originally released by Simply Red back in the '80s, this new hit version is by popular Canberra cover band Simply In The Red.

Forever in Blue Jeans: from its unforgettable opening lines, this popular Neil Diamond song has long baffled financial experts with its peculiar assertion that 'Money talks, But it don't sing and dance and it don't walk'. Says long-time fan Scotty from Music Marketing: 'Of course money can sing and money can dance! Money will do whatever you want it to do so long as you keep on borrowing more and more of it! That's the beauty of the government's latest trillion-dollar JobSinger, JobDancer and JobWalker packages designed to pump as much free money as possible into the money-making, er, I mean music-making industries.

I Should Be So Lucky: chirpy hit from the Singing Budgie herself, this delightful ditty is the perfect song to whistle along to as you head down to the local Centrelink on your way to grab a soy latte before hitting the beach for a busy afternoon of catching up with friends and soaking up the sunshine.

Get a Job: trite nonsensical song with completely meaningless lyrics for today's young music lovers, although the chorus is quirkily quaint: 'Sha na na na, sha na na na na, Sha na na na, sha na na na na, Yip yip yip yip yip yip yip, Get a job, sha na na na, sha na na na.'

Working for the Man: brilliantly insightful song by the late, great Roy Orbison about the only way to be a successful business entrepreneur these days is either by designing some dodgy internet App that gets picked up by some big-spending government agency (I don't remember that bit in the song—ed) or else by marrying the boss's daughter.

The Carnival is Over: new Australian national anthem, recorded by The JobSeekers.

Googling Google

24 October 2020

As the Trump administration launches legal action against the world's dominant search engine provider with a massive anti-trust lawsuit, *The Fin*'s Big Tech correspondent Ms Rowena 'Cookies' Clickbait tries to find out exactly what the company is accused of having done wrong by, er, googling related subject matters. Here is a screen grab of Rowena's recent search history:

Google (verb): to engage with the world's most popular and intelligent search engine in order to find out all the information you are looking for without any bias or anti-competitive algorithms whatsoever.

Google (noun): a popular and highly competitive internet search engine platform that's in healthy competition with all the many other search engine companies such as, er, anyway, Google allows users to immediately find what they are looking for even when they have no idea what they are looking for.

Google (advertising): GoogleAds is a popular advertising model that makes use of sophisticated but entirely harmless algorithms that assist users in being helpfully directed to those advertisers whose name for whatever reason happens to randomly without any assistance from us whatsoever pop up first in the queue.

GoogleAd: hey we couldn't help noticing that you're looking for a Search Engine with incredible advertising capabilities!!! Look no further!

GoogleAds has all your needs!! You'll never have to go looking for customers again!!! Click here NOW!

Trust: the ability of a human to have faith that his or her interests are being looked after in a responsible and ethical manner.

Trust in Big Tech: confidence that large and powerful online organisations that have unprecedented access to an individual's private lives and private thoughts would never misuse that power, no way, no siree.

Anti-trust: I'm sorry, it looks like there aren't any matches for your search. Did you mean ANTI-TRYST?

No, I mean anti-trust.

I'm sorry, it looks like there aren't any matches for your search. We have re-directed you to ANTI-TRYST: noun meaning the opposite of a romantic meeting between two lovers.

I don't want anti-TRYST I want anti-TRUST!

GoogleAd: Feeling lonely? just had your heart broken by a trusted loved one? Looking for a little bit of love on the side? Find the partner of your dreams at Trysts-R-Us!! Click here NOW!

Anti-trust: I'm sorry but it appears that this page has been deleted. We have re-directed you to ANTI-TRUMP.

I don't want anti-Trump I want anti-trust!!

Anti-Trump: a completely understandable and common emotion of antipathy verging on outright loathing and disgust towards any individual with the surname Trump (see TRUMP).

Trump (top searches): Trump racist Trump sexist Trump spreads diseases Trump related to Adolf Hitler Trump pays no income tax Trump dies of Covid Trump colludes with Russia Trump pulls the wings off insects Trump descended from Attila the Hun Trump snorts cocaine in gay snuff movie…

President Donald J. Trump: I'm sorry, it looks like there aren't any matches for your search. Google Tip: why not try using these words in a way that might actually appear on the page that you're looking for, such as 'Why I am voting for Joe Biden to become PRESIDENT rather than that idiot DONALD J. TRUMP.'

Why is Trump attacking Google?: I'm sorry, it looks like there aren't any matches for your search.

Monopoly: popular board game invented by the Parker Brothers during the Great Depression.

Google monopoly: I'm sorry, it looks like there aren't any matches for your search.

Search engine monopoly: I'm sorry, it looks like there aren't any matches for your search. Google Tip: try using words that might actually appear on the page that you're looking for, such as: 'Google is the only SEARCH ENGINE I would use if I was looking for clever strategies on how to play the board game MONOPOLY'.

GoogleAd: looking for the best discounts on board games!!! You'll find all your favourite games including MONOPOLY at rock bottom prices right here at BoardGames-R-Us!! Click NOW!

Competition: quaint and out-dated concept whereby individuals or organisations try and 'compete' with each other to see who is best, i.e. by dancing, running, playing darts, selling cars etc.

Internet competition: I'm sorry, it looks like there aren't any matches for your search.

Search engine competition: I'm sorry, it looks like there aren't any matches for your search.

Search engine optimisation competition: I'm sorry, it looks like there aren't any matches for your search.

Competition watchdog: standard variety of household canine commonly used for domestic security purposes, see Doberman, Alsatian, Rottweiler, etc.

GoogleAd: Scared of burglars??? Need a WATCHDOG?? Top breeds available at Pooches-R-Us. Click NOW!

Bing, Yandex, CCSearch, Swisscows, StartPage, Gibiru, DuckDuckGo, OneSearch, etc: Huh? Never heard of any of them. Try googling 'Google' instead.

Hallowe'en.

Horror show

31 October 2020

It's Hallowe'en tonight, but what on earth should the kids all dress up as? In this exclusive guide to modern gothic horror, *The Fin*'s special spectral correspondent Ms Rowena Broom-Hilda conjures up a witch's brew of the best costumes available if you really want to scare the neighbourhood witless.

Joe Biden & Kamala Harris twin set masks: the ideal scary double act, and indeed the stuff of nightmares. And so easy to make! All you need is two simple black strips of cloth and a couple of rubber bands and hey presto! you're instantly transformed into a terrifying leftist freak show. For added dramatic effect, why not get Joe to come creeping out of next door's basement and pretend he has no idea where he is! And who needs a witch's cackle when you've got Kamala's fake laugh to spook the neighbourhood with?

Greta mask: a couple of pigtails, a permanent frown and away you go! With doomsday, Armageddon, the apocalypse and the End of the World only 18 months / 5 years / 12 years (take your pick) away, a Greta costume has the added advantage that all the school kiddies are already scared half to death by her. And in case some skinflint neighbour doesn't give you enough delicious treats, there's nothing like an angry 'How dare you!?!' to put a guilt-ridden grown-up in their place.

Albo mask: hours of endless fun tricking the neighbours with this scary two-faced mask— also known as the 'each-way Albo'—with a ghoulish 'green' Albo on one side and a grubby 'blue-collar' Albo on the other. But how do you know which one you should pretend to be to get the very best treats as you knock at each door? Here's a clue: if there's a battered-up Ute with some dirty tools and equipment in the drive-way, go blue-collar Albo. But if it's a large pristine 4-wheel drive covered in 'No More Coal' and 'We Heart Zali' stickers, well… it's gotta be green Albo.

Kevin Rudd & Pink Bat twin set masks: there's nothing that says Hallowe'en quicker than bats, so why not one of you dress up as Kevin Rudd and the other as his pink bat? You could even sneak upstairs and hide in the neighbour's attic! (Manufacturers warning: pink bat may spontaneously ignite.)

Kevin Rudd & Julia Gillard twin set masks: hells bells! you want to give the neighbours a laugh, not make them slam the door in your face!

Dan Andrews mask: available with a whole host of scary accessories including fake jug ears, sinister horn-rimmed glasses and black masks, the kit also comes with an *#IScareWithDan* twitter handle and drone technology guaranteed to keep the kiddies within 5 kilometres of home.

Chris Bowen mask: a perennially favourite scary freak, the Chris Bowen mask comes in a plethora of discontinued varieties, from 'Terrifying Treasurer' to 'Ghoulish GroceryWatch' and includes a special discontinued 'Franking-stein's Credit' with a free tee-shirt emblazoned with the horror Hallowe'en slogan 'If you don't like Labor's tricks or treats, don't vote for us'. (Update: Chris Bowen masks now come with free fake chocolate hydroxychloroquine pellets to terrorise all your Covid positive friends with.)

Simon Birmingham mask: now you can really scare all your conservative friends by turning up at their house disguised as the new Finance Minister.

Gladys & Daryl twin set masks: ideal for sneaking around the neighbourhood after dark for years on end with nobody knowing what you're getting up to.

The ABC launches a new cultural channel.

The Dreadful Works of Leonardo da Vinci

27 November 2020

Accused of overt political bias and an obsession with identity and Green politics, the ABC announced this week that it is launching an entire new arts channel devoted to restoring its reputation as the nation's leading cultural broadcaster. In a world exclusive, *The Fin*'s media and entertainment guru, Ms Rowita Rosebutt, gets a sneak look at the ABC's new line-up of classical arts programmes.

The Dreadful Works of Leonardo da Vinci: In this must see 10-part series, a panel of experts explore the militant white supremacy within the drawings of this Renaissance-era arms dealer, who was single-handedly responsible for inventing the helicopter, the tank, the submarine and other aggressive machines responsible for five centuries of European oppression and enslavement of people of colour, w*mmin, gays, lesbians, the disabled and other minority groups. In Episode 1, da Vinci's most reprehensible work, the so-called 'Vitruvian Man', is critiqued for its unique combination of misogyny, sexism and genitalism. As one experienced ABC presenter notes, the idea that a cis-gender man disgustingly displaying overtly non-binary genitals with arms and legs outstretched is somehow at the centre of all mathematical shapes such as a circle or a square is of course typical of the transphobic Euro-centric thinking of this renowned right-wing agitator and war-monger. Episode 2 explores the domestic violence and coercive control behind the forced half-smile of the Mona Lisa, the long-suffering spouse of the so-called Italian 'nobleman' Francesco del Giocondo, who disgracefully insisted his wife pose for hours on end for the pleasure of a lecherous old white man with a beard only to be leered at by five centuries of oppressive white male 'art critics'.

Meeting Michelangelo: A creative re-imagination of the life and times of repressed homosexual and queer activist Michelangelo di Lodovico Buonarroti Simoni. In this multi-media experience, the audience is invited to walk in Michelangelo's own footsteps as he struggles to come to terms with his identity and is forced to seek friendship and love in the most unlikely places, including the public baths in Florence and behind the cloisters in the Duomo. In a world-first for digital interactive technology, the audience is then invited to create their very own new set of Michelangelo Masterpieces, including the spectacular Sistine Chapel Ceiling Graffiti App which allows the user to re-design this problematic piece of religious propaganda in a more eco-friendly and progressive style in keeping with today's more acceptable values.

The Disabilities of Vincent: A must-see doco on one of the world's most revered artists, the Dutch post-impressionist Vincent Van Gogh who was forced to create over 2,000 works of art whilst suffering from acute mental depression, catastrophic near-blindness and dysmorphic aurisphobia (fear of one's own ear). The documentary shatters the popular myth that Van Gogh's use of vibrant colours and impulsive brushwork was revolutionary in the field of modern art and instead points to the disgraceful state of mental health facilities in mid-nineteenth century Holland with explosive revelations about the shameful lack of a properly-funded public healthcare system and draws terrifying parallels with the Liberals plans for Medicare if they win the next election.

Mozart Goes to Paris: Music-lovers will delight in this modern interpretation of the fascinating story and inspiration behind Mozart's delightful compositions such as *Concerto for Flute and Harp*, *Piano Sonata in A minor* and *Symphony No. 31*, all of which were written on a train trip to Paris as he flees Salzburg determined to attend the 1778 Climate Change Conference and persuade Australia (surely Austria?—ed) to re-double our efforts under the Paris Agreement. In a unique fusion of past and present, Mozart's incomplete ditties have been vastly improved by being set to several speeches by Greta Thunberg, also a child genius and prodigy who, just like young Amadeus, is determined to save the planet before it's too late. In a chilling finale, Mozart composes his *Requiem for a Dying Planet* as rising ocean waves lap at his feet in his gloomy Prague attic.

Beethoven's Life Matters: In this challenging and confronting new six-part documentary filmed around the world from Bonn to the Bahamas to Botswana, proclaimed Instagram blogger Alaysha Brown journeys into the dark past to explore the most dramatic discovery in classical musical in over a century; namely, that the opening bars of Beethoven's *Eroica* when played backwards and at twice the normal speed are eerily similar to the ancient tribal rhythmic dance songs of the Aciore people of the Kalahari who for centuries lived in amazingly sophisticated settlements before being kidnapped by ruthless white colonialist slave traders and sold into a lifetime of servitude culminating in Donald Trump's America and poses the tantalising question: was Beethoven black?

A high-profile woman becomes Chairman of the
Sydney Opera House board.

Tossa

5 December 2020

In exciting news, it was announced this week that the wife of a former
prime minister has been appointed Chair of the Sydney Opera House.
In this world exclusive, *The Fin*'s culture buff Ms Rowena Utzon-Hughes
takes a sneak preview at the exciting operatic feast we can now look
forward to:

Verdi's 'La Turnbullata': the tragic tale of a young boy destined for
greatness whose cold and heartless mother runs off to join the circus leaving
the lonely boy with nothing but his extraordinary gifts and talents and the
prophesy of his wealthy grandmother that he will grow up to become the
smartest person in the room. With its infectious melodies, this gem of an
operetta captures the delightful aristocratic air of self-indulgence of the
'bien pensants' of Sydney's 'belle époque' of the early 1960s.

Stravinsky's 'The Bligh's Progress': inspiring opera which follows the
journey of a talented and gifted young man sent to a cold and heartless
boarding school where he is quickly singled out as the smartest boy in
the dorm. He discovers he has a remarkable gift for kayaking, and soon
dazzles his contemporaries as an outstanding law student and journalist
before winning a scholarship to Oxford where he woos the great love of
his life 'mia moglie Lucia' and as the final curtain falls the audience rises
to its feet in wild and ecstatic applause.

Mozart's 'La Goanna': delightful operetta where a bright young man destined for greatness returns home from his studies abroad and falls into bad company defending the wealthiest man in the land who has been besmirched in the sinister royal Costi-Gan Tutti commission.

Verdi's 'Catcher of the Spies': This magnificent opera begins and ends with the memorable libretto 'Economico con la verità' ('economical with the truth'), a superb vocal duet between a stuffy old British representative of the Crown who is thoroughly outwitted by the sparkling intellect and unmatchable charisma of the smartest lawyer in the courtroom.

Rossini's 'Il Mercante di Banchieri' (The Merchant Bankers): our flawed hero, destined for greatness, gets tossed out of Heaven but overcomes the ignominy of his downfall by setting up his own merchant bank with a little help from his friends Nifty Nev and the son of the legendary god Gough.

Wagner's 'OzEmandias': one of the lesser-known operas of the gargantuan Ring Cycle, this epic gothic saga follows the tale of a talented merchant banker (das Rheingoldmann) who mysteriously stumbles upon a letter written on a magical piece of paper that flies through the air all by itself when you press 'send'. Recognising that this could bring him untold wealth and power, he buys up half the company but as fortune would have it his glamorous wife the ravishing beauty Lucy tells him to 'Sell! Sell! Sell!' just moments before the tragic Götterdämmerung—the crashing finale of the Dotcöm boom.

Rogers & Hammerstein's 'The Queen and I': this inspirational musical tells the uplifting tale of a brave man who single-handedly sets out to overthrow the stuffy, old-fashioned monarchy and replace it with a progressive and compassionate republic with himself as its Head. There's not a dry eye in the house when his noble dream comes crashing down, leaving the crushed protagonist ruefully singing in a trembling vibrato to the cold-hearted Monsignor Howard that 'you broke this nation's heart'.

Puccini's 'Malcolma Butterfly': one of the most beguiling of Puccini's operas, this gentle and restrained tale in two acts tells the story of a man who is deeply in love with himself but flits like a butterfly from one political party to the next, unable to decide whether his great gifts and talents are best suited to him joining the Guild of Labor or the cold-hearted Librettos.

Verdi's 'La Mano Nera' (The Black Hand): one of the bloodiest of operas, this grisly story tells the gory tale of the hugely talented Narcissisto who spends his time prowling the corridors of power flanked by an obsequious lady in red stilettos and a mincing poodle plotting and scheming and stabbing anyone who stands in his way in the back.

'South Pacific': musical pantomime set against the backdrop of war in the South China Seas where the protagonist commissions 12 French subs with his friend 'the Dame' but it turns out they won't be ready for 50 years and then sink because they don't have any engines.

Puccini's 'Tossa': this dreary opera tells the turgid story of the miserable ghost of a brilliant journalist, lawyer, banker and republican destined for greatness who is tragically brought down by his own ego, sorry, by an evil cabal known as 'Cielo dopo il tramonto' (sky after dark). Based on the obscure fantasy novel 'A Bigger Tossa'.

*As Covid restrictions are lifted, China takes umbrage at Australia
and starts boycotting our products. And Mathias Cormann heads
for the OECD.*

A danceable solution

12 December 2020

With the easing of social distancing restrictions across the land, licensed
venue-owners and fun-loving economists are excitedly talking about a
'dance-led' recovery. But what will the new dance crazes look like? In this
world exclusive, *The Fin*'s physical gyrations expert, Ms Rowena Travolta-
Astaire kicks off her heels and hits the dance floor to check out the latest
fashionable moves and grooves:

The Albo Twist: made popular by the hit 'I Did it Each-Way', this
spine-twisting routine sees the dancer gyrate in such a contorted fashion
that he or she appears to be going in two opposite directions at the same
time. For beginners, practice by shuffling your feet firmly to the left and
at the same time spinning your torso to the right. Then swap over. Repeat
again and again until your caucus calls it a day.

The Funky Jinping: lots of fun, in this energetic dance you pretend
to be a chicken, or if that's too hard, pretend to be a Jinping. The trick is
to look as mean and aggressive as you possibly can in order to express
without words your extreme displeasure with your partner. Next, flap your
arms around, kick up a fuss with both your feet and refuse to touch any of
their beef, lamb, barley, lobster or wine. Repeat until your dance partner
falls to their knees and begs for your forgiveness.

Last Tango (in Brussels): deceptively simple traditional Belgian folk dance where the male dancer exerts as much effort as he possibly can to ensure he can leap safely in one bound from dreary old Canberra straight into a starring role in the finest dance halls of Europe.

The Matt Kean Mambo: best known for its intricate and fancy footwork, the Matt Kean Mambo originated in communist Cuba and has since spread like wildfire, sorry, bushfire, across the globe. Easy to perform when the lights are out (which is pretty much guaranteed), the dancer simply keeps shifting further and further to the left until he or she has completely run out of energy or fallen off the stage. (Gigantic batteries not included.)

Up the Watusi 2.0: popular in the Jindabyne area, this bizarre dance move involves dancers repeatedly squatting down on their haunches and at the same time thrusting their hands upwards, palms open flat, mimicking the action of somebody desperately trying to push water uphill.

The Jerk: wildly popular in Victoria, this dance originated around railway crossings and roundabouts but has since become a favourite anywhere within 5 kilometres of your own home. For added fun, the female partner prances around the living room in her pyjamas while the male, wearing a seductive mask, attempts to wrestle her to the ground and handcuff her.

Doing the Time Warp: creepy dance where ex-Prime Ministers suffering from Relevance Deprivation Syndrome bob up and down every five minutes on the ABC. Cringe factor 11.

The Smashed Avocado: updated version of the Mashed Potato, in which men with wispy beards and ponytails on top of their heads pretend to be cycling home with each other after consuming copious quantities of decaffeinated soy chai lattes in order to save the planet.

Gangster Style: popular dance craze made famous by an eccentric

North Korean pop star with a pudding bowl haircut where rows of ultra-thin dancers march in goose-step in formation together clutching fake rifles over their heads making jerky movements prior to dropping dead from starvation.

Lap-Top Dancing: popular in seedy Ukrainian and Chinese nightclubs especially among oligarchs and cocaine billionaires with important political connections, laptop dancing evolved from a locked down basement in downtown Delaware before taking over the entire world.

Walk like an Extinction: dancers lie in the middle of the road as if they have been glued to the tarmac and wait for the end of the world.

Christmas. And one Labor MP decides maybe coal isn't all that bad.

Self-help books

19 December 2020

Stuck for last-minute pressie ideas for those impossible-to-buy-for relos? Never fear, at this time of year there's nothing more popular than Lifestyle and Self-Help books to fill the most difficult stockings. But which ones? In this week's world exclusive. Ms Rowena Chakra-Guru checks out the latest self-help books that may have escaped your attention.

The Each-Way Secret: throughout his life, the author struggled to reconcile who he has to be with who he really is until he had a life-changing realisation: why bother? In this gripping narrative of self-discovery, popular perceptions expert Dr Antonio 'Albo' Al-Banese says you can be all things to all people simply by adopting the 'Each-Way Albo' mantra! 'Just learn to say whatever they want you to say', is one of the key insights in this astonishing book. 'You can be a greenie one moment and a coal-miner's bestie the next!' Just free yourself of all those pesky deeply-held convictions first!

Coming Out: throughout his life, the author has always played second fiddle to people far less talented than himself. 'But why on earth should I do that?' he asks himself as he embarks upon a searing journey of self-discovery in search of his inner-blue-collar worker through the marginal electorate of the Hunter Valley. 'I can be anyone, maybe even the leader!' is the astonishing conclusion to his enthralling quest.

Failing Upwards: throughout her life, the author has always failed at everything she ever touched. Biggest election loss in NSW history? Yep, that was her! Four low-rating TV shows all dumped? Yep, her again. Spectacular loss in the Bennelong by-election? Yep, her again! But now self-esteem self-help guru Ms Kristina K. Neely has learnt to embrace her inner failure. 'The more I fail, the more successful I am,' is the riveting conclusion to this powerful journey of self-discovery. 'At this rate I'll be PM by 2023!'

Two Rules for Holidaying: for decades now we've been told that travel broadens the mind and that it's important to get some family time alone with the kids away from work. Forget that! In this deeply meaningful and insightful set of rules for enjoying a productive and stress-free annual holiday, the author Dr Sco 'Mo' Morrison concludes. 1. Never go to Waikiki. 2. Or Honolulu.

Printing Money: this is the only money guide you will ever need, say the publishers, and they're not wrong! In this tell-all journey of self-realisation, former conservative Treasurer Mr Joshua Frydenkeynes discovers that rather than, for example, keeping your promise to return to surplus, all you need do is put everybody on a universal wage dressed up with fancy names, preferably with the word 'Job' in the title. Even better, make sure the cash you give them for doing absolutely nothing is more than what they were getting when they actually worked! 'It's all about giving' is one of the author's key insights. 'And then giving some more.'

Kean to be Green: in this mesmerising work of deep personal reflection, the author realises that he is living a lie. 'I was sitting there in my ministerial office inside a successful Liberal government that had been voted in on its conservative credentials, when suddenly it hit me: is this really who I am?' asks the author in a moment of breath-taking self-awareness. 'I threw my question out to the lobbyists and it came back with a resounding "No". From that moment on, I have devoted my entire life to the sole purpose of propping up the renewables investment industry.'

Choosing a Partner: for too many years, women were told to choose men who are reliable, honest and good-looking. What a joke! In this deeply moving journey of self-discovery, lonely hearts columnist Gladys Berry Jaykleen finds romance can flourish in even the most unlikely places.

Deep Sleep Therapy: in this awesome study of the power of positive thinking, the author disappears into his basement for six months barely communicating with a living soul and emerges six months later as the most powerful man on earth.

2021–the Year Democracy Dies

As Australia descends further and further into a spiral of lockdowns, curfews, protests, police brutality and vaccine hysteria, the prime minister abdicates all responsibility as how best to handle the virus to power-drunk premiers and their unelected bureaucrats. With livelihoods and businesses being destroyed on a whim, Australia becomes the laughing stock of the free world for its police brutality and totalitarian lockdowns.

Meanwhile, the unlamented Miserable Ghost and his doppelgänger Kevin 07 continue to prowl the corridors of the leftist media looking for opportunities to create mischief.

As the year draws to a close, there appears to be light at the end of the tunnel. Or is it just the fast-approaching Glasgow Climate Change Express?

Covid vaccines hit the market. And Cricket Australia decides not to celebrate Australia Day.

Vaccines

23 January 2021

Confused about all those vaccines currently being rushed out onto the market? Do any of them actually work? How dangerous are they? In this world exclusive, *The Fin*'s very own viral load-shedding expert Dr Rowena Wuhan-Batsoup checks out the likely efficacy of the plethora of pinpricks soon to be available from your local government health department.

AlboZeneca: two years in the making and widely heralded as the perfect antidote to the disastrous failure of its predecessor, the rapidly abandoned Shorten WiV vaccine, the AlboZeneca has so far failed to live up to early expectations and has indeed performed extremely poorly in all randomised trials, except in those inner-city enclaves where the spread of a deadly new strain, commonly called the wokevirus or WoKe21, is at its most virulent. Expected to be replaced very soon by either the attractive new PL-iBEr-Sek shot in the arm or perhaps even the extremely long shot of the Joel-fit-Zeneca vaccine, which is currently being trialled with mixed results on elderly working class voters in rural coal-mining districts where the wokevirus is virtually non-existent.

Morrisona: developed last Christmas during the Australian bushfire season (and coincidentally just a few weeks before the outbreak of the Wuhan bat-soup virus) at a beachside location close to the Hawaiian Institute for Crisis Control and Media Management, and tested widely on focus groups within the hot zones of the NSW south coast, the Morrisona vaccine works on the simple principle that the best cure for a bad dose of opinion polls is for the sufferer to be seen standing on the spot swatting flies or drinking beer even if he's not actually doing anything. The Morrisona vaccine is at its most effective when stored within national medicine cabinets.

Tr-UMp-24: hugely popular vaccine used specifically to treat against rampant political correctness and hardcore climate hysteria, it has now been discarded since its daily delivery method (Twitter) shut the experiment down altogether. Expect to see it back on the market in about four years' time.

Joe BI-dn: manufactured over many long months in a dingy basement in Delaware, it has never actually been tested on any living human beings. However, the manufacturers are confident that the extraordinary results from the recent November 3rd Placebo Ballot Trials held across five key American mid-western test states indicate that at least 80 million doses of the ballots can be easily manufactured out of thin air and can even bring dead people back to life.

kA mA-LA: heavily marketed as the perfect antidote to white supremacy and toxic masculinity, this Indian-Jamaican combination is believed to be potentially lethal when accidentally swallowed by vulnerable or doddery septuagenarian white males who have recently moved from their basement into a spectacular white marble-clad new nursing home.

Kri-Sti-NA (K-Neally): following a 15-month experimental trial as the premier vaccine in NSW that flopped dramatically with the worst trial results in NSW history on 28 March 2011, the manufacturers Pfizzer decided that Kri-Sti-NA was a, er, fizzer. However, the mutant strain within the Sussex Street DNA led to the vaccine being trialled again several times over, always with the same disastrous results, most notably in the Bennelong cluster. Pfizzer are not giving up, however, and there are rumours the K-Neally strain is going to be trialled yet again later this year as an alternative to the failed AlboZeneca (see above).

BoW-eN: highly non-contagious and ineffectual vaccine that the manufacturers attempted to market with the snappy slogan 'If you don't like our untried and untested vaccines, don't inject them.' To the surprise of the shadow health minister at the time, Mr Chris Bowen (Lab), the public didn't touch them or his party with a barge pole.

DNA-Andrews: highly toxic mutant version of the standard Labor vaccine that has been modified to give senior politicians complete immunity to any form of prosecution whatsoever from highly infectious hotel quarantine inquiry findings. The DNA-Andrews strain is rumoured to have escaped from a Manchurian laboratory experiment in China.

GL-adYs (DA-ryl): following secretive trials in confined spaces (parliamentary lifts, underground car parks, hotel lobbies, phone booths, etc) using pseudonyms and fake disguises, this unusual and hitherto unimaginable combination was discovered to kill the romance bug stone dead.

Austral-Day-26-1 vaccine: virulent and toxic strain of left-wing dogma based on hitherto unknown secret Indigenous herbs and remedies that invades the body politic and attacks the common sense synapses. In clinical trials conducted within the boardroom of Cricket Australia patients universally displayed extreme symptoms of insincere virtue-signalling.

Pornographer Larry Flynt kicks the bucket.

Porn

13 February 2021

With the tragic news this week of the death of Larry Flynt, the ninth-grade dropout who revolutionised the pornography industry with raunchy publications such as *Hustler*, strip clubs and 'adult' shops, libidinous voyeurs have been thrown into agitated despair, asking: what next for porn? In this world exclusive, *The Fin*'s adult entertainment correspondent, Ms Rowena Lovelace-Moneyshot, details the exciting new categories of porn that are now available:

Alboporn: strictly for the fetishists, Alboporn features explicit and graphic images of the bizarre love-in between Labor leader Anthony 'Each Way' Albanese in a shiny leather Akubra hat and gnomic, bearded Kevin 'Pink bitts' Rudd as they try to hustle innocent young and unsuspecting voters and lure them into their sweaty Labor tryst. Highlights include a steamy cameo by former leader Bill 'Shorty' Shorten complaining about Albo's 'tiny' policy agenda.

Climateporn: get all hot and bothered as you flagellate yourself for your sinful fossil-fuelled indulgences, submit yourself to the terror of the approaching apocalypse, drool over the imminent doomsday and try to restrain yourself to net zero emissions before gluing yourself to the pavement.

Joelporn: secret hidden video cameras reveal former Labor 'hard man' Joel Fitzgibbon confessing to his innermost fantasies, including his deep-rooted desire to dress himself up in a 'blue-collar' pair of denim overalls and parade down the main drag of Cessnock covered in filthy coal dust.

Conspiracyporn: whip yourself into a feverish state of daring and excitement by logging onto the 'dark web' of Craig Kelly's Facebook page and expose yourself to the most shameful and vile blasphemies and dirty, degenerate conspiracy theories such as, er, ivermectin works as a prophylaxis and, er, renewables are a rort.

Kristinaporn: hot blonde bombshell and former cable TV babe Kristina will tickle you in all the right places as she indulges her deepest desire to avoid at any cost having yet again to face the cruel and sadistic punishment meted out to her over and over again by angry NSW voters and instead fulfil her passion for hard-hitting political engagement and fluffy media coverage by keeping both feet firmly planted in the Senate.

JobKeeperPorn: get goosebumps as you devour all manner of earthly delights in this current fetish for earning lots and lots of money without actually lifting a finger. Lie back on your bed and watch as sweaty Pacific islanders toil picking fruit in the back-breaking fields and farms of rural Victoria while you help yourself to another delicious round of taxpayer-funded self-indulgences.

Wuhanporn: starring beefcake Dr Tedros and his macho World Health Organisation, Wuhanporn satisfies an insatiable compulsion within globalist circles to handcuff yourself to Mistress China and then never blame her for doing anything naughty, no matter how wickedly she behaves. Hardcore fanatics are known to indulge in pangolophilia where they lie prostrate in front of a ruthless dictator and smear themselves with baby bat soup before stripping themselves of any credibility whatsoever..

Clusterporn: you'll be drooling over every salacious detail as yet another cluster of Covid cases is discovered in some hot and steamy quarantine hotel or even better at the local throbbing, pumping beachside RSL full of sweaty bodies breathing all over each other in a maskless orgy of social intercourse (also known as 'dancing').

Davosporn: 'You'll own nothing and you'll be happy' is the sado-masochistic promise of the devilishly indecent 'Great Reset' perversity designed to strip individuals of their property rights and enslave them in a more natural state to a 'sustainable' future. Highlights include lustful 'Davos' man flaunting his excessive wealth and green goddess 'Greta' giving even the most powerful men and women in the room a severe tongue-lashing.

DanAndrewsPorn: how he keeps it up for so long, hour after hour, is a mystery, but lovers of Dan Andrews porn will quite happily spend each and every day watching the same limp performance as he attempts to convince us all that he is not responsible for the hotel quarantine disaster and Victoria is doing a great job containing the virus.

Kyrgiosporn: also known as Aussie open porn, this usually involves two men, both of whom may or may not be Greek, spending literally hours thrashing around, grunting, swearing and abusing each other in the most degrading fashion until one of them collapses in a pool of dripping sweat and savagely kisses the ground before being declared the winner.

Serenaporn: similar, but with women.

Crownporn: watch with irresistible pleasure as one by one the wealthiest men in the land are brought to their knees, shamed and disgraced.

Insurrectionporn: these hardcore video tapes aren't for the faint-hearted, showing hour after hour of revolting footage as deranged Trump supporters wander up to the Capitol building and, er, wander on in.

The hapless Dan Andrews government declares another lockdown during which it decides to place black bin liners over the heads of Covid detainees in transit.

Bin liners

20 February 2021

The world of innovation was rocked to its core this week with the exciting and astonishing announcement that the Victorian government has finally found a way to stop the Coronavirus dead in its tracks: by sticking a black plastic bin liner over the head of any suspected carrier. But why stop there? Surely there are myriad political uses for this humble Aussie product? *The Fin*'s innovation correspondent, Dr Rowena Garbo-Stringpull, investigates potential other uses for the much-maligned black bin liner.

The Albo Maxi-Super Strength Bin Liner Policy Holder: contrary to those vindictive taunts that you only have a 'tiny' policy agenda, what better way to demonstrate to those snivelling caucus colleagues of yours that you in fact have an absolutely gargantuan policy agenda than by lugging a bulging black plastic bin liner crammed full of all your amazing ideas into parliament each week? Those factional warlords will never dare look you in the eye again!

The Bowen Binned Brain-snaps Commemorative Collection: looking for a handy gift pack to commemorate your best years in politics? Wondering how to package up for posterity all those brilliant, ahead-of-their-time yet disgracefully overlooked ideas of yours such as 'Grocery Watch', 'The Malaysian Solution', 'Franking Credits Tax' and snappy slogans like 'If you don't like our policies, don't vote for us.'? Yours for only $2.99 (incl postage and packaging) the Complete Chris Bowen Policy Commemoration Legacy Souvenir Pack comes in its own shiny black plastic bin liner complete with stylish yellow plastic pull-strings so you can keep the lot tightly secured together in the one place where they truly belong and give future generations the tactile fun of rummaging through them in an appropriate manner.

The Fitzgibbon Hunter Valley Coal Mining Personalised Political Protective Gear: if a bin liner can ward off COVID-19, then protecting you from coal dust and political blowback should be a doddle! What better way to demonstrate your support for clean coal mining at the same time as promising to clean up the planet than by parading up and down the main drag of Cessnock fully kitted out in your own protective Joel Fitzgibbon autographed bin liner?

The Binjuggal Binjuggal Liner: at last we have the proof! As has been well established by the ABC, Labor politicians, actors and authors, among others, and contrary to white mythology, pre-colonial Indigenous Australians DID in fact build massive cities, harvested frozen peas, ate McDonalds, drank coffee from Nespresso pods, invented dental floss and rolled their own cigarettes among many other long-overlooked achievements, all of which has now been conclusively shown to be true thanks to a pre-settlement black bin liner discovered in a recent archaeological dig adjacent to an ancient Bendigo tip.

The ScoMo Odourless Bin Liner: what to do with all that embarrassing baggage in your past? Such as being punted from the tourism gig, being Malcom Turnbull's closest ally and stabbing Tony Abbott in the back, stabbing Dutton in the back, stuffing up superannuation for all time and going on hols during the bushfire season? Pack it all up into one

2021—THE YEAR DEMOCRACY DIES

single odourless ScoMo Bin Liner and all that whiffy rubbish magically disappears just in time for the next election!

The Dan Andrews Discarded Holidays Almanac Bin Liner: sometimes you get so busy cancelling public holidays and destroying any sense of community and history that you forget just how many events you have thrown onto the scrap heap in the one year. Now you can gather all the remnants of what was once a thriving, bustling Victorian community and store the happy memories safely in one place in the Dan Andrews Discarded Holidays Black Bin Liner Bag. You'll have hours of fun remembering such destroyed delights as Easter, Mother's Day, Father's Day, the Melbourne Show, the AFL Grand Final, the Melbourne Cup, Valentine's Day, Chinese New Year, the Rip Curl Pro, Moomba and literally thousands of family and community events.

And while you're at it, don't forget to also order your **Dan Andrews Smelly Leftovers Bin Liner:** an absolute treat for all those Victorian restaurants, cafes and other small businesses that have disappeared under Dan, the latest offering from Dan Andrews Garbage is a complete bin liner stuffed with your favourite selection from the rotting lobsters, salmonella shellfish, decaying dumplings, melted chocolates, malodorous meatballs, fetid falafels, putrid Peking Duck, rancid risotto and other such Victorian delicacies that all had to be binned last weekend thanks to Andrews' pointless five day lockdown.

The Michael McCormack Career Path & Nationals Leadership Trajectory Black Bin Liner: a must-have for every (OK, we got the gag thanks—ed).

Green eggs

6 March 2021

The world of children's nursery rhymes was rocked to its core this week following the banning of several books by Dr. Seuss. *The Fin*'s children's literature correspondent Dr Rowena Grinch-Ham has updated some of the author's classic works to keep them more in tune with contemporary values:

the sun did not shine.
the wind did not blow.
so we sat in the house
with the heating turned low.

I sat there with Angus.
we sat there, we two.
and I said, 'how I wish
we had nuclear too!'

too wet to go out
and too cold to play ball.
so we sat in the house.
we did nothing at all.

and then something went BUMP!
how that bump made us jump!
we looked!
then we saw him slink in like a cat!
we looked!
and we saw him!
it was Matt with no hat!
and he said to us,
'why do you sit there like that?
I know it is dark
and the wind is not blowing.
but we can have fun
if the Snowy is flowing'

'I know some good tricks I can play,
on the Nats
with windmills and panels,'
said Matt with no hat.
'a lot of good tricks.
I will sell them to you.
and Gladys will not mind at all if I do.'

then Angus and I
did not know what to say.
it was that or no telly
for the rest of the day.

but our fish said, 'no! no!
make that man go away!
tell that Matt with no hat

you do NOT want to pay.
he should not be here.
he should not be about.
he should not be here
when the lights are all out!'

'now! now! have no fear.
I'm ever so keen
I'm saving the planet,
I'm ever so green.
I'll harness the sun
and the wind just like that
There's never a blackout'
said Matt with no hat

but the fish looked so sad
And tried not to frown,
saying 'why on earth
did you shut Liddell down?'

'why, that was my plan
it was always my wish,
to play a game I call
Pushing Up Fish!'

'it's a game we can play
All night and all day
It's a game that's fun
Even when there's no sun
I've bought a new pump

and that pump makes you jump!
There's a battery too
For a minute or two!
I can push water uphill
and push you up too
then you'll swim back down
what else would you do?'

'this is no fun!' said the fish.
'put me down'!
'I do not want to play
'I do NOT wish to drown!'

'but I'm saving the planet!
I'm ever so green.
with panels and turbines
I'm ever so keen!
I've saved the koalas
I've locked up the trees ·
I've racked up your bills
I've paid lots of fees
It's not just a hobby
I play in the lobby
It makes the world better
Ask my friend Greta
I ran it past Trent
And Dave Sharma too
And Jason and Michael
Said it's what we must do'

Then that Matt with no hat
said with a grin
Being keen and being green
Is never a sin

It's worth going broke
To say you are woke
We can play for as long as your mother is gone
So long as we never switch anything on!'

Harry and Meghan accuse the royals of being racist in a chat with Oprah.

Racists in the Palace

13 March 2021

The world of interracial royal marriages was rocked to its core this week following the shocking suggestion by Harry and Meghan that a senior member of the British royal family might once have queried 'how dark' any offspring of theirs would be. In this world exclusive, *The Fin*'s royal correspondent Lady Rowena 'Saxy' Coburg-Mountbatten answers the question on the entire world's lips: who is the royal most likely to have made such a comment, and what were the circumstances in which they said it?

Princess Anne: 'Do tell, Harry, who was that young filly I saw you with on the television the other night? American actress, they said. Well, no offence, but Windsors and Americans do not mix, if you get my drift! Remember Wallis, that's all I say! Can she ride? Does she have her own horses?' Harry: 'Er, Wallis…what…? I don't think so, no, er, we… we didn't chat about anything like that, she…' Anne: 'Well, I jolly well hope you don't intend breeding, I remember the time we sired that gorgeous American Saddleback with a Windsor Red! Turned out blacker than an Arabian! What a calamity! Couldn't give it away!'

Prince Edward: 'I say Harry, charming young lass I saw you with on the old gogglebox the other night! An American actress they said! Are you two an item, then?' Harry: 'Well, Uncle Eddy, it's early days yet, but you never know!' Edward: 'Jolly good show! You know, I was thinking, we could do with someone like her in the next "It's A Royal Knockout!". To add a bit of colour, as they say, and movement!'

Prince Andrew: 'I say, Harry, who's that tasty bit of crumpet I saw you with on the telly the other night? Corrrr… she's a bit of alright, know what I mean?' Harry: 'Um, just a friend, Uncle Andy. An American actress on a show called *Suits*. Andrew: 'Well, she can slip into one of my suits anytime she likes! Get it!? My birthday suit! Ha ha ha! Tell her if she's looking for her Prince Charming I can help her get a bit of skin in the game, if you know what I mean! Ha ha ha! Just depends how dark it is! Ha ha ha!'

Prince Charles: 'Harry, please listen up, I'm so depressed because of this wretched global warming! It's all I can think about these days! Entire eco-systems are burning up and we will all have to evolve physiologically or we'll all be frazzled and the entire human race will be wiped out!' Harry: 'Um, Dad, I actually just wanted to ask what you thought about my new American girlfriend…' Charles: 'What I think is that your children and grandchildren will be much darker skinned or they simply won't survive!'

Camilla: 'I say, Harry, who was that exotic young temptress I saw you with on the TV the other night?' Harry: 'She's African American. Her Mum's black and her Dad's white.' Camilla: 'How nice for her! But how can she be sure? Nobody can ever be one hundred per cent certain who their father really is, can they now Harry?'

Kate: 'Harry, can you hear me? It's a dodgy line, you keep dropping out. I just wanted to say I think you'll need to renovate the cottage. If you and Meghan are having a baby Wills and I are worried it will be way too dark. Hello?'

Prince Philip: 'Dear boy, do tell, who was that exotic creature you were gadding about with on the idiot box? Looks like she's descended from pirates!' Harry: 'She's an American actress, grandpa, in a show called

Suits.' Philip: 'Well, I hope she doesn't have to wear one, that's all I can say! Give me a dusky girl in a grass skirt any day of the week over some pasty Earl's daughter in a Coco Chanel suit, as old Bunty used to say on safari in Botswana. You know, old chap, I've often wondered how many brown-skinned royals there are out there!'

Queen Elizabeth: 'Dear Harry, do sit down. Now I know you like to play the field and you young men must have your fun and all of that but it's high time you settled down. I'm told you were filmed with a beautiful African American actress on the television the other night and that you two look so happy together. Excellent! Personally, I'm thrilled! Keep it to yourself, but I'm especially keen on the idea of introducing a bit of diversity, as they say, into the Firm's gene pool. Imagine! A good-looking Windsor baby with gorgeous dark curly hair and beautiful brown skin! Instead of all that horrid red hair and ghostly whiteness! I can't think of anything better for the future of the Crown!'

Sex scandals continue to plague Canberra.

The Canberry Tales

27 March 2021

The world of shocking stories of carnal lust and debauchery was rocked to its core this week following the discovery of the missing fragments from Chaucer's masterpiece, *The Canberry Tales*. In this world exclusive, *The Fin*'s medieval literature expert Professor Rowena de Cameron translates:

> When March's flooding rains have pierced the drought
> Of fields right to the root, and bathed each sprout
> Upon the ramparts of the privileged tower
> It brings forth the desire to deflower;
> Now in that season it befell one day
> In Kingston at the tavern where I lay,
> As I was all prepared for setting out
> To Canberry with a heart devout,
> That there had come into that hostelry
> At night some twenty-nine, a company
> Of sundry revellers who did drink and laugh
> For Liberals were they all and long of staff
> So onward up the hill to Canberry we rode
> Into the darkness to unburden each our load.
> Through the gated pass we merry men did slide,
> The chambers and the tables there were wide,

One lay himself upon the fair damsels desk

And by the time the sun had gone to rest

All manner of appetites had been consumed

Within that dark and musty room.

But nonetheless, while I have time and space,

Before proceeding further here's the place

Where I believe it reasonable to state

Something about these staffers to relate

And also what array they all were in.

And with this tawdry tale I must begin.

There with us was a chap, a solitary man

Which is oft how such debauchery began

He was a valiant warrior for his lord;

No man had pierced more with his sword.

He emptied from his pouch an oriental powder

As pure and white as any flower

And pass it around we did one by one

In order to facilitate the evening's fun.

Now he had brought his friend, a youthful squire

A lover and night bachelor to admire.

His locks were curled as if set by a press.

His age was twenty years or so, I guess.

He was a courteous, humble lad and able,

Who performed with agility and grace upon that table.

He sang or else he fluted all the night;

In showing all we sinners no respite.

Beneath his belt positioned handily

He tended to his gear most yeomanly.

There also was a girl so finely dressed

She came from Fyshwicke, we all guessed,

And tightly laced, she had a nice new pair

Of shoes. Her face was botoxed, smooth and fair.

She looked so young, but was no youth

No need to ask her how, but it's the truth.

Of table manners she had learnt it all,

For from her nose she let no morsel fall.

There was a staffer in her company

Whose moustache was lily-white as could be,

A devotee of all delights that lure us,

He truly was a son of Epicurus.

Alas, I do not recall this staffer's name.

A spinning merchant with a forked tongue also came,

Dressed in a suit. Tall and proud he sat

Upon his Lady's desk. A pink beaver hat

He wore, and boots most elegantly wrought.

He spoke with pomp on everything he thought,

And boasted of the earnings he'd collected

and how the PM's good name must be protected.

It seemed a shame, and caused me some chagrin,

To see he still had powder on his chin.

There was a staffer hailing from the west,

The selfies he took I'd rank with the best.

He'd been to university I'd allow.

He was as fiercely woke as he knew how.

There also with us was a minister

Who liked to do things somewhat sinister

So pimply was his skin, eyes puffed and narrow.

He was as hot and lecherous as a sparrow.

With black hand, scabby brows and scanty beard,

He had a face that all the MPs feared;

And when with wine he was quite well infused,

Gay indeed was that minister's mood.

The supplier was a slender, choleric man.

He shaved his beard as closely as one can;

He surely was a festive sort of fellow;

Many a pilfered wine draught made him mellow

Why, he'd be willing, for a quart of wine,

To let some rascal have his concubine

For one whole year, excusing him completely.

He well could 'pluck a bird' (always discreetly),

While drinking more Bordeaux, this staffer snoring

had no use for conscience, thought it boring.

From near Darlinghurst a rent-boy came;

He was a little shy, which was a shame.

But not for long, he was soon aroused

To sing and dance for us, to carouse.

His plucked his lute and sang his sonnet,

'Where's the minister's desk? Let me frolic on it!'

As Nicolle Flint calls it quits, Scott Morrison reshuffles his Cabinet.
With the emphasis on 'women'.

Prime Minister for Women

2 April 2021

The world of Westminster-style politics was rocked to its core this week following the exciting news that the Prime Minister has reshuffled the entire concept of representative democracy. In its place Scott Morrison has restructured his Cabinet to more adequately reflect the priorities of his government, including new portfolios of Women's Safety, Women's Security and Women's Safety and Security. In this week's world exclusive, *The Fin*'s recently appointed Editor-in-Chief-of-Women and Chief-Women's-Political-Correspondent, Dr Rowena Shelia-Quotas, explains that this week's reshuffle was only the beginning, and outlines the exciting newly re-named ministerial portfolios we can expect to see unveiled in coming months.

Minister for Schoolgirl Safety and Protection Against Toxic Schoolboy Masculinity: responsible for introducing mandatory weekly school assembly apologies by all schoolboys to all schoolgirls for staring at them, making eye contact with them, winking at them, flying a paper dart over their head, writing their name on a desk inside a sexually-suggestive heart with an arrow through it, offering to buy them a Coke, asking for their phone number or offering to walk them home.

Minister for Safety of Women in Pre-Marital Entertainment Industries: responsible for guaranteeing the safety of soon-to-be-married women by ensuring that all Male Strippers at Hen's Parties are first vetted for Covid or any other communicable diseases, viruses, or other off-putting toxic masculine traits including excessive body hair, masculine body odours or bad breath, squinty eyes, unimpressive crop of hair, unimpressive torso or any other inappropriate physical shortcomings.

Minister for the Safety of Women in the Workplace and the Eradication, Prevention and Incarceration of all Alleged Upskirting Crimes (including any and all forms of inappropriate iPhone behaviour): responsible for ensuring mandatory prison sentences for any photographs taken by men of women in any situation that have not formally been vetted and approved beforehand by the Women's Safety Committee on Appropriate Use of a Mobile Phone Camera in the presence of Women.

Minister for Health, Safety and Financial Security of Women in Fashionable Cosmetic Enhancement Parlours: responsible for ensuring adequate access by women to high-quality beauty and self-esteem-enhancing products including federally-funded Covid financial stimulus compensation schemes such as Josh Frydenberg's recently announced BotoxSeeker, YouthKeeper and NipTucker packages.

Minister for Women's Safety and Security in Toxic Checkout Queues: responsible for ensuring women who have been forced to endure the indignity and disrespect of having to do the household shopping once a week are not further intimidated by having to stand in a queue behind a toxic, boorish masculine shopper reeking of stale booze and cheeseburgers by supplying federally-financed Express Women Shopper's Safety Lanes in all supermarkets.

Minister for Women's Safety and Job Security in the Public Broadcaster: responsible for ensuring safe and secure representation at the ABC of all diverse and inclusive female presenters, producers and on-air talent by, er, getting rid of all the men.

Minister for Road Safety and Security of Women Drivers: responsible for developing a more amenable road and traffic network system that prioritises women driver's safety and reduces female stress and lack of self-esteem behind the wheel by criminalising toxic male verbal aggression and inappropriate and offensive facial expressions (including the raising of eyebrows or open-mouthed staring) in everyday common female driving experiences such as accidentally turning the 'wrong' way down a one-way street or inadvertently parking across two parking spots.

Minister for Safety and Security of Women Walking Home At Three in the Morning After a Night on the Tiles Down a Back Alley in the CBD: responsible for introducing 6pm curfew for all males within 100km radius of major CBDs… anyone got any other ideas?—Scott.

Minister for Safety and Security of Women in Contact Sports: responsible for ensuring women and girls are not subject to physical harm by being tackled by transgender women who in all likelihood are much stronger and physically more challenging than… oh, hang on, er, on second thoughts maybe we'll give this one a miss—Scott.

Minister for Safety and Security of Women in the Defence Forces: responsible for ensuring that when Women Soldiers and Officers are in front-line combat situations they are given non-discriminatory equal opportunities to participate with their male colleagues in all events, such as being taken captive, blindfolded, held hostage in a dark cave by a bunch of marauding jihadists, tortured, and, er, OK maybe we need to re-think this one—Scott.

Minister for the Safety of Women Liberal Candidates in the crucial seat of Boothby: responsible for ensuring full support for all female candidates who are being harassed by GetUp!, Greens or Labor supporters to the point where we call out the Labor party and demand… actually, scrap this one, can't be bothered—Scott.

A former PM gets appointed to a cushy job–
and then fired 48 hours later.

101 uses for a defunct PM

10 April 2021

The world of Malcolm Trumble was rocked to its core this week following the devastating news that the former prime minister, former opposition leader, ex-Australian Republican Movement chief, former merchant banker, ex-autobiographer, former journalist, former ABC personality and ex-lawyer has been discarded from his latest job in record time, even for him. Said a spokesperson for someone who once sat near Mr Trumble in a Chinese restaurant: 'It is perfectly common for Mr Trumble to be casually discarded—much like a soggy dumpling on a lazy Susan I believe he once likened it to—but it usually takes a bit longer than 48 hours.' Said another spokesperson for a different person who once rubbed shoulders with Mr Trumble in a lift at No. 1 Bligh Street speaking on condition of anonymity: 'The beauty of appointing Mr Trumble to any senior key leadership role is that you know you will never have to worry about long service leave or splashing out on a gold watch.'

In this week's world exclusive, *The Fin*'s short-term employment and career advice correspondent Ms Rowena Gigs-Galore suggests an array of temporary jobs that the owner of one of Sydney's most prestigious harbourside mansions could now try his hand at:

Lazy Susan designer: with his proven skill in swapping positions and rotating roles, what better job for Mr Trumble than designing an innovative and agile new range of portable Lazy Susans? Coming in a shade of eco-designs from deep Guardian green to pale Liberal-lite aqua, the Trumble Patented Lazy Susan Range offers the perfect gift for those who enjoy a bit of late night take-away dumplings with colleagues over a spot of after-hours plotting and scheming in any modern office or Queanbeyan back yard shed.

Great Barrier Reef Tour Operator: with the imminent demise of the Great Barrier Reef by the end of the decade due to catastrophic global warming and, er, some jellyfish, what better short-term gig for the former PM than hosting his own Last-Minute Luxury Reef Tours of this doomed and fast-disappearing world heritage landmark? As an added bonus, snorkelers will get to go on a mystery 'deep dive' looking for that magical $400 million treasure chest of taxpayer's money that was tipped into those pristine waters during a casual lunch.

Celibacy advocate: with his universally-applauded and highly successful patented 'bonk ban', Mr Trumble could easily have a successful career as a self-help guru and celibacy advocate offering handy tips to ambitious and horny young male and female staffers who are keen to get to the top without actually having to shag the boss.

Leather Jacket designer: with his nifty fashion sense and stylish appearance, Malcolm's Leather Attire could easily become the go-to name in men's fashion design. After all, what woke young man about town could resist a shiny black leather jacket with subtle Tony Jones-autographed gold-leaf embroidered Q&A logo?

Professional culinary utensil and cutlery endorser: what better marketing tool for a sharp blade manufacturer than boasting that your entire range of knives comes with the stamped seal of approval from the man who successfully knifed every political rival who stood in his way? From the Titanium Tony blade to the Brendan Backstabber to the Peter King Stainless, these knives are guaranteed to get the job done!

Plumber: with the former PM's proven ability to push vast amounts of water uphill in defiance of gravity, what better qualification for a domestic plumber or drain cleaner? The unique patented Trumble High Rise Hydro System will revolutionise modern skyscraper plumbing designs, with water tanks in the basement miraculously delivering water pressure all the way up to the penthouse dunny whilst generating abundant energy on the way back down again!

Sturdy interior furniture maker: fed up with wobbly table tops that aren't fit for purpose? Why not check out the new range of Trumble Tables—uniquely designed to continuously have things put on and then taken off again, no matter how cumbersome or unwieldy they may seem. From banking policies to raising taxes to cutting super to a carbon tax to an ETS, nothing is off limits when it comes to the Trumble On-and-Off-and-On-the-Table Table.

Poltergeist psychic: worried your home is haunted? Not anymore! Now with the Trumble Miserable Spectre Diviner, your ghosts will scurry back to the afterlife as fast as their plasma will carry them rather than put up with the aggravation of listening to Trumble whinge for the rest of eternity.

Waffle maker: what better Father's Day gift than a unique patented Trumble Waffle Maker? Comes complete with innovative and agile additional extra's and for Mum's Day there's even a My Wife Lucy Waffle Maker matching set.

A former Defence Minister realises there is a military threat to our nation.

Pyne family tree

17 April 2021

The world of former defence minister Christopher Pyne was rocked to its core this week with the realisation that Australia might end up in a war with China within the next five years. 'I would have to say that the possibility is more likely than it was [when I was defence minister],' he told a group of students. 'Not a cyber war, but a real one involving loss of life, destruction of military platforms, with aggressors and defenders on different sides.'

Who'd've guessed? In this world exclusive, *The Fin*'s forward thinking correspondent Madame Rowena de Claire-Voyant looks at the long line of famous Pyne's who have similarly been gifted with such extraordinary powers of prescient vision.

Christeus Pinilios, Troy, 1194 BC: speaking at the foot of a large abandoned wooden horse that he immediately recognised as a wonderful gift from the gods, this insightful Trojan general explained to a crowd of students that it paid to be vigilant and to never let your guard down. 'I would have to say that the possibility exists that at some point in the next five years the Greeks may well figure out a way to cunningly infiltrate our impregnable city,' he warned, 'but not on my watch!'

Cicero Pyneus, Rome, 44BC: former imperial general with a fondness for libertine Roman orgies and Commander of the Black Hand Brigade,

Pyneus famously declared to a group of students that he was 'in the winner's arena', before predicting that Julius Caesar may one day stand for election to the Senate. 'The possibility is that one day Caesar may tire of soldiering. Indeed, I gather he has already crossed the Rubicon, which clearly indicates his desire to return to Rome for a peaceful career within our democratic system.'

Kristogoth the Pine, Asian Steppes, 406 AD: visionary leader with a flair for wild parties and an advocate of mixed Hun-Slavic marriages, Kristogoth was noted for purchasing a fleet of advanced Viking wooden ships specifically modified to his own design which involved removing the cumbersome Scandinavian oars and replacing them with his own unique bamboo paddles. The final words of Kristogoth's most insightful speech were never completed when, speaking before an enthusiastic crowd of students he famously proclaimed that 'I would have to say that there is always the possibility that within the next five years Attila may undertake the odd spot of rape, pillage and…' just as a flaming spear lodged itself in his throat.

Lord Blackhand of the Longstaff, Pyne Castle, Nottinghamshire, 1215 AD: popular aristocratic landowner who famously convened the Knights of the Winner's Circle, a group of frolicking friars dedicated to achieving marriage equality between nuns and monks throughout Christendom. Lord Blackhand was well-known as a favourite in the court of King Malcolm the Usurper, a paranoid narcissist who lived a ghost-like existence in his lavish harbourside palace before being discarded like a soggy dumpling on a 13th century lazy Susan (is this last bit historically accurate?—ed). Speaking to a group of yeomen, Blackhand warned that a band of disgruntled pickpockets and archers hanging out in the nearby forest posed no immediate threat to rich landowners and, besides which, they would only ever be interested in robbing the poor.

Christophorus Pynumbulus, Genoa, 1488 AD: seaman and navigator who designed a fleet of submersible vessels with which he intended to conquer the New World. The original design for the fleet was purchased from the French on the specific instructions that the work all be done in Genoa to convert the vessels to Pynumbulus's own unique design replacing the traditional French sails with a novel underwater-oar propulsion system.

Leonardo da Pinci, Florence, 1512 AD: colourful Italian polymath of the High Renaissance renowned as a painter, sculptor, architect, draughtsman, theorist and gay marriage activist whose notebooks contained designs for some of the most advanced weaponry ever conceived, including a submarine powered by an original Da Victa lawnmower engine.

Jean-Christophe du Pin, Pâtissier, Bastille, Paris, 1788: renowned pastry chef who was a favourite with the residents of Versailles, a swish suburb to the south of Paris, who couldn't get enough of his pastries. Famously reassured his nervous clientele that all the baying, howling, angry mobs would be satisfied with a slice of cake.

Albert Pynestein, Zurich, 1915: German-born theoretical physicist widely acknowledged to be one of the greatest scientific minds of his time, Pynestein pioneered two great discoveries, the ability to push water uphill in defiance of the laws of gravity for political reasons only and the quantum mechanics of installing diesel-powered engines into nuclear craft in order to hold your seat. Speaking to students in 1939, Pynestein opined that at some distant point in the future it was a theoretical possibility that Hitler might begin the second world war but it was highly unlikely.

Best we forget

24 April 2021

This Anzac weekend, Australians gather to commemorate those who
sacrificed so much to create the freedoms we enjoy today, under the
slogan 'Lest We Forget'. However, due to an unfortunate typographical
error *The Fin*'s nostalgia columnist Dr Rowena Memory-Laine thought
she'd been asked to write a column entitled 'Best We Forget'. *The Fin*
apologises for this misunderstanding.

Dear Ed,

Here are my top 'Best We Forget' moments from the last two decades.
Trust this is what you were after. Love Rowena

Best We Forget Election: In a flurry of excitement Australians
overwhelmingly decide that Prime Minister John Howard is way past his
use-by-date, out of touch, stale, unimaginative, old-fashioned, over the
hill, yesterday's man, useless, incompetent, a loser, a no-hoper, a relic of a
bygone era and… opt for Kevin Rudd instead.

Best We Forget Summit: Gathering in the nation's capital, a thousand of the
nation's finest minds and eminent persons put their brains together to solve
the complex problems facing the future of the nation. Luminaries assembled
include an overpaid movie star, an out of work scriptwriter, a failed comedian,
a couple of professors and, er, that's about it. After millions of dollars and
weeks of feverish activity the Summit comes up with… nothing.

Best We Forget Federal Plan to Lower Grocery Prices: Chris Bowen's
GroceryWatch.

Best We Forget Federal Plan to Lower Fuel Prices: Chris Bowen's FuelWatch.

Best We Forget Edge-of-Seat Political Decision-Making Moment: The 17 minutes during which Rob Oakeshott tells us who his 9-year-old daughter has chosen to run the country.

Best We Forget Backfiring Political Stunt: Tipped off by a Labor staffer that opposition leader Tony Abbott is dining in a nearby restaurant, an angry activist mob surround the venue leading to chaos as Prime Minister Julia Gillard, who is also lunching there, has to be dragged to safety.

Best We Forget Cunning Political Strategist: John McTernan.

Best We Forget Immigration Policy: Unveiled to much fanfare, Labor's Malaysian Solution is a brilliant and insightful plan to reduce the numbers of asylum-seekers flooding into Australia by swapping each one of our most unwanted illegal aliens for, er, four of Malaysia's most unwanted illegal aliens.

Best We Forget Immigration Minister: Chris Bowen.

Best We Forget Treasurer: Chris Bowen.

Best We Forget Strategic Last Minute Election Eve Commitment: 'No cuts to the ABC or SBS.'

Best We Forget Conservative Prudent Small Government Self-Reliance Initiative: The Abbott government's Paid Parental Leave scheme.

Best We Forget Political Acumen and Media Savviness in front of a camera moment: munching on a raw onion.

Best We Forget Political Coup: Following widespread outrage at a Liberal Prime Minister embracing such disgraceful policies as eating a raw onion and knighting a Prince, conservative commentators en masse urge conservative Liberal MPs to overthrow conservative Tony Abbott in favour of, er, Malcolm Turnbull.

Best We Forget Prime Minister: Malcolm Turnbull.

Best We Forget Election Campaign: Prime Minister Malcolm Turnbull shows his commitment to women's issues by lunching at a Gentlemen-only club and demonstrates his empathy with the working man by knocking off at noon each day.

Best We Forget Magnanimous Election Night Victory Speech: Having spent the evening sulking in his harbourside mansion, a furious Malcolm Turnbull blames the Labor party for the fact that he has totally wiped out Tony Abbott's huge majority.

Best We Forget Plan to Deliver Cheap Reliable Renewable Energy: Convinced that the normal laws of physics and gravity do not apply when there's a quid to be made, Prime Minister Turnbull concocts a scheme that involves pushing water uphill in the middle of the night and then letting it run back down again during the day.

Best We Forget Excuse for Being Dumped by your own Party: 'It's clear the Liberal party got rid of me because they feared I was going to lead them to victory at the 2019 election'.

Best We Forget Post-Prime Ministerial Career Commitment: 'What I won't be doing is hanging around like a miserable ghost'.

Best We Forget Election Campaign Platform: Convinced of imminent victory, the Australian Labor party offers to tax self-funded retirees' franking credits and offers an exciting plan for mandatory electric vehicles.

Best We Forget Election Prediction: To a man and a woman, the mainstream media in Australia predict a Bill Shorten victory at the 2019 election (except for the author of this book).

Best We Forget Christmas Holiday Destination Choice: As Australia heads towards a balmy summer, Prime Minister Scott Morrison and his wife flip through a handful of glossy brochures advertising tantalising family holidays in delightful tropical resorts in Hawaii.

Best We Forget Covid Protection Scheme: Convinced that federal authorities and the Army don't know how to organise an effective quarantine scheme, Dan Andrews calls in a bunch of randy unemployed nightclub bouncers instead.

Tensions with China rise, as the new defence minister admits war is a possibility.

Art of War

1 May 2021

The world of Chinese military strategies was rocked to its core this week following the discovery in an ancient tomb in the remote mountainous Shandong province of a set of bamboo scrolls containing what is believed to be the missing final chapter of Sun Tzu's *Art of War* written in ancient Mandarin. In this world exclusive, *The Fin*'s oriental expansionism expert, Professor Wuhena Tan-Ming translates:

Chapter 14: Vanquishing the White Barbarian of the Southern Isle.

Sun Tzu said: The time shall come to send a host of a hundred thousand men vast distances across the oceans to seize the Great Isle of the South rumoured to contain wealth and minerals beyond our wildest imaginings and farms and lands of great openness and fecundity. But sending armies on leaky wooden vessels will entail heavy losses and a drain upon the Emperor's resources. Instead, a wise general will float a thousand coral reefs from the depths of the seas, pouring onto them copious amounts of sand and stone and position upon them great armies visible only to the birds of the air.

Hostile nations may try to sail their vessels of barbaric trade over or even under these waters but fear not. It is a trick. Vessels that sail beneath the waves from the South are a distant fantasy built by those who eat the legs of frogs and shall contain useless cheap engines no more powerful than those normally designed for the trimming of lawns. The weak general who enters into an agreement to purchase such a fleet of sinking vessels is of kind that would have men marry men and women marry women.

Move not unless you see an advantage. For a few hundred ounces of silver, the wise leader will purchase a leasehold of some five score years (minus one) of the mighty southern Port of Dah-Win giving ample time and opportunity to make preparations for the Emperor's arrival.

Unhappy is the general who lands his army in foreign lands across the seas only to be met by surly locals with hostile glances and unappreciative murmurings beneath their breaths, including unclean swear words. Thus, the wise soldier tills the soil before his approach, purchasing the loyalty of the new subjects with scholarships and seats on prestigious boards, teaching the wisdom of Confucius in the centres of learning to soften up the citizenry for the Emperor's arrival.

Knowledge of the enemy's dispositions can only be obtained by befriending their officials or living as a merchant amongst them, gifting them gold and silver such as might be hidden in large sacks obtainable from Aldi. Doomed is the fate of one who tries to win his battles without first cultivating the chattering classes; for the result is a waste of time and general stagnation.

A barbarian army that allows its soldiers to become women through a cut of the blade is not an army any wise general ever need fear.

No ruler should put his tools upon a new terrain without first having snapped up as much of it as he can through extensive acreage purchases, merchant acquisitions and the buying of fine mansions perched upon the foreshores of their harbour.

Hence the saying, there is none so weak as a Foreign Barbarian with green greed in his pale blue eyes. Offer up to such a weakling unattainable riches, including tacky household devices made by the peasants of Guangdong or the slaves of Xinjiang.

With subtle ingenuity of mind, the wise general first unleashes upon his foe a terrible sickness, such as might be found festering in a bowl of baby bat soup.

The enlightened ruler subdues his vassal states in a manner that is more effective and subtle than the deadliest blade. For in every land there is a puny leader, treacherous and cowardly, who would lock up his own people and force them to cover their faces with cloth and hide in their homes for fear of the bat soup sickness. This ruler can easily be persuaded through gifts of trade and baubles, so long as he vows to tie himself to the Emperor's belt and travels faithfully upon the Emperor's road.

Do not hesitate to take back those islands and glittering harbour merchant cities that are rightfully yours.

In preparation for the final attack, the victorious ruler confuses his enemy by refusing to partake of their lobsters, wine and other delicacies.

A wind that rises in the daytime lasts long, but a night breeze soon falls. So too does the sun shine brightly during the day but its power is lost during night. Convince those you seek to conquer to rely solely upon the sun and the wind, while you harness all the mighty power of coal and fire, and your swift and final victory is assured.

The new mooted schools curriculum places even more emphasis on Indigenous culture.

First curriculum

8 May 2021

In exciting news this week, a leading expert in pre-colonial Indigenous education standards has given the thumbs up—a traditional Indigenous sign of showing approval—to the new national curriculum. Head of First Peoples Studies Professor Roweena Cashcoe of the University of Wagga Wagga, who identifies as part-Pitjantjatjara-Walpiri-Luritja takes a close look at the new curriculum and praises its recognition of the educational norms common throughout the First Nations prior to the Genocidal Invasion of 1770. The new curriculum includes:

First Maths: an in-depth study of the beautifully simple and pragmatic mathematical formulas used by the First Peoples who lived in peaceful and harmonious egalitarian agrarian communes in which everybody had as much of everything as they could possibly want or need and nobody ever took anything from anybody else. Says Professor Roweena: 'Colonial mathematical concepts such as addition and subtraction are clearly the product of white supremacy, with 'numbers' being used to 'take away' items—such as the lands of Indigenous peoples—and 'adding them' to the possessions of the colonisers. The idea that you can subtract something from one column and add something to another column and that this somehow ends up with an 'equal' sign is as obscene as it is racist. Worse, it's obvious that the so-called 'plus' symbol, which they call a 'positive' sign, is in fact extremely negative because it is identical to a well-known toxic European religious symbol, namely the cross. But worse than all of that is the appalling 'division' sign which is blatantly and unapologetically a symbol of, er, division. How divisive can you get!?'

First Geography: students are encouraged to express their individual creativity and innate spiritualism by drawing lines on a blank map of the pre-colonial continent of Gondwanaland and giving the spaces in between the lines evocative names representing those of the First Nations, such as Peaceland, Harmonyland, Utopianland, etc. Says Professor Roweena: 'One of the most vile aspects of the colonial invasion was the systematic destruction of the spiritual and psychological boundaries that clearly existed between the gentle, peace-loving First Peoples of the First Nations who lived together with mutual respect for each other's safe spaces and personal boundaries and had no need of the artificial European concept of "borders".'

First Biology: in this empowering and inclusive new course, the diverse rainbow genders of the First Peoples are scientifically explored through a re-interpretation of ritual dance, art forms and smoking ceremonies to explore the rites of passage for traditional First Lesbians, First Gays, First Queers, First Bisexuals and First Transgenders incorporating multiple art forms and story-telling. Says Professor Roweena: 'Is it really a coincidence that the First Peoples worshipped a Rainbow god? I think not! And it is well-known that the colonisers deliberately poisoned the blankets of genderqueer First Peoples with toxic masculinity in order to stop them sleeping together so as to impose a misogynistic, sexist, transphobic and cis-gendered new "normality" upon what was a traditionally feminist and tolerant matriarchal society of First Wom*n.'

First Physics: an in-depth scientific look at the physics of colonial invasion, including vivid computer-generated modelling and graphic visual demonstrations of how a wooden ship containing a toxic white gang of determined, armed and aggressive, er, botanists can easily overpower hundreds if not thousands of tranquil, harmonious, peace-loving, well-fed and prosperous agrarian and egalitarian sustainable communes. Says Professor Roweena: 'What is clear is that the leaders of the First Nations had an advanced appreciation that arming themselves with dangerous weaponry such as bows and arrows and gunpowder was a sure-fire way to create endless division and rivalry between the peace-loving and communal tribes that existed prior to the colonial invasion so they didn't bother.'

First Medicine: in which students are encouraged to explore traditional pre-colonial vaccination programs including Pfizer, AstraZeneca, Moderna and, er, the others. Says Professor Roweena: 'It is abundantly clear from all the available evidence that the Coronavirus was unheard of in pre-colonial invasion days throughout the entirety of the First Nations. Modelling by Imperial College clearly shows that COVID-19 arrived here on 26 January in Captain Cook's First Fleet.'

First Climate Science: as a mounting body of evidence now shows, pre-colonial invasion Indigenous First Peoples had already determined the dangers of anthropogenic global warming and had roundly rejected the idea of mining fossil fuels for their energy supplies and had instead embarked on a more sustainable approach using renewables that involved relying upon the sun for warmth and the wind to cool themselves down. Says Professor Roweena: 'It is clear that the First Nations were light years ahead of their European counterparts in appreciating the need to live in harmony with nature in order to prevent the annihilation of the planet thanks to catastrophic climate change.' (Where's the satire?—ed.)

The Treasurer releases his Liberal budget. But what does it all mean?

Josh's thesaurus

15 May 2021

The world of synonyms was rocked to its core this week following the description by the Treasurer Josh Frydenberg of his Budget—the highest spending budget in Australia's history that will leave Australia with trillion-dollar debts for years to come—as 'a Liberal budget'. To help readers navigate the exciting new world of 'Liberal values and principles', *The Fin*'s conservative correspondent Ms Rowena Lenin-Marx has helpfully compiled the brand new Frydenberg Liberal Thesaurus.

Budget: noun 1 sales pitch, political opportunism, election manifesto, spruiking leadership credentials, never let a good crisis go to waste, beat the lefties at their own game, skewer Albo and Chalmers, thrill the Guardian, titillate the ABC, win the next election, etc.

Budget: noun 2 ideal personal public relations exercise, chance to show off leadership skills, not-to-be-missed opportunity to portray oneself as a typical Aussie family man, battler, everyday bloke, just as much of a knockabout daggy Dad as that guy from the Shire, see also: being filmed taking the kids to the park, swinging on monkey bars, playing touch footie, eating an ice cream, diligently working on important financial papers at home while Mum prepares lunch.

To budget: verb 3 loosen the purse strings, empty the wallet, splurge out, splash out, shell out, put your hand in someone else's pocket, burn a hole in the nation's pocket, spend like a Lord, spend like a drunken sailor, do a reverse Costello, do a triple Swannie with double pike, spend like even a Labor Treasurer wouldn't dare, see also: kick the can down the road, stick it on the credit card, stick it on the never-never, you can't take it with you, let the grandkids pick up the tab, it's all just zeros on bits of paper anyway.

To budget: verb 4 to get your priorities straight, to make important financial choices, to sacrifice one thing in order to prioritise an…. oops, sorry, scratch that, should read: to prioritise everything under the sun, to have your cake and eat it too, to grab the whole swag, to give 'em the lot with bells on, Easter show bags, Christmas in May, welfare happy hour, economic smorgasbord, eat 'til you drop, help yourself to the lot, enough is never enough etc.

Budgeting: verb 5 checking the data and crunching the numbers, checking the latest financial markets, checking the latest polling data, double-checking the latest polling data, checking the Covid focus groups data, checking the latest border closures data, re-doing the polling numbers, ticking all the boxes, leaving no group without a handout, etc.

To budget: adj. 6 generous, spendthrift, extravagant, politicised, spin, PR exercise, advertising campaign, marketing, Scotty, lipstick on a pig, polishing the turd, gilding the lily, papering over the cracks, etc.

Money: noun 1 numbers written down on spreadsheets by Treasury officials, fantasy figures, blank sheet, lefties, hacks, bureaucrats, substance that grows on trees, cheap as chips, not worth the paper it is printed on, down the gurgler, in the poo, see also: wheelbarrows, Weimar republic, Venezuela.

Money: noun 2 stimulus, handout, keynesianism, social justice, modern monetary theory, marxism, collectivism, corporatism, oligarchism, build back better, climate change, alarmism, great reset, fourth industrial revolution, authoritarianism, totalitarianism, orwellian, socialism, communism, tyranny, slavery, total collapse of society, war, death.

To monetise: verb 3 to turn a negative into a positive, to create a good impression, unbridled optimism, paint a rosy picture, fantasy land, la la land, tell 'em they're dreaming.

Money: adj 4 monopoly, money bags, money tree, on the money, truckloads of money, print money, in the red, in hock up to one's eyeballs, cashless society, broke, penniless, not my problem, money, money, money, it's a rich man's world, abba, money (that's what I want) beatles, money, it's a gas, grab that cash with both hands and make a stash, pink floyd, take the money and run, steve miller band, money for nothing and your chicks for free, dire straits.

Dire straits: see also: precarious position, hopelessness, up sh-t creek without a paddle, stuffed, rooted, cactus, history, done in, finished, all over bar the shouting, Australia's future.

Value: noun 1 value for money, valuable political asset, value your input, valuable commodities upon which our entire future prosperity depends, see also: iron ore, iron ore, and, er, iron ore.

Liberal: adj. 1 values, principles, ideals, philosophy, boring.

Modern Liberal: adj 2 trendy, luvvy, woke, fabian, socialist, climate, alarmist, turnbullite, treacherous, etc.

Thrift: noun 1 out-dated, old-fashioned concept that has no place in the modern Liberal party, see also: thatcherism, reaganism, howardism, conservatism, caution, frugality, prudence, belt-tightening, balancing the books, surplus, back in black, austerity, cut-backs, living within one's means, cutting one's coat according to one's cloth, you can't spend what you don't have, day of reckoning, etc.

Victorian Budget

22 May 2021

Australians were shocked to learn in the Victorian Budget this week that many Victorians have suffered serious deprivations and health ailments over the past 12 months thanks to the pandemic. In this world exclusive, *The Fin*'s in-house self-help author and wellness guru Dr Rowena Balmy-Oils identifies some of the common complaints she has observed pop up during the course of the pandemic and offers some helpful tips on the best ways to remedy them.

Sore back syndrome 1: it is not uncommon for typical hardworking Victorians during a pandemic when they are overburdened by having to attend their four-hundredth press conference in as many days to have a momentary lapse of concentration when going down a set of steps and find themselves incapacitated at the bottom of the stairwell. Dr Rowena's self-help remedy: 'Sufferers are advised to immediately retire to the safety of their bedroom and avoid any bright popping journalists flashlights or intrusive questions until the Budget is well and truly out of the way and the focus group results are in.'

Sore back syndrome 2: over the course of the pandemic an unfortunate group of some 27 weak and enfeebled Victorians have complained that they are suffering from acute feelings of inadequacy and confusion compounded by the irritable sensation of not actually possessing a spine every time they sit down on the Opposition benches. Dr Rowena's physio tips: 'Sufferers are advised to try something novel such as standing up for something they actually believe in or if that fails attempt to hold some genuine conservative principles, otherwise a painful electoral death is inevitable in about 12 months' time.'

Quarantine claustrophobia: many Victorians these days suffer from an acute imaginary fear of being trapped indoors in a dingy Melbourne hotel for a period of up to fourteen days with no physical companionship or anybody to cuddle up to. Dr Rowena's holistic wellness treatment: 'In this day and age it should be possible to find someone who is working in close proximity to you to come and share your personal space or even share intimate moments with, including offering an all-over therapeutic body massage. Known colloquially as 'Victorian private security guards', these helpful individuals are easily identifiable by their willingness to accompany you all the way to your empty double bed in order to assure you strictly observe social distancing rules.'

Fluffy pyjama syndrome: common during pregnancy, this novel self-esteem issue is typically found in the suburbs surrounding Ballarat, where anxious Mums imagine that they are standing at home in their pyjamas making a cup of tea for their hubby in front of their kids when a fully-armed SWAT squad of Victorian brownshirts (surely 'police'?—ed) suddenly kick the door down and arrest and handcuff them for spreading anti-government propaganda on Facebook. Dr Rowena's self-help suggestion: 'Never, ever open the front door to a woke Victorian cop'.

Injection aversion syndrome: many Victorians these days are displaying feelings of nausea and profound distress when confronted by 'Safe Injecting Rooms' wherever they turn, particularly outside school playgrounds and busy shopping centres. Dr Rowan's explains: 'Safe Injecting Rooms are well recognised as an extremely safe and efficient way for a Labor government to shore up support from fanatical Greens and other hardcore radical left-wing activists.'

Euthanasia paranoia: These days it is not unusual that elderly and retired individuals, particularly if they happen to be loaded or live by themselves in a beautiful large Toorak mansion, express concerns that their immediate family have been encouraging them to pop in for a visit to one of Victoria's exciting new 'assisted departure' clinics. Dr Rowena suggests: 'The moment they drop any fancy-looking brochures with butteries and pretty flowers on the cover in your lap, sell up super quick and move to New South Wales.'

That's-A-Bit-Rich List

29 May 2021

As the world of envy and jealousy is yet again rocked to its core by the publication of the AFR's annual Rich List, *The Fin*'s lists editor Ms Rowena Clique-Bates is proud to publish the top entries in our equally important 2021 That's-A-Bit-Rich List. In order to qualify, entrants must demonstrate a proven ability to inspire a filthy look accompanied by the muttered phrase 'that's a bit rich':

Dan Andrews: having ignored federal offers of help to manage Victoria's hotel quarantine security back at the beginning of the pandemic, Mr Andrews is a clear favourite in the That's-A-Bit-Rich stakes for his brilliant and insightful decision to ignore proven skilled army and police officers and employ instead randy private security nightclub bouncers from firms hand-picked exclusively for their Indigenous, diversity and union-affiliated credentials.

Joe Biden: a multiple performer in this year's That's-A-Bit-Rich List, Joe rose from being a bumbling no-hoper hiding in his basement who couldn't organise a rally larger than a Delaware chook raffle to becoming the most powerful man in the world. Among Joe's many That's-A-Bit-Rich credentials are: accusing Donald Trump of spreading wild conspiracy theories about the Coronavirus originating in a Wuhan biotech lab several months before launching an investigation into whether the Coronavirus originated in a Wuhan lab; accusing Donald Trump of being racist in closing the US borders to China several months before closing the borders to India; and accusing Donald Trump of locking up a handful of children in cages on the Mexican border several months before locking up a massive influx of children in cages on the Mexican border.

Anthony Blinken: a new entrant into this year's That's-A-Bit-Rich List, Mr Blinken distinguished himself over the last few days by lecturing Israel on the need to stop retaliating against Iranian-supplied Hamas rockets and missiles at the same time as his boss is busy helping the Iranians re-arm Hamas with rockets and missiles.

AMP: it's rare for an organisation to secure a coveted spot on the That's-A-Bit-Rich List, but wealth giant AMP rocketed up the charts for its genius policy of deducting insurance premiums from the superannuation accounts of more than 2,000 customers despite having been notified of their deaths.

Scott Morrison: streaking up the That's-A-Bit-Rich charts, Scott Morrison earned himself high marks for his superb denunciation and sacking of Christine Holgate for wasting $12,000 dollars of Australian taxpayers money on a couple of Cartier watches at the same time as he and his mate Josh were working out how to waste over a trillion dollars of taxpayers money on far more expensive baubles (without even any decent watches to show for it.)

Mark Butler: federal Labor factional warlord and firebrand MP who blames the federal Liberal party for the Victorian Labor party's disastrous handling of the Coronavirus resulting in over 800 deaths.

Anthony Albanese: following the devastating result for Labor in the Hunter Valley by-election because the party is viewed quite correctly by their former blue-collar base as implacably opposed to coal and jobs, Mr Albanese, who is implacably opposed to coal and jobs, claimed that 'there is a message for federal Labor' in the devastating result.

Paul Barry: a favourite for many years as a struggling That's-A-Bit-Rich

Lister, Barry—whose primary qualification rests on the fact that he earns around a quarter of a million dollars a year for fronting a quarter-of-an-hour of tediously derivative TV each week—this year raced up the charts with his astonishing backflip with double pike this week on the causes of Covid. Last year Barry famously lambasted Sky News for their 'wild conspiracy theory' in suggesting the virus may have come from a Wuhan biotech lab when he now admits that the virus may have come from, er, a Wuhan biotech lab.

The entire population of Victoria: A last impressive entry into the That's-A-Bit-Rich List from the entire population of Victoria who upon learning that the government they elected is yet again putting them all into lockdown to prevent outbreaks of the Coronavirus immediately decided en masse to up stakes and escape to Covid-free New South Wales, bringing with them, no doubt, the Coronavirus.

*China's fifth column of, er, columnists are instructed to make China
appear more loveable.*

Uncle Cuddles

5 June 2021

The world of biting satire was rocked to its core this week following the
revelation that Chinese communist party dictator-for-life Xi Jinping
has asked his propaganda arms working within the Western media to
make China appear more 'loveable' to the rest of the world in their daily
columns. Due to an unfortunate accident involving his brain being fried
by a short-range microwave weapon of unknown origin, our regular
columnist Rowan Dean has been replaced at short notice by his eager
young intern Ms Luweena Lu-ling who has filed today's column in his Lu,
er, lieu:

'Thoughts, Observations and Meditations Upon the Role of Loveable
Chinese Leadership in an Era of Western Hegemonism.'

It was a beautiful, glorious sunrise that greeted me as I stepped off the
train from Beijing and placed my fragrant foot for the first time onto the
bounteous, lush soil of Xinjiang Autonomous Province. All around me
the birds were singing a melodious tune and rays of sunlight glistened
off the sparkling dew as I made my way past the excited and perfectly
formed rows of happy smiling Uighurs who had shaved their heads in
the customary fashion and come to greet me with petal blossoms and
quaint folk dancing performances which involved lying face-down on the
platform with their hands behind their necks as a simple but heartfelt way

to show their gratitude for the loveable kindness bestowed upon them by Emperor Xi. Later on, I popped into a local produce store where I picked up a home-made pair of Nikes and a freshly-made iPhone for next to nothing!

To many, of course, Great Leader Xi is a fearsome figure, a towering presence of strength and resolve, a proud Father and Hero of the Nation, a visionary who understands the needs of his people and who sacrifices himself daily to the task of creating a Paradise for All on this temporal Earth in line with his Celestial Mandate from Heaven and, of course, in keeping with the key principles outlined in his must-read best-seller 'The Thoughts of Xi Jinping' which had given me such solace on the long but serenely calm train journey across the cloud-dappled mountains of Fujian. But to me Chairman Xi will always be known simply by the nickname he bestowed upon himself when I first met him when I was just a bright young Beijing schoolgirl keen to come Dux of my school—Uncle Cuddles.

Could there be a kinder or more inspirational man in all of China than Uncle Cuddles? I remember back in Year 2 when I was struggling to comprehend some of the more complicated protein molecular formulae of cymothoa exigua in 'Series 4 of Advanced Oceanography and Plankton Ecology, Volume 17', Uncle Cuddles arranged for the whole class to take a day trip to one of his Peaceful Marine Parks in our loveable Spratly Islands! On a clear, sunny morning we landed on a smart, shiny new runway which he had lovingly constructed right on top of a delightful coral reef and in no time we were splashing around in the pristine waters collecting colourful seashells and preserving the biodiversity of the reef through our careful and sustainable use of lovingly-developed Chinese solar panels and wind farms.

Later on, as we were flying home, Uncle Cuddles gave us an impromptu geology lesson about how the continents were formed and how the earth's plates are constantly shifting and to demonstrate this he pointed to a large teeming island in the sea directly below us which, he explained, would very soon be part of mainland China again.

History, too, was a subject that I excelled in thanks again to the loving guidance that Uncle Cuddles bestowed upon our school. Has there ever been a man more concerned about easing the sufferings of his fellow countrymen and women by righting the wrongs of our unjust colonial past? Eager to reward us with a quick shopping trip last year, Uncle Cuddles took us to a large harbourside town with glittering tall buildings that had been liberated only very recently by him from the tyranny of the deceitful and treacherous Treaty of 1997, a vile document imposed upon the sovereign Chinese nation by the racist capitalist slave owner Margaret Thatcher who had kidnapped the people of Hong Kong and forced them to live in bondage and servitude for 99 years. But no longer! As the crowds danced and cavorted in feverish excitement and highly explosive festive fireworks lit the night sky, young people screamed with delight at the entertaining sound of popping gunfire and coughed themselves silly gasping for air as the celebratory plumes of tear gas wafted across the evening's fun-filled festivities.

Even Uncle Cuddles had tears in his eyes.

World leaders, including Scott Morrison, get together for the G7 in Cornwall.

Seven go bonkers in Cornwall

12 June 2021

The world of spiffing adventures and lashings of globalist elitism was rocked this week by the discovery of the lost manuscript of Enid Blyton's unfinished masterpiece 'Seven Go Bonkers in Cornwall'. The book is the final instalment in the long-running children's series that follows the adventures of the 'Gee! Seven Secret Society' who get together during holidays to save the world from rotters and bounders:

Scotty jumped out of bed. What an exciting day! It had been a long journey all the way from Singapore and he still felt squiffy from the chilli crab he'd been forced to eat at the silly old grown-ups function. But today was a very special day because he had been asked if he would like to join the Gee! Seven Secret Society. At last! Scotty had immediately said yes, because that's the sort of chap he was. What japes they would have! But it still puzzled him. Surely if he joined, wouldn't they have to re-name it the Gee! Eight Society? But there was no time to ponder such imponderables, because already Scotty could hear the excited activity coming from the room next door where Boris and Carrie were having a pillow fight. BOING! BOING! went the bedsprings. Scotty could picture them jumping up and down on the mattress! What larks! But then… SMASH! Scotty froze, his instincts immediately alert to danger. Had someone dropped a plate? Scotty, with his forensic skills, deduced it must be a piece of Cornishware… they were in Cornwall, after all. Someone was in for a real spanking, that's for sure, Scotty surmised.

But before he had time to further consider the source of the mysterious noise, his instincts alerted him to an eerie wailing sound coming from the garden. 'Ommmm!'

Scotty pulled back the chintz curtain and saw the lonely little Canadian boy, Justin, sitting cross-legged on the lawn dressed like an Indian. 'What are you doing?' called out Scotty. 'I'm getting in touch with my vibrations and my chakra,' replied Justin, 'because my pal Greta says that our house is on fire and we only have a few months left to save mankind, er, I mean womankind, from perishing in the burning flames!'

Scotty didn't make any comment because he knew Justin was imagining things and that if the house was really on fire somebody would have called the fire brigade by now. On top of which Scotty knew that Justin had grown up in a very troubling household where his father was actually a secret communist dictator in Cuba and his mother liked to sleep in a bed full of rolling stones.

There was a nervous tapping on the door. Scotty pulled it open and was excited to see Angela and Emmanuel with the shy Oriental boy Yoshi he'd met on the train. 'We have to save the planet! There's no time to lose!' said Angela staring angrily and somewhat rudely at Scotty—as if it was all his fault! Emmanuel nodded in agreement. 'Eet ees ze end of ze world!' he hissed.

'I know!' said Scotty. 'And I think I know who is to blame!'

The others all looked startled. 'Who?' said Mario the Italian boy, who had mysteriously appeared from the kitchen.

'It's the Emperor of China!' said Scotty, excitedly. 'He wants to rule the world all by himself! He won't even buy our lobsters anymore! And won't even touch our barley…'

Yoshi nodded excitedly. 'It's true. Let's all gang up together! Or else it's the end of the planet!'

'But it's already too late!' called out Justin from the garden. 'Greta says the globe is burning! Even though it's snowing like billy-oh!'

'Stop whining!' interrupted Angela rudely. 'We have to find Joe. Is he still hiding in the basement?'

But just then the door flew open and Boris came stomping out, still in his pyjamas and rubbing the large red bump poking out of his scruffy hair. 'Would you believe it, chaps,' he said, 'she hit me over the head… with THIS!'

'What is it? asked the others. 'A saucepan?'

'Cornishware!' yelled Scotty triumphantly, secretly pleased at his logical reasoning, the hallmark of any good detective.

'No, no, no. Nothing like that, chaps,' said Boris. 'She walloped me over the head with this Net Zero Green Emissions scheme of hers! We're going to build back better and save the whole world!'

'How?' said the others excitedly.

'Easy!' said Boris. 'We turn off all the lights, turn off all the heaters, shut down all the factories, stop driving cars and aeroplanes, only eat tofu and insects and live in the dark! It's the only way to save the spiffing planet, chaps!'

There was a hush, as the Gee! Seven all shuffled nervously. Finally Scotty spoke up. 'Let's do it' he said, excitedly. 'Sounds like a jolly good plan!'

As the shortlist for a major book prize is announced, Barnaby Joyce makes a comeback, the Queensland chief health officer has a change of heart and a new strain of the virus appears.

Book Prize

19 June 2021

With the highly-anticipated shortlist for Australia's most prestigious literary prize having recently been announced in the NSW State Library, *The Fin*'s books editor Ms Rowena Franklin-Myles wades through the contenders to see who will take the crown of contemporary Australian fiction.

The Mask that Slipped: a lonely country doctor working among the cane fields of rural Queensland discovers she has a knack for closing down schools for weeks on end, driving local businesses into the ground and decimating the booming tourism industry simply by donning her 'magic mask' and whispering 'lockdown' into the ear of the nearest Premier. But all hell breaks loose when a mysterious vaccine that causes teenage boys to drop dead of blood clots in the streets threatens to become widely available and she discovers she is in fact a committed anti-vaxxer who escaped over the border from a hippy commune in Nimbin. Spoiler alert: in the end, her conscience gets the better of her and she decides to pack it all in and become a humble Governor instead.

The Bonker's Revenge: set among the beetroot fields of northern New South Wales, a struggling accountant discovers he has a gift for the gab and a knack for retail politics that drives the lefties insane and he quickly becomes the nation's most despised Deputy Prime Minister. But all hell breaks loose when he falls in love with a female journalist and she gets pregnant and they decide to keep the child and get married and live together as a normal couple. Incensed and outraged, the local media stalk the pregnant woman up and down her street until the Prime Minister agrees to sack Barnaby and impose a permanent Bonking Ban. Spoiler alert: in an entirely predictable twist, Barnaby triumphs and Turnbull looks like a goose (again).

Straining Delta: when popular Aussie girl-next-door singer-songwriter Delta wakes up one morning, she discovers she is all over the newspapers for all the wrong reasons with headlines screaming: 'Deadly Delta!', 'Delta Strain Decimates!' and 'Death at the Hands of Delta!' Has she committed some heinous crime? The nightmare only worsens when she realises she is being accused of being a highly infectious new strain of the Coronavirus and is directly responsible for the death of millions of people across the planet! How will she cope? Will it affect her record sales? What will her fans think? Will she ever write a hit song again? Spoiler alert: in the end, the even deadlier new Kylie strain of Covid appears and Delta returns to being a humble judge on a reality TV music show.

Albino Emu: set in a remote Indigenous community in the outback, a young albino man grows a bushy beard and discovers people think he is aboriginal. One day he follows a magical emu and stumbles upon a long-lost aboriginal civilisation with viaducts, skyscrapers, the internet, airports, restaurants, cafes and a gullible taxpayer-funded national broadcaster who swallow his whole yarn. However, things start to unravel when two highly-qualified archaeologists start looking into his claims…

The Man with No Convictions: set in the sterile corridors of Manuka and Barton in downtown Canberra, this political thriller sees a former marketing man with no genuine political convictions rise to the very top simply by being a master manipulator of the art of factional dealings and telling the public what they want to hear. Pure fiction, of course.

Many a Slip: a man goes to a weekend beach party on the Mornington Peninsula and falls down the stairs. Soon all hell breaks loose and the rumours are flying thick and fast! Was he blind drunk? Was he pushed? Was he stabbed in the back by his Deputy? Did the Chinese do it because of the cancelled Belt and Road? Did he get beaten up with a baseball bat because he tried to crack onto his host's teenage daughter? In this exciting contemporary novel, the reader gets to write the ending themselves to avoid the author being sued.

Chow Mein Kampf: set on an endangered great barrier reef in Far North Queensland, a lonely Chinese dictator from a remote palace in Beijing discovers he has a knack for conquering the world but first has to conquer his own fears of inadequacy by building a wall of steel and invading Hong Kong and Taiwan. But all hell breaks loose when he accidentally spills a vial of High Grade Plutonium-Enhanced Bio-Weapon-Grade Gain-of-Function Ebola-Flavoured Coronavirus into a bowl of Bat Soup Chow Mein in a Wuhan wet market and then successfully exports it all around the world during feverish Chinese New Year festivities. Spoiler alert: In the end he invades Poland, murders six million Uighers and launches World War III.

The NSW department of education comes under cyber attack.

Bo and Zhang

10 July 2021

In shock news this week it was reported that a widespread cyber attack on the NSW Department of Education networks had forced it to shut down a number of its internal systems. Meanwhile, in a remote and nondescript building in the outer suburbs of Beijing, a group of highly sophisticated cyber-espionage operators held their daily morning briefing.

Zhang: Great news, comrades! After months and months of tireless work involving the noble efforts of hundreds of dedicated Party members both here and in the Great Southern Vassal Province of Sydney, Operation Glorious Infiltration of a Thousand Schools has had its first great success! As Comrade Xi has himself said many times, to know your enemy's education system is to know your enemy's thinking and to know your enemy's thinking is to know your enemy's weakness! Having infiltrated the highest and most important learning centres of knowledge within the largest education system of The Great Southern Island of Natural Wealth and Resources will give us unparalleled access to the very essence and roots of their most critical strategic defensive conceptualising! Please enlighten us, dear comrade Bo, as to the educational highlights of your successful infiltration?

Bo: Er…

Zhang: Please, please… don't be shy…

Bo: Well, ah, we've just finished, um, downloading it all, sir, so, ah… it's early days, Comrade Zhang…

Zhang: Come come, no need to be modest. I'd hate to think you were holding anything back...

Bo: No, no, of course not, sir, it's just that, ah, there's a lot of complicated material that we need to, um, analyse from a, er, an analytical perspective... um, a bit more analytically, sir, we're not quite sure exactly, what, um, perhaps...

Zhang: Snap to it! It can't take that long! You must have learned something already, just from the chapter headings, for example. History? What are they teaching in History? The causes of World War Two? The Opium Wars? The Glorious Revolution? The rise and fall of the Roman Empire? Democracy and Ancient Greece? The silk road and the trading routes and the...

Bo: Er, um, no, no, nothing about any of that, um, but there's quite a bit here... a lot actually... about how the Aborigines invented, um, agriculture, and, er, had massive great big villages, apparently...

Zhang: Maths, then!! What level of mathematics have they achieved?

Bo: Er, ah, yes, that's a bit of a tricky one, too... we couldn't actually find any maths as such, not what we would call maths at any rate, although there is a pie chart...

Zhang: The children are studying Pi? At what age...

Bo: No, not Pi, that doesn't get a mention anywhere, this is a, er, a pie chart...

Zhang: A chart? What of? Military capacity? Industrialisation and manufacturing? Grain harvesting and storage capacity? Population movements and dispersal of natural resources?

Bo: Er, um, no, no, nothing like that, it's, er, we had to double check the translation, sir, apparently it shows, um, the fifty-four different genders...

Zhang: The 54 what???

Bo: Um, apparently apart from boys and girls there are, um, fifty-two other, you know, er, fiddly bits, sir...

Zhang: English, then!!! What are they studying in classical literature?? Shakespeare? Tennyson? Dickens? Salinger? Or more imperialist works? Hemingway? Vonnegut? Kipling?

Bo: Um, er, no… ah, we haven't spotted anything like that, sir, although this week's Year 12 Recommended Reading is, er, a 'creative novelette' entitled 'Me and My Two Dads Go To The Mardi Gras' by someone called, ah, Rainbow Frillyshorts.

Zang: Chemistry, then!!! What are they studying in chemistry??? Biological weapons? Immunology? Viral enhancements and gene therapy??

Bo: Oh yes! just a second, glad you mentioned chemistry, sir, I saw it in here somewhere, ah, yes, here it is… it's a School Project, for, um, seniors, sir, two choices '… Build Your own Meth Amphetamine Lab' or 'Design Your Own Safe Injecting Room'.

Zhang: Geology, then? The movement of the tectonic plates? The defensive capabilities of mountain ranges and oceans? Mining rare earth minerals???

Bo: Not quite, but I did see something about 'mining', hang on, oh yes, here it is: 'How to Stop Adani Mining'. It's a day trip to Queensland where they practice, um, painting placards and, er, vandalising shop fronts…

Zhang: Geography??

Bo: No, ah, no, sir, not as such… although there is a lengthy study guide here on 'Stolen Land and Why We must Give it all Back'.

Zhang: Give it back? Who to? Economics, then? What are they studying in their Economics courses? How to manipulate market forces? Monopolising supply chains? Controlling critical infrastructure?

Bo: Er, um, no, this one did take me by surprise, sir. There's only one text that they teach in Economics, sir. It's called, um, 'Das Kapital' by, er, Karl Marx.

Zhang: Karl Marx?? Nobody reads that crap anymore.

Chinese cyber warfare ships appear on the horizon.

Bo and Zhang 2

17 July 2021

Following the news last week that the NSW Department of Education came under an intense cyber attack, it was reported this week in even more shocking news that China's top surveillance vessel, the Tainwangxing, is prowling off our coast spying on Australian-US military war games.

Meanwhile, in a nondescript building in the outer suburbs of Beijing, China's top cyber-espionage decoders once again held their daily morning briefing.

Zhang: Great news, comrades! After weeks of tireless work involving the noble efforts of our finest seamen in the pristine waters off the Great Southern Vassal Province of the Thriving Barrier Reef, Operation Glorious Code Breaking of a Thousand Enemy Vessels has been an outstanding success! As Comrade Xi himself said, to listen in to your enemies most cunning plans and whispered strategies is the swiftest path to defeating them! Please enlighten us, dear Comrade Bo, as to what codes you have cracked to unlock the secrets of the military might and defensive capabilities of the Foreign White Devil Barbarians?

Bo: Er…

Zhang: Come, come. Don't be shy…

Bo: Sure, ah, well, of course, lots of different codes to, er, decode, and…

Zhang: Snap to it! No secrets around here, ha ha!…

Bo: Er, of course not. Well, um, yes, there is… that is to say, it appears that the Australian Defence Force has developed some, er, terrifying new weapons, sir, it's just that we haven't quite cracked…

Zhang: Such as? A cold fusion hydrogen-based quantum fissile kinetic depth charger? An interceptive point-to-point reactive proton missile? A satellite-based oceanic submersible early-warning system? You have to be more precise!

Bo: Of course!… ah, we just need to crack that first all-important code, sir, you know… like in the Enigma Code movie, haha!

Zhang: This is no laughing matter, comrade.

Bo: Ahem, no, of course not. Our code-breakers are working around the clock, sir. We're downloading every meeting, every conversation, every email, every power point presentation! Interestingly, they all begin with an identical set of codewords…

Zhang: Excellent!

Bo: …which unfortunately we have yet to decipher…

Zhang: Why not?!?

Bo: Well, um, every morning the entire crew get together and, um, burn some gum leaves, sir…

Zhang: Burn some gum leaves??

Bo: Yes, we think it is an extraordinary new advanced technological strategy to carbonise the atmosphere in order to disrupt our microwave thermal imaging interceptors, sir. They are clearly using a chemical compound derived from eucalyptus oil at high temperatures, sir, to evade our advanced surveillance mechanisms. Our top mass spectrometer team are currently breaking down the molecular structure of burnt gum leaves to see…

Zhang: Yes, yes! What else?

Bo: Well, then they speak in code, sir, about 'acknowledging custodians of the land they're on…'

Zhang: But they're on the water!

Bo: Precisely! That's how we know it's a subterfuge. Then they deliberately jumble up their words, like 'the Buluguyban...'

Zhang: 'The Buluguyban' What's that? A hidden underground missile network?

Bo: Possibly, sir. But it changes up and down the coast. Yuwibara... Dharumbal... it's a mystery.

Zhang: Not for long, I trust, Comrade Bo. I'd hate to see you transferred to our Uighur Re-enlightenment program in Xinjiang... what have you learned about the enemy's operational capabilities?

Bo: Ah, yes, I was just getting to that bit, sir... clearly their main defensive strategy, in fact, their only defensive strategy, is codenamed Operation Diversity and Inclusion. It's all the top brass ever talks about...

Zhang: Surely you mean Operation Diversify and Intrusion? That's basic Sun Tzu... diversify your troops in order to make your intrusion more...

Bo: Um, yes that would make sense, sir, but we've double-checked and it's definitely 'Diversity' and 'Inclusion'. It appears to be, um, some highly advanced, uniquely colour-coded strategic operation designed to, er, 'combat and ultimately defeat all vestiges of white oppression'.

Zhang: Combat what?

Bo: White oppression, sir. Our experts suspect it uses white noise in order to suppress electronic communications in order to oppress any violent dissent... As I said, the entire Operation is built around this complex code of colours and a rainbow motif prominently displayed throughout all enemy vessels, frequently accompanied by a set of random letters that are clearly the key to the code. We've noticed the repetition of L, G, B, T and, er... Q.

Zhang: A rainbow code?

Bo: Yes, sir. We currently have our mass spectrometer team working on the unique electronic properties of the colour white in order to determine how this form of radioactive oppression can be harnessed to our own advantage…

Zhang: Any hint of bio-weapons?

Bo: Um, just one reference, sir. It's a deadly new toxin they're working on.

Zhang: Codename?

Bo: Toxic Masculinity, sir. Apparently the Australian Navy has plans to completely obliterate it!

A university professor is convicted of writing abusive letters to herself.

Self-abuse

24 July 2021

With the news that a UTS professor has been found guilty of posting threatening and abusive hate letters to, er, herself, *The Fin*'s in-house psychologist Professor Rowena Freudian-Slipps wonders if the art of writing yourself letters full of self-loathing and self-criticism might in fact be healthier than we think.

Dear Smugface, you miserable, pathetic, snivelling, grovelling, Mummy's-little-boy! I saw you today at that so-called joke of a press conference and you made me want to spew with that cringeworthy snotty little apology of yours! Snotty Scotty!! That's what they used to call you back at kindy, didn't they!! Thought we'd forgotten, did you!?! I never forget!! Call yourself a marketing guru?!? The only thing you've ever sold is your soul, mate!! And don't forget, pal, I even know where you live (it's called the Lodge!) Yours in disgust, ScoMo.

Dear Little Miss Spinster, there you go again! No wonder you can't even keep a steady boyfriend! Now the whole of NSW has fallen out of love with you too! What is wrong with you?!? There you were riding high in the polls and everyone in the entire frigging country saying how much they loved you coz you were the gold standard and the best in the land and the only one with any common sense and so much better than those dolts in Victoria and WA and Queensland! And what do you go and do!?!

You blow it!! The whole thing! Now even the tradies can't stand you! And will you take that stupid black mask off it makes you look like the Grim Reaper! Miserably yours, Gladdie.

Dear Moron, listen to yourself, will ya? You got dementia or what? You can't even string a goddam… er, what's it called when a bunch of words and stuff are placed one after the other and there's a verb in there somewhere?… oh yeah, a sentence, that's it… you can't even string a goddam sentence to… I mean come on, man… where was I? oh yeah, what I was saying was when I was a kid the little black kids used to hop into the pool and rub my legs and… er… and, er, anyway this is the biggest environmental welfare homeless jobs package in the world and the point is if you listen to the President, I mean Donald Trump, I mean… where's that black Indian woman, what's her name again? Yours, Joe.

Dear Dopey, are you kidding me? You fell down a set of stairs? As if! Come on, why not face up to what you really did and be a man for once! Dan the Man, remember?!? That's supposed to be you!!! So admit it— you had a few sherbets too many coz you were hobnobbing with all the squillionaires and they were telling you how great you were and how you should be in the Lodge or running the UN or something and you let it go to your head and you thought well this single malt Scotch stuff is pretty damn good and next thing you know you got a bit fresh with some of the sheilas but hey you were only kidding around I mean what's the point of going to a frigging piss-up if you can't let your hair down? What are we all now, a bunch of Catholic monks or something? Jesus! Damn my ribs hurt. Yours in agony, Daniel.

Dear Moneybags, there you go again! Can't help yourself, can you?!? Spend, spend, spend!!! What is it this time? A billion here? A billion there? All for what?!? Splurge, splurge, splurge!! I mean, it's only money after all! And it's not as if it actually belongs to anybody! Not really. Let's be honest, it's just a bunch of zeroes and commas on bits of paper! It's not like it's actual real cash or anything like that… is it?!? Surely we can just print some more? Josh.

Dear Haystack-Head, you look like an upside-down mop with that stupid hair-do of yours!! Worzel Gummidge had more style and panache than you ever will! Why do you always look like you just got out of bed having shagged Carrie senseless for the past twelve hours?!? Don't you even own an ironing board? Can't somebody buy you a decent Saville Row suit?? Why can't you be well-groomed like a proper resident of Number Ten?? Like Winston? Or Hugh Grant?? Then you could really pull a few tasty young birds!! Now that would be more like it!!! Then you could get rid of that mad Greenie chick!! Yours in disgust, BoJo.

Dear Kevin, you absolute legend you! Words fail me when it comes to praising not only your superior intellect but… (not sure this one qualifies—ed.)

After a large anti-lockdown rally in Sydney, the police clamp down.
And Australians start spying on each other.

DobSpotters

31 July 2021

With fears that this weekend may see more anti-lockdown rallies in our major cities, NSW Police Commissioner Mick Fuller has urged the public to do their civic duty and dob in anyone they know who may have attended these events so that the police can hunt them down. But how does a dobber know exactly who to dob in without going to the rally itself? In this handy cut-out-and-keep Dobber's Dobspotting Guide, *The Fin*'s East German correspondent Fraulein Rowena Snitch-Snoops offers up her tips for spotting those tell-tale signs that help identify any anti-lockdowners in your midst.

The suspicious flatmate: have you noticed how your flatmate has been unusually self-absorbed during this lockdown? Why does he or she spend so long in the bathroom? How come they never laugh at your jokes about Craig Kelly anymore? Why do they never take their headphones off whenever you want to have a chat?!? And why do they walk out of the room every time you switch on the ABC??? These are sure-fire signs that your flatmate does not appreciate the benefits and virtues of lockdown... better nip it in the bud and call DobSpotters!

The creepy next-door-neighbour: let's face it, for far too long you and your partner have had to put up with that weird old grumbling guy next door mowing his lawn at unholy hours on a Sunday morning (like before noon!), not to mention the way he sits on his patio listening to homophobic talkback radio. Then there was the time he tore down your tinsel fence decorations just before Mardi Gras! What a disgrace! But it gets worse! Remember the night you peered through his curtains and caught him watching Alan Jones! Time to call DobSpotters!

The right-wing sibling: OK, so you haven't seen your Trump-loving half-brother since that big family climate change stoush back in 2016, but that's no reason not to be suspicious of him. Come to think of it, remember when you were kids and you went snorkelling up on the Gold Coast and guess who threw a tantrum and refused to wear a mask?!? What sort of a sicko refuses to wear a mask when we all know that masks save lives! Just coz he's vaguely related to you doesn't mean you shouldn't call DobSpotters!

The unappreciative boss: Cast your mind back to that last Zoom meeting where your brilliant idea for a new Lockdown Home Exercise Wellness Workout Self-Harmony App was turned down flat by your miserable boss. Wasn't it a bit suspicious how he taunted you about your lack of imagination? And—think carefully now!—didn't he mention that he was 'otherwise occupied' this coming weekend? Time to call DobSpotters!

The ambitious work colleague: One of the beauties of lockdown is that it gives you time to reflect at leisure upon some of the more egregious insults you had to put up with back in the miserable days when you shared a cubicle with one particularly unsavoury and overly-ambitious individual. The guy who was always sucking up to the boss! Greasy black beard and dandruff on his beanie! But… hang on! Wasn't that him just there on the telly?!? Behind that placard! Certainly looked like him! Better call DobSpotters!

The stuck-up shelf stacker in the supermarket: Fortunately you were well-prepared for this lengthy lockdown when you headed into Aldi six weeks ago and stacked up on dunny paper and Spag Bol! Such foresight and clever planning. But what about that stuck-up cow stacking the shelves in aisle six who snootily told you it was rude to horde? Well, look who's laughing now! She would definitely be the sort of selfish individual who would go to an anti-lockdown rally! Probably an anti-vaxxer to boot! What was her name again? Aileen. That's right! Aileen at Aldi. Shouldn't be too hard for the cops to hunt her down! Quick, call DobSpotters!

The psychopath in the park: Remember that time you were harmlessly walking Scruffles in the park and that crazy man who lives near the swings suddenly rushed out and started berating you for not having picked up pooch's poo-poos? As if! You were merely practising healthy social-distancing and it was hardly your fault the mutt crapped in the kiddies playground! Worse, this deranged psychopath threatened to call the council and said he 'knows where you live'! Well, two can play at that game!! Better call DobSpotters.

The overpriced butcher: Remember that Nazi who laughed at you when you asked if he sold any vegan kale sausages?? Well, turns out he was shut on Saturday morning at the exact same time as the rally! If that ain't suspicious, what is? Better call DobSpotters!

Jobs for the girls

21 August 2021

As New Zealand Prime Minister Jacinda Ardern urges the Taliban to be nice to women, spokesperson for the Taliban Zabihullah Mujahid proves that he 'gets it' by promising that women in Afghanistan will be well looked after providing they 'stay within the framework' of traditional Islamic teachings and values, saying 'Women are a key part of our society and they are going to be working with us shoulder to shoulder'. Excited by the prospect of a new, tolerant and modernised Taliban, the Fin's 'Middle East diversity and inclusion' correspondent Ms Rowheena Sharria-Lore uncovers the exciting new job prospects that await eager young modern Afghani women keen to work shoulder-to-shoulder with their Taliban menfolk under the benevolent and woke leadership of Mullah Baradar.

Burqa embroiderer: For far too long the customary Afghani burqa has been seen as a symbol of male oppression of Afghani women and girls. No longer! From now on modern Afghani women will be invited to participate in the design, manufacturing and embroidering of new improved and modernised Afghani burqas including a new diverse range of inclusive colour choices such as Helmand Lilac (blue), Kandahar Aqua (blue) or Pashtun Purple (blue), as well as being involved in applying their individual skills to ensuring a wide choice of intricate weave of our latest eco-friendly facial covering mesh fabric (fine, very fine, very, very fine or totally impenetrable).

Burqa fitter: Eager to move away from the traditional 'one-size-fits-all' approach adopted by previous misogynistic Afghani regimes, the more enlightened Taliban of Mullah Baradar has established inclusive new burqa-fitting boutiques to replace the now abandoned and burned-out decadent fashion houses that used to adorn the Kabul CBD. Sensitive and well-educated modern Afghani women can now be safely fitted in a custom-made Taliban-approved Burqa Fitting Room by young, well-educated female burqa-fitters who will ensure that the burqa complies with traditional values, such as ensuring that not one single square inch of naked female flesh is visible to any male eyes. (Disclaimer: The Taliban refuses to accept responsibility for any libidinous Afghani males who may be carnally provoked by catching a glimpse of female flesh due to poorly-fitted burqas.)

Limb selector: In what was once an exclusively male domain, the modern Taliban now invites eager young women to apply for the highly coveted job of Limb Selector. Keeping within the framework of traditional Taliban values, any convicted felon may choose as a suitable punishment whether to have his (or her! we are inclusive after all!) foot or hand surgically removed. But how to decide which limb you can best do without? What's the better punishment for the modern Afghani pilferer: to stop them playing soccer or playing guitar? Our modern highly-trained selectors will carefully guide you through this potentially momentous and life-changing decision!

Taliban stonemason: In the primitive and, er, stone-age days of the old-fashioned Taliban, the ritual stonings of wanton adulteresses and treacherous fornicators were crude and ugly affairs involving coarse and cumbersome chunks of rock being hurled indiscriminately at those women who brought shame upon their male relatives by stepping outside the framework of traditional Taliban teachings. No more! Today's modern Afghani woman can choose from a range of environmentally-friendly eco-

stones, including Jalalabad river pebbles, smooth Oasis sandstone, Hindu Kush granite or glittering Nimruz limestone to enhance the occasion. Why not select your own custom-made mixture for a truly diverse stoning to remember?

Interior decorator: In keeping with traditional Taliban values, modern Afghani women will be required to spend a great deal of time indoors. What better opportunity to hone your feminine interior designer skills? You'll be amazed what a difference having a good eye (well, at least one) can make to your everyday home environment. Learn how to creatively re-arrange those AK-47s in the corner of the bedroom, and why not hide those bloodstains on the kitchen wall with a carefully chosen Laura Ashley print?

Cane grower: With an increase in the frequency and intensity of lashings and canings these days, why not put your entrepreneurial skills to good use and grow your own canes? For judicial canings, we recommend a sturdy variety of thick rattan, whereas of course a lighter bamboo such as China Dwarf or Timor Black usually fetch a good price and are ideal for more mild taboos and offences.

Rooftop rentals: While most modern and progressive Kabul households have obviously been fitted out with subsidised solar panels to help reduce emissions and meet international requirements to get to net zero and save the planet from catastrophic climate change, there's no reason why you can't also make a quick buck by leasing out your rooftop terrace for the occasional gay tossing exercise—the higher your apartment the better the price you can charge!—working shoulder to shoulder with the menfolk strictly within the framework of traditional Taliban teachings.

Rolling Stones drummer Charlie Watts passes away. Sydney is in lockdown. Vaccine passports are all the rage. And I predict the end of Gladys Berejiklian's time as Premier.

Charlie Watts

28 August 2021

With the sad death of Rolling Stones drummer Charlie Watts, *The Fin*'s Swinging Sixties correspondent Ms Rowena Ruby-Tuesday discovers that the band's songs still resonate to this day:

(I Can't Get No) Vaccination: With its hard-hitting riff written by Keith Richards after spending three weeks lying in his bed staring at the ceiling during lockdown, and with the snarling vocals of a bored and petulant Mick Jagger, this classic rocker tells the story of a young man desperate to get vaccinated so he can enjoy all the hedonistic joys that western Sydney has to offer. The subversive lyrics perfectly capture the angst of socially alienated young Middle Eastern men keen to evade Covid restrictions at the same time as avoiding getting jabbed: 'When I'm drivin' in my car, Outside the 5k zone, Cop stops and asks to see, my Covid information, supposed to have my inoculation, But I can't get no… I can't get no… I can't get no vaccination! I try and I try and I try and I try! Can't get no… no no no!'

19th Nervous Lockdown: Classic Stones single that mocks the older generation of chief medical officers for their single-minded and out-dated reliance on restrictions and lockdowns as the only solution to society's Covid problems. The song is also famous for Bill Wyman's so-called 'dive-bombing' bass line towards the end, inspired by the dive-bombing ratings of Gladys Berejiklian towards the end of her time in government: 'You were stuck at home and all alone because they closed the schools, And after that you turned your back on Brad and all his fools, On my first trip I tried to drink my coffee from a flask, But then I realised I couldn't sip it through my mask, Had to stop! Get back inside! Here comes my nineteenth nervous lockdown! Here comes my nineteenth nervous lockdown!'

As Fears Go By: A haunting baroque-flavoured ballad that tells the poignant story of a hopeless government that is so determined to scare its population into submission and terrify everybody witless about a flu-like virus that it shuts everything down including all the playgrounds, even though children aren't at risk from the disease. The song which reached number six in the charts was famously written by Mick Jagger and Keith Richards for their girlfriend Marianne Faithfull (this is sloppy journalism, Rowena, how can she be the girlfriend of both of them?—ed. It was the '60s—Rowena). 'It is the evening of the day, I sit and watch no children play-ay-ay-ay, Smiling faces I can't see, They're laughter-free, I sit and watch, As fears go by-y-y-y.'

Dear Doctor: An amusing pastiche of the over-the-top tragic love stories that typify country 'n' western songs, Mick Jagger sings in a faux American accent the tale of a lapsed anti-vaxxer who is secretly relieved when his fiancée ditches him on their wedding day which has been postponed yet again due to Covid restrictions. 'Oh help me, please doctor, I'm dizzy There's a pain where I once had a heart, It's myo… carditis… did it come from the jab? Are you certain the vax played no part?'

Ventilator blues: A heavy blues number from the band's famous double album *Exile on Macquarie Street*, the song has been repurposed by the NSW government's ad agency as the perfect jingle for its latest COVID-19 scare campaign: 'When your spine is cracking and your hands, they shake, Heart is bursting and your head's gonna break, Nurse's cussing, temperature soared, Feels like murder on the Covid ward, Unless you got your vaccination, everybody's gonna need more ventilation.'

It's All Over Now: The band's third single and their first number one, this jaunty cover of the Bobby Womack original is still the most famous version. The song tells the story of a popular premier who people adored because she trusted them but then suddenly she betrayed them by imposing unbelievably harsh lockdowns with dire results: 'Well, Gladys used to stay up all night long, She made us proud, she made us strong, She topped the polls and that's no lie, But tables turn and now it's her turn to cry, Because I used to love her, but it's all over now!'

Gimme shelter: This iconic song from *Let It Bleed* captures the sheer violence, mayhem, chaos and utter helplessness of one of the most turbulent periods in American history, namely Joe Biden's disastrous evacuation of Kabul: 'Rape, murder, It's just a shot away, It's just a shot away, yeah, The Taliban is threatening, my very life today, Gimme, gimme shelter, Or I'm gonna fade away.'

Goats Head Soup: Famous Stones album named after the new staple Afghan diet under the Taliban.

After a disastrous capitulation to the Taliban in Kabul, Joe Biden declares, er, victory.

Victory in Afghanistan

4 September 2021

With US President Joe Biden excitedly boasting of his stunning victory in Afghanistan, *The Fin*'s revisionist historian Dr Rowena Sliding-Dawes ponders how much better things could have turned out if only Joe Biden had been in charge of other troubling conflicts.

Publius Quinctilius Bidenus, 9AD: 'Last night in the Teutoburg Forest, I successfully ended 600 years of Roman expansionism. We completed one of the biggest transfers of strapping young men from soldiering into slavery that the modern world has ever seen. Moreover, we managed to find an environmentally-friendly new way to clear and then fertilise a vast wooded section of that forest for future agricultural purposes. The bottom line: only a tad over 99 per cent of the legion are now dead or enslaved. In fact, just yesterday, the Visigoths and the Huns passed a resolution to send a clear message that the entire community of Vandals expects to visit Rome at the earliest possible opportunity.'

King Harold Bidwenson, 1066: 'Last night on the outskirts of Hastings, I ended 12 long hours of exhausting battle. We completed one of the biggest transfers of arrows through the air that the world has ever seen. Moreover, we have discovered an entirely new way to remove cataracts. The extraordinary success of this mission was due entirely to my, er, piercing eyesight. The bottom line: only 95 per cent of the Norman invasion has succeeded. In fact, just yesterday, the Holy See passed a resolution to send a clear message that the entire Christendom expects William the, er, Conqueror to, er, pack his bags and head home at the earliest possible opportunity.'

Biden Inca, 1533: 'Last night in Cajamarca, I ended 300 years of building roads and sacrificing children to the Sun god after I bravely tossed a Bible on the floor and stubbornly refused to swear allegiance to the King of Spain. The bottom line: at least somebody's finally taken away all those tawdry baubles and other kitsch junk that was cluttering up the basement. In fact, just yesterday Ferdinand V passed a resolution to come back and clear out the rest of it at the earliest possible opportunity.'

Napoleon Bidenpart, 1812: '*Zut alors!* Last night on the outskirts of Moscow, *ma Grande Armée* ended five long weeks of waiting patiently in the snow for the city to fall. Now I am proud to announce that more than 100,000 men are happily heading home towards the warm bosom of Mother France. No nation, no nation has ever done anything like this! Only the glory of France had the capacity and the will and the ability to do it! The bottom line: only 98 per cent of our men and horses will perish. In fact, just yesterday, the Imperial Security Council passed a resolution to send a clear message that the entire Holy Roman community expects the Russian Empire to help move us, er, forwards back towards the Rhine—notably, by providing blankets, heating, hot water bottles and mugs of steaming cocoa. In fact, just yesterday an excited group of marauding Cossacks passed a resolution to come and physically assist us in every way they can at the earliest possible opportunity.'

Lord Bidigan, 1854: 'By Jove, last night in Crimea I completely ended traditional European warfare as we know it with the shortest cavalry charge in history! Just 25 spiffing minutes and it was all done and dusted! My rather rash assumption that the damn Russkies wouldn't use their cannons against swords and steeds turned out to be not an entirely accurate one. But let me be clear, we got a damn good poem out of this malarkey thanks to that Tennyson chappie and if you ask me future generations will thank us. 'Storm'd at with shot and shell, Boldly they rode and well; Into the jaws of Death, Into the mouth of Hell, Rode the six hundred. C'mon man, that's just beautiful!'

First Lord of the Admiralty Winston Bidenhill, 1916: 'Last night in the Dardanelles I ended eight long months of war with the Turks. The bottom line: the Aussies now have a national identity.'

Dwight D. Bidenhower, 1945: 'Last night in Berlin, I ended war with the Soviet Union before it had even begun! We completed one of the biggest transfers of traumatised citizens from one murderous totalitarian dictatorship to another ever recorded in human history! The bottom line: we only had to hand over 100 per cent of the population of eastern Europe in order to appease the commies! In fact, just yesterday, the Politburo passed a resolution that those who suffered under the tyrannical boot of Nazism can now enjoy the exact same level of bureaucratic co-operation that they are accustomed to under the new arrangement with the Soviets, including gulags, famines and mass starvation at the earliest possible opportunity.'

Scott Morrison ditches the dodgy French submarine deal and opts for a new alliance with Britain and the USA in order to get some new nuclear subs.

Submarine names

18 September 2021

The world of submarine warfare was rocked to its core this week with the explosive (is that the right word?—ed) news that Australia has torpedoed (or this?—ed) its diesel submarine deal with the French and instead commissioned a fleet of nuclear submarines as part of its freshly re-minted alliance with Britain and America. But what will the new subs be called? And will they be named after those who did the most to bring about this exciting new development in Australia's defensive capabilities? In this world exclusive, *The Fin*'s defence correspondent Ms Rowena Reynolds-Payne unveils the new fleet:

HMAS *My Wife Lucy*: with a propulsion system fuelled by its massive twin Goldman Sachs bank accounts (surely 'nuclear engines'?—ed), the *My Wife Lucy* is in a class all of its own, capable of operating in all harbourside conditions and performing extremely deceptive manoeuvres under the cloak of darkness at the deepest depths of treachery (surely 'the ocean'?—ed). Fans of this particular vessel claim it is clearly the smartest sub in the pen but critics complain that the 'character' and 'personality' of the vessel suffer due to numerous fatal flaws in the original design, such as an extremely thin-skinned hull which is likely to overheat and implode at the first whiff of electoral disaster (surely 'underwater battle'?—ed).

HMAS Pyne: sister ship to the *My Wife Lucy* and named after the much-maligned former Defence Procurement Minister Christopher Fixer-Pyne, this submarine proudly boasts a fashionable rainbow colour camouflage pattern cunningly designed to make it look like a giant tropical fish in order to sail undetected through the pristine coral reefs of the South China Sea and sneak up and say 'Boo!' to those naughty Chinese sailor-boys! Other highly impressive features include the new design of the Cherry Bar (surely 'bridge'?—ed), featuring the unique 'black hand' leather helm grip with mirrored flashing disco ball periscope unit which ensures that whenever the Captain is in the Winner's Circle the vessel automatically swerves to the far left before sinking without a trace.

HMAS Snowy 2.0: unique submarine design commissioned by the Snowy Mountains Renewable Submarine Energy Company which uses the latest cutting-edge solar power and wind technology combined with Turnbull-designed hydro pumps (patent still pending) to power the submarine for indefinite periods deep beneath the ocean by simply pumping sea water in at one end in the morning then pumping it back out again at night.

HMAS Emmanuelle Macron le Magnifique le Fantastique le Noble le Généreux le Superbe le Sage: named in lieu of paying hundreds of millions of dollars of compensation to the French for cancelling their squillion-dollar subs contract.

HMAS Albo: capable of travelling in opposite directions at the same time, this vessel is fitted with the latest anti-detection technology, allowing it to travel for months on end without leaving any trace whatsoever of having actually been anywhere or done anything.

HMAS Kristina: with its blonde-haired, blue-eyed, all-white, Caucasian female crew, this vessel is a supreme example of the Navy's commitment to diversity and inclusion. Originally expected to be called the Tu Le in order to attract former Vietnamese boat people whilst patrolling the waters surrounding the western Sydney electorate of Fowler, the vessel is in fact simply a cheap refit of the failed *HMAS Bennelong* which itself was a dodgy paint job of the failed *HMAS Sky News Anchor* which was itself a quick respray of the failed *HMAS Premier* which was of course originally known in the docks around Circular Quay as the *HMAS Puppet*.

HMAS *Thérèse Rein:* named in honour of the immensely talented (surely 'wealthy'?—ed) wife of the former Prime Minister of Australia the Honourable Krudd Oh-Seven, this submarine is moored off the glittering waters of Noosa in a specially-designed 17-million-dollar berth from which it fires salvos at the crowded beaches of Sydney demanding police arrest any sweltering Sydneysiders who dare go anywhere near Bondi beach during lockdown.

HMAS *Rat Effers:* designed to strike fear and terror into the Chinese Xi-Class submarine fleet, this vessel's highly sophisticated communication's equipment has been uniquely programmed by a crack team of Sinologists and social media linguists to intercept Chinese sub-to-sub communications and cunningly replace them with abusive and vile Australian swear words.

HMAS *Andrews:* with the most up-to-date submersible technology, this vessel is capable of remaining locked down on the ocean floor for months and months on end. Vaccine passports mandatory for anyone who wants to go to the pub, er, sub. (Warning: beware of steep slippery stairs.)

HMAS *Malcolm:* named in honour of the man who forced Australia to get real about China by making the worst and most expensive submarine purchase in maritime history in order to save a few seats in Adelaide.

Civil unrest in Victoria as the lockdowns and curfews continue and Victoria Police find a new enthusiasm for batons and rubber bullets.

Genesis

25 September 2021

Genesis 13:21 And so it came about in the days of Daniel King of Sodom and Gomorrah and of all the territory that lay in between and extended even to the beachside suburbs that a mighty City rose upon the edges of the Bay, and in his wisdom did Daniel decide to spend vast amounts of gold and other treasures that he took from the hands and pockets of his people in order to cancel the construction of an unholy tunnel that passed beneath the City Gates from East to West and instead did deliver at the intersection of every dusty pathway a multitude of Camel Crossings replete with flashing lights and bells and other such manifestations of his earthly powers.

Genesis 14:14–16 But verily the Lord remained sceptical and gazed down upon the City with displeasure, beholding the sinners and their merry-making, their debauchery and their drunkenness, even as some who were born as man declared themselves woman and even as some who were born as woman declared themselves man. Now it was said that the high priests of Sodom were exceedingly wicked and did forsake the Word of the Lord and instead built great temples and other forms of worship to the gods of the Paganites, and did place upon the rooftops of the Unbelievers panels of glass and other such shiny baubles so as to pay tribute to the false god of the Sun and given witness to the false Angels of the Wind and bow down before the turning of giant blades and turbines which they proclaimed in their ignorance and wickedness as the True Almighty Power and Sustainer of All Life on Earth.

Deuteronomy 29:23 And the Lord said, 'I am a jealous God and I take pride in my handiworks and I certainly do not take kindly to the suggestion that it is Mankind who can control the rising of the oceans and the melting of the ice caps, who can prevent the floods and ease the droughts, who can stop the rivers swelling and the earth from cracking. That's my job, and mine alone. Nor do I look kindly upon the notion that the warming of my Creation is caused by the farting of camels and the burning of goat's dung and the digging up of coal such as is used to heat homes and cook food in winter times.'

Isaiah 19:3 But Daniel ignored the warnings of the Lord, and did continue to urge his people to pray to the Pagan gods, even to the Green gods of the forests and the mountains and the streams and to the Rainbow gods full of pride in their shiny new Temple and the Merchants of Despair in their Safe Injecting Rooms, and the Teachers of Fluidity preaching to the innocent young children in their Safe Schools, and the fornicators and the blasphemers and even those who would worship at the woke altars of Diversity and Inclusion.

Jeremiah 13:14 Then in his despair and his dissatisfaction, the Lord did punish Daniel and his people with a pestilence in the form of a fearsome plague, verily so that the streets of the City lay bare and the people huddled inside their homes for months on end, lest the soldiers in black come knocking on their doors. And the people did tremble in fear and did marvel upon the daily preachings from Daniel and his Chief Apothecary

Brett who reassured them all was well, even as the fornicators took it upon themselves to guard the Quarantine Gates, and much merriment and fraternisation took place among the sinners in the hotel corridors.

Ezekiel 16:44-58 And so it happened that Zoe the daughter of Ballarat whilst of child and still in her fluffy pink pyjamas did turn to her Facebook and dared to gaze upon a post which was a message to attend an anti-lockdown rally at the weekend. And in his anger Daniel the Unjust had her arrested and dragged away in handcuffs before the eyes of her distraught husband and her own wailing children. But soon the people took to the streets to overthrow Daniel, and did tear asunder their flimsy papyrus masks and refuse the mandatory passports of tyranny, even as they dressed in hi-vis vests and proclaimed their adherence to the laws of the land. But Daniel was a cruel and wicked King who turned a deaf ear to the pleadings of the hungry and those out of work, of the tired and the mentally depressed, and instead sent more soldiers dressed in black to punish and hurt the people and drive them back into their unrighteous confinement.

Lamentations 11 At which point the Lord said, 'Stuff it, I'll try an earthquake instead.'

How would cancel culture cope with the Beatles?

Johnny's birthday

9 October 2021

It's John Lennon's birthday! The man who declared himself bigger than Jesus Christ before later declaring that he WAS Jesus Christ; the man who scribbled down the lyrics 'Imagine no possessions, I wonder if you can' in the back of his chauffeur-driven psychedelic Rolls Royce on the way to his Surrey mansion; and the man who retired from being a superstar in order to take drugs and bake bread for his son would today turn 81. Could there be a pop star who was more enlightened or progressive? Perhaps not. But how would his lyrics stand up in today's world of cancel culture and woke identity politics? One can only, er, imagine.

I Want to Hold Your Hand: The opening lines in this repugnant song are both patronising and deeply offensive as the singer condescendingly suggests to a woman that she is intellectually his inferior ('Oh, yeah, I'll tell you something, I think you'll understand…') before immediately making overtly inappropriate suggestions about groping her. As the song goes on the abusive behaviour continues with the singer incessantly pleading to 'touch' her because it makes him 'feel happy inside', even going so far as to encourage her to break normal social distancing and hygiene restrictions by holding hands.

A Hard Day's Night: With its priapic lyrics glorifying the patriarchy, this unbelievably misogynistic song suggests that women are only good for one thing and have no place in the modern workforce. 'It's been a hard day's night, and I've been working like a dog… But when I get home to you, I find the things that you do, Will make me feel alright.'

Norwegian Wood (This Bird Has Flown): Extremely inappropriate song that has been widely condemned for its sexist lyrics in which the singer refers to a young woman as a 'bird' (suggesting she is little more than his pet in a cage). Worse, after making it clear he failed to obtain written consent for their sexual relationship by boasting 'I once had a girl!' the singer quickly backtracks and reveals his toxic masculinity with the ancient anti-feminist trope that she was in fact the perpetrator of the sexual encounter ('… or should I say, she once had me.') After sneering at the woman because she is less financially privileged than him ('I looked around, and I noticed there wasn't a chair') he admits to drinking her wine and biding his time, the classic prelude to a date-rape scenario. Finally, when the woman reveals she is a victim of the gender wage gap who has to get up earlier than he does in the morning to go to work he bizarrely boasts about 'crawling off to sleep in the bath' in what is an obvious reference to the aftermath of an ugly domestic violence incident.

I Am the Walrus: Not only an extremely specie-ist diatribe in which the singer pretends he identifies as an animal, in this case a walrus, one of the most endangered creatures on the planet thanks to catastrophic global warming, the song goes out of its way to mock mental illness ('Sitting on a cornflake, Waiting for the van to come') and the agony of depression ('Stupid bloody Tuesday Man, you been a naughty boy, You let your face grow long' before poking fun at gender confusion in a vile transphobic tirade of classic hate speech ('Crabalocker fishwife, pornographic priestess, Boy, you been a naughty girl, You let your knickers down').

A Day in the Life: Vile Murdoch-inspired rant in which the singer repeatedly sucks up to News Corp ('I read *The News* today, oh boy') and revels in the right-wing media's incessant promotion of white male privilege ('… about a lucky man who made the grade… nobody was really sure if he was from the House of Lords'). In the final stanza, after glorifying tobacco products ('Found my way upstairs and had a smoke') the singer praises four thousand fracking mines in Blackburn, Lancashire, the original home of coal. 'And though the holes were rather small, They had to count them all,' he gloats in true capitalist-exploitation style.

Imagine: In this disgusting anthem of climate denialism the singer fraudulently claims that there is 'No hell below us', ignoring the Science which states that there is indeed a hell below us, namely, the hellish fossil fuels directly responsible for the imminent destruction of the planet. Unbelievably, he then says that there is 'above us only sky', a direct contradiction of the latest IPCC report which states that concentrations of CO_2 in the atmosphere are at an all-time high.

Polythene Pam: Hideously transphobic song ridiculing gender dysphoria and economic deprivation: 'See Polythene Pam, she's so good-looking but she looks like a man. See her in drag, dressed in her polythene bag.'

I Want You (She's So Heavy): Obscene fat-shaming song. Disgraceful.

Jealous Guy: 'I began to lose control, I didn't mean to hurt you, I'm sorry that I made you cry…' Oops, might give this one a miss.

Woman is the N***er of the World: Bloody hell, where do we start?

Finally some good news; New South Wales has a new conservative Premier. (But the catch is his ghastly choice for Treasurer.)

The Doms dominate

16 October 2021

The world of abrupt leadership changes was rocked to its core this past fortnight with the sudden elevation of Dominic Perrottet to one of the most powerful leadership positions in the land, Premier of New South Wales. But who is this man really? Where does he come from? Have there been any other famous Dominic's in world history? In this explosive exclusive, *The Fin*'s Catholic-with-six-kids correspondent Lady Rowena Dominique-Pirhouette explores the rich family heritage and genealogy of the man known simply as 'Dom'.

Dom Corleone: known to many simply as the Godfather, or even just as God, Dom Corleone was reputed to be the head of the dreaded Cosy Nostril, a secretive organised crime gang of, er, Catholic Dads with six kids who control all the car pools and share pick-ups to footy on Saturday morning throughout the mean streets of Epping, Baulkham Hills and Beecroft. Dom Corleone is immortalised in a trio of Oscar-winning films by Frances Ford Coppalot which chronicle his rise from humble West Pennant Hills lawyer and 'consigliere' to the original Irish mafia Godfather 'Fingers' O'Barrel, who got gunned down in an Italian restaurant by a violent gang of corruption investigators because he 'forgot' to pick up the tab for a $3,000 bottle of red wine, through to when Dom is anointed head of the Liberal family and Premier of New South Wales after his sister

Gladdie elopes with a clay-pigeon shooter from Wagga Wagga. In the final bloody scene, Dom can't believe it when he is mercilessly betrayed by his own adopted son and recently-appointed Family Treasurer, 'Lucky' Matteo Kean, played by a barely recognisable Greta Thunberg with prosthetic nose and shaved head.

Dom Juan: legendary, swashbuckling, dashingly handsome, tall, dark-haired fictional libertine (don't you mean Liberal?—ed) from Castille Hill whose life of seduction inspired a wealth of books, poems, plays, movies and operas. In all the tales, Dom Juan becomes notorious for his ability to woo men and women of all voting ages and polling stations in life, and often disguises himself as a moderate or a conservative in order to do so. Dom Juan's famous motto is 'Tan largo me lo fiáis', or 'What a long term you are giving me!'. Alas, that would have been the case had Dom not foolishly opted to try and seduce the greenies by hopping into bed with Matt Ever-so-keen. When taxpayers realise that Matt has been squandering the state's precious treasures by pumping cash into madcap schemes to syphon carbon dioxide out of the atmosphere Dom is cast out and goes straight to hell on the opposition benches at the next erection, er, election.

Dominic Voting Machines: notorious machines linked to the internet which caused mayhem during the NSW 2021 Presidential Election with accusations of dubious late night activity in Macquarie County. Critics such as Mr and Mrs Stokes of Pittwater have repeatedly complained that the machines were rigged to give all the votes to Dominic Perrottet and none whatsoever to, er, Rob Stokes.

Iron Dom: unique mobile all-weather defensive missile system developed in a bunker in Macquarie Street designed to intercept and destroy incoming flak from terror cells of journalists hiding in underground bunkers in Ultimo and Pyrmont. When a salvo is launched—typically a deadly Clennell-style warhead which normally approaches with only a few seconds warning straight out of the Sky, sometimes even after dark, the Iron Dom is instinctively activated giving the Premier and his advisers ample time to duck for cover.

Dom Pérignon (1638–1715): distant ancestor to the new NSW Premier Dom Pérrottét, Dom Pérignon was a 17th century monk at the remote Benedictine monastery in the forests of Epping-sur-Road. In 1677 Pérignon was unexpectedly promoted to Premier Cellar Master when his Mother Superior, the Eastern Orthodox nun Sister Gladys, was found cavorting in a haystack with Daryl the Dodgy, a cart dealer from Parramatta-sur-Rive. However, history records the shocking mistake Dom Pérignon made on his first day on the job when he insisted on putting one extremely noxious variety of ultra-green eco-organic grape into his most treasured new batch of wine which soured and then poisoned the entire barrel forcing Dom Pérignon to ditch the lot and start all over again.

Dom Pérignon (2021): Famous brand of premier champagne developed by a 17th century monk (see above) which is now regarded as one of the finest and most prestigious brands in Australia (surely 'the world'?—ed). With its effervescent personality combined with strong oak characteristics, dry sense of humour, beautifully integrated acidity, excellent length and strong mineral backbone, this top drop—although in its infancy—should age quite well. The palate is crisp and clean, matched with an exquisite nose.

About the Author

Rowan Dean has been the weekly political satirist at the *Australian Financial Review Weekend* for the past decade as well as being one of Australia's leading media commentators. He is the host of the top-rating *Outsiders* show on Sky News Australia and a regular commentator on other shows. Rowan is also the editor-in-chief of *The Spectator Australia*, the sister publication to *The Spectator* in the UK, one of the world's oldest and most respected publications. Rowan is also the author of several books, including the novel *Corkscrewed*, a tale of hedonism and ambition in the heady days of 1980s advertising.

Rowan's documentary *Death of the Aussie larrikin?* was a major hit on Sky News Australia and Rowan was also one of the original panellists on the ABC's *The Gruen Transfer*. Prior to that he was an advertising creative director and filmmaker responsible for many top Australian and international ad campaigns. As an Australian copywriter in London, Rowan was responsible for one of the most successful alcohol launches ever—the Fosters Lager campaign featuring Paul Hogan—as well as co-writing an ad that has repeatedly been voted one of the top ads of all time, Hamlet *Photobooth*.

For more information go to rowandean.com.au or follow Rowan on Twitter @rowandean